Crimes Against Humanity and Civilization
THE GENOCIDE OF THE ARMENIANS

Go, Melanie/Emily —
A chapter of
each per day.
Yes You Can!

Jan

Facing History and Ourselves, Inc.
Brookline, Massachusetts

FACING
HISTORY
AND
OURSELVES

The image on the cover of *Crimes Against Humanity and Civilization: The Genocide of the Armenians* was painted by the artist Arshile Gorky. It is based on a photograph of Gorky and his mother, Shushan der Marderosian, taken in 1912. Although Gorky is generally identified as an American artist, he was born Vosdanig Adoian near the city of Van in what was then the Ottoman Empire. A few years after the photograph was taken, Gorky and his mother were victims of the Armenian Genocide. While he survived, Gorky remembers his mother dying in his arms. As an artist Gorky returned to the subject of the 1912 photograph many times throughout his career.

Photo courtesy Lennon, Weinberg Gallery

Acknowledgment of photographs and other images accompany the images throughout the book. Acknowledgment of the many documents and other quotations included in this book may be found at the end of each chapter. Every effort has been made to trace and acknowledge owners of copyrighted materials, but in some cases that has proved impossible. Facing History and Ourselves would be pleased to add, correct, or revise such citations in future printings.

Cover Painting by Arshile Gorky, *The Artist and His Mother*, ca. 1926-1936, courtesy of the Whitney Museum of American Art, New York.

Jacket and book design by Sandy Smith-Garcés

Facing History and Ourselves, 16 Hurd Road, Brookline, MA 02445
(617) 232-1595
www.facinghistory.org

Printed in the United States of America
3 4 5 6 7 8 9 10
March 2017

ISBN 978-1-940457-26-0

This book is dedicated to

Dr. Charles K. and Beverly J. Achki.

Among those who have known them, they have set a compelling example

of human decency and respect for others that embodies the principles taught

in Facing History and Ourselves.

Given in their honor by

Tom Blumenthal and Lisa Achki Blumenthal

and their children.

TABLE OF CONTENTS

PREFACE

In 1939, just before the invasion of Poland and the beginning of the Nazi Holocaust, Adolf Hitler asked his generals, "Who today still speaks of the massacre of the Armenians?"[I] He was referring to the systematic murder of the Armenians by leaders of the Ottoman Empire during World War I. Within a generation, the heinous crime had faded from public memory. Hitler learned a lesson: he could act with impunity.

During the genocide, Henry Sturmer, a journalist for the German newspaper *Kolnische Zeitung*, was outraged. He wanted Germany to use its influence as an ally of the Ottoman Empire to stop the systematic extermination of the Armenians. When they failed to do so, he wrote:

> *The mixture of cowardice, lack of conscience, and lack of foresight of which our government has been guilty in Armenian affairs is quite enough to undermine completely the political loyalty of any thinking man who has any regard for humanity and civilization.*[II]

In July 1915, Henry Morgenthau, the U.S. ambassador to the Ottoman Empire, similarly frustrated, begged the State Department to take action against what he called the "race murder" of the Armenians. Instead, the nation chose to remain neutral. While his government remained silent, Morgenthau pleaded for the lives of Armenian children, women, and men. Mehmet Talaat, the Minister of the Interior for the Committee of Union and Progress, asked Morgenthau, "Why are you interested in the Armenians anyway?" He continued, "You are a Jew; these people are Christians. The [Muslims] and the Jews always get on harmoniously. We are treating the Jews here all right. What have you to complain of? Why can't you let us do with these Christians as we please?" Morgenthau replied, "I am not here as a Jew but as American Ambassador [...]. I do not appeal to you in the name of any race or any religion, but merely as a human being."[III] What Morgenthau understood is essential to the work of Facing History and Ourselves, for we ask, how do children develop what sociologist Helen Fein calls a "universe of obligation"— the circle of individuals and groups "toward whom obligations are owed, to whom rules apply, and whose injuries call for [amends]?"[IV]

What have we learned about responding to genocide and prevention of violence in the 90 years since the Armenian Genocide that can make a difference as we "witness" genocide today? How do we help students answer the question, "How do I make a difference?" After a study of responses to 20th century genocide, journalist and human rights scholar Samantha Power concluded that we need to develop a toolbox with a range of possible responses to genocide. Facing History and Ourselves believes that prevention begins by developing an informed compassionate citizenry—it is our mission.

As we witness the ongoing genocide in the Sudan and the resulting refugee crisis, teachers worldwide are looking for ways to engage their students in a study of history that illuminates how things could have been different. What can we learn from the past to guide our responses? How has the moral, political and legal landscape changed since world leaders first described, "crimes against humanity?" The story of the Armenian Genocide and its legacies is told in Facing History's newest resource book, *Crimes Against Humanity and Civilization: The Genocide of the Armenians*. It is a history that is as relevant today as it was when the Nazis began their march through Europe. It raises important questions about our own responsibilities as individuals and as members of groups and nations to those beyond our borders. And it is also raises important questions about the rule of law and education in bringing understanding about past genocide to citizens today. In fact, Michel Mazor, a survivor of the Warsaw Ghetto, recalled: "During the terrible days of July and August 1942, we often spoke of the fate of the Armenians by the Turks in 1915." He wondered if "the gas chambers and crematoria of Auschwitz and Treblinka" would have come into being if "at the end of the First World War, a 'Nuremberg Tribunal' had convened at Istanbul."

These questions have long been central to the work of Facing History and Ourselves. Soon after the founding of the organization in 1976, Manoog Young of the National Association of Armenian Studies and Research approached us with the idea of creating a study guide on the Armenian Genocide as a companion to *Facing History and Ourselves: Holocaust and Human Behavior*. He and others in the Armenian community were eager to tell the story of what was then a "forgotten genocide." Our research marked the beginning of our work with the history of the Armenians in the Ottoman Empire.

Our long association with professor and historian Richard Hovannisian at the University of California at Los Angeles heightened our awareness of the genocide and its legacies. At our workshops and institutes, he describes how the failures to bring the perpetrators to justice and Turkey's evolving denials of the massacre have complicated our understanding of not only genocide but also guilt and responsibility.

We could not have produced *Crimes Against Humanity and Civilization: The Genocide of the Armenians* without the support of so many friends and scholars. We are grateful to Carolyn Mugar for the grant to support this project that funded our research, and scholars Samantha Power, Peter Balakian, and Henry Theriault for their guidance and advice in creating this valuable resource. Special thanks to Thomas and Lisa Blumenthal, whose generous grant supported the printing of the book and its dissemination to educators. Facing History and Ourselves would also like to acknowledge the efforts of Senior Historian Mary Johnson in creating the first drafts of the book; Adam Strom who researched, wrote, and edited the final manuscript; Marc Skvirsky and Margot Stern Strom for their leadership; Sandy Smith-Garcés who designed the book; Chris Stokes, Cynthia Platt, Brooke Harvey, and Jennifer Gray for helping to turn this manuscript into a book, as well as Karen Lempert, Sarah Gray, Melinda Jones-Rhoades, and Tracy O'Brien for their work in the library overseeing permission requests.

NOTES

I.   Samantha Power, *A Problem from Hell: America and the Age of Genocide* (New York: Basic Books, 2002), 23.
II. Deborah Dwork and Robert Jan van Pelt, *The Holocaust: A History* (New York: W.W. Norton & Co., 2002), 39-40.
III. Henry Morgenthau, *Ambassador Morgenthau's Story* (Plandome: New Age Publisher, 1975), 339.
IV. Helen Fein, *Accounting for Genocide*, (Free Press, 1979) 4.

INTRODUCTION

Over ninety years after the outbreak of the Armenian Genocide, its legacy still has power to prompt moral reflection, deep questioning, and even anger. As we prepared this resource book, a number of Turkish and Armenian scholars were meeting, both online and face-to-face, to make a joint inquiry into their past, finding ways to acknowledge and discuss a history whose denial by some, feels to others like a gaping wound. This discussion was energized by an ongoing debate about Turkey's relationship to the European Union, with some current members arguing that official Turkish recognition of the genocide should be a prerequisite for membership. These debates serve as a reminder that history, even with the passing of generations, continues to shape the way people think about themselves and others.

At the same time, genocide and genocide prevention are now understood as among the primary challenges of our day. Many politicians and scholars hoped that the end of the Cold War would usher in a new era of democracy and human rights; instead the eruption of mass violence in East Timor, the Balkans, and parts of Africa makes it clear that finding the tools to prevent genocide is as urgent as ever. In the twentieth century more human beings died through genocidal violence and state-sanctioned murder than on that era's countless bloody battlefields.[V] The twenty-first century is not looking much better. Even when violence abates, cities and towns are uninhabitable, refugees live in the most squalid conditions, and, as rebuilding begins, fear of retribution and revenge prevails while myths and misinformation threaten to precipitate new cycles of violence. Before long these are no longer regional issues, children scarred by conflict sit in classrooms across the world, images of genocide flash across television screens and computer desktops while reporters count the dead, and, increasingly, politicians find themselves questioned about the ways that they respond.

Facing History and Ourselves believes that education can help to shape new a generation of leaders who can make a difference. As you read the accounts in this resource book you will find historical echoes. The dilemmas faced by those who worked to protect Armenians in the last years of the Ottoman Empire, and during the genocide itself, are not so different from the challenges facing those who respond to genocide today, whether it is in Bosnia, Rwanda, or Sudan.

In 1915 journalists, politicians, and ordinary people considered how best to respond to the accounts of "horrors" and "outrages" in Turkey's Anatolian desert. Unable to remain silent, local and national leaders challenged tradition by boldly proclaiming that responsibility for human life does not stop at national borders. Their solutions set important precedents for international law. In fact, the phrase "crime against humanity," made famous as one of the counts at the post-Holocaust Nuremberg Trials, was first used to describe the massacres of Armenian civilians in the spring of 1915.

As the pillaging of Armenian villages continued, diplomats debated questions of national sovereignty. In the absence of military intervention, coalitions of individuals, religious groups, and voluntary associations were able to raise millions of dollars to house and feed refugees from the slaughter. While those efforts saved many, humanitarian relief alone could not stop the mass murder of women, children, and men. In the wake of the genocide, official promises to hold the perpetrators accountable faded, as did support for the new Armenian state.

To many who had followed the bloody history of Turkey's campaign against its own people, the impunity enjoyed by those who had ordered and carried out the killings was unbearable. One of them was Raphael Lemkin, a Polish Jew and a law student. Lemkin confronted one of his law school professors. He asked, "Why is the killing of a million people a lesser crime than the killing of a single individual?"[VI] His professor used a metaphor to explain that courts did not have any jurisdiction: "Consider the case of a farmer who owns a flock of chickens. He kills them and this is his business. If you interfere, you are trespassing." But, replied an incensed Lemkin, "the Armenians are not chickens."[VII] Lemkin dedicated the rest of his life to finding a way to make sure that the law would recognize the difference. In 1944 Lemkin coined the word "genocide" and later he drafted the United Nations Convention on Genocide. The convention was ratified on December 9, 1948, one day before the adoption of the Universal Declaration of Human Rights.

Although this convention requires that its signatories take whatever steps are necessary to prevent genocide, too often the international community does little but stand by while mass killings continue in places like Sudan and the Democratic Republic of the Congo. In his role as a columnist for the *New York Times*, Nicholas Kristof warns readers about the consequences of silence. "There is something special about genocide," he writes, "When human beings deliberately wipe out others because of their tribe or skin color, when babies succumb not to diarrhea but to bayonets and bonfires, that is not just one more tragedy. It is a monstrosity that demands a response from other humans. We demean our own humanity, and that of the victims, when we avert our eyes."[VIII]

This resource book recounts the story of the Armenian Genocide and its painful legacy through primary sources, witness testimony, literature, and historical analysis. We hope that these powerful stories will help a new generation to understand that genocide is a threat to all of us: it is indeed a "crime against humanity."

NOTES

V.   "Institute for the Study of Genocide-International Association of Genocide Scholars," *http://www.isg-iags.org,*. (Accessed on December 18,2005).

VI.   Raphael Lemkin, *Totally Unofficial Man: The Autobiography of Raphael Lemkin, in Pioneers of Genocide Studies*, ed. Steven L. Jacobs and Samuel Totten (New Brunswick, NJ: Transaction Books, 2002), 371.

VII.   Robert Merrill Bartlett, *They Stand Invincible: Men Who Are Reshaping Our World* (New York: Thomas Y. Crowell Company, 1959), 97.

VIII.   Nicholas D. Kristof, "A Tolerable Genocide," *The New York Times*, November 27, 2005, *http://select.nytimes.com/search/restricted/article?res=FA0A17F83C550C748EDDA80994DD404482* (Accessed on January 20, 2006). 2005.

REFLECTIONS ON THE ARMENIAN GENOCIDE

The Armenian Genocide forcibly removed a people from its homeland and wiped away most of the tangible evidence of its three thousand years of material and spiritual culture. The calamity, which was unprecedented in scope and effect, may be seen as the culmination of the ongoing persecutions and massacres of Armenians in the Ottoman Empire, especially since the 1890s. Or it may be placed in the specific context of modern nationalism and the great upheavals that brought about the dissolution of a multi-ethnic and multi-religious empire and the emergence in its place of a Turkish nation-state based on a mono-ethnic and mono-religious society. The approaches are not mutually exclusive and should be examined in the context of the plight of the Armenians in the nineteenth century and their ultimate elimination from the Ottoman Empire in the first part of the twentieth century.

A critical issue in the Armenian case that has general application is the way traditional-bound societies react to change or attempted change. If the Armenian quest for equality and security in the Ottoman Empire was viewed by the dominant element as a serious threat to its accustomed way of life, one need look no further than the reactions in the United States to the civil rights movement in the second half of the twentieth century to see certain comparisons in the strong, sometimes violent, response to impending change. There are, of course, fundamental differences that must be noted as well. If in the U.S. case the government intervened to enforce legislation and change, in the Armenian experience, the sultan's government was directly complicit in obstructing the very reforms to which it had acceded, at least on paper.

One might consider whether there was anything that the Armenian people or their leaders could have done to escape their fate in face of an emerging militant nationalism espoused by the Turkish rulers. Was there any real way for the Armenians to have kept their identity, their religion and culture, and still survived in the changing geopolitical, ethnic, and economic environment? Could they or should they have avoided intellectual and political currents that emanated in Europe and gradually made their way eastward? In what ways did their own cultural, educational, and economic progress affect their relations with the dominant group and impact on the course of their history?

It is important also to consider the role of foreign governments that intervened from time to time in the Armenian Question. What circumstances could have made the results of external intercession more favorable? And what was the role of bystander governments during the period from the 1890s to the 1920s? How did the demonstrated vulnerability of the Armenian people make the perpetrators all the more audacious?

A common feature of most genocides is denial by the perpetrator side. In the Armenian case, the question should be raised as to why, long after the Ottoman Empire has been succeeded by the Republic of Turkey, does there continue to be such adamant rejection and denial of the truth. Were there conditions that made the aftermath of the Armenian Genocide radically different from the post-Holocaust period? And why do powerful countries such as the United States participate in trying to cover up or obscure the magnitude and significance of the Armenian Genocide while fully recognizing the crimes of Nazi Germany and the genocidal policies of that regime?

Students should also consider the effects of the trauma and of post-traumatic stress, the ways in which survivors live with painful memory and react to denial, and how the trauma manifests itself in subsequent generations. As for legal recourse, one may ask how victim groups, especially those that are also dispossessed of their goods, properties, and even homeland, can place their case before national and international bodies that tend to be made up of mutually-protective nation-states? Might the outcome for the Armenian victims and survivors have been different if the international tribunals that now operate in the Hague and elsewhere been empowered at the time? Finally, how is it possible to seek legal recourse and to have truth prevail over perceived national interests? Is it possible to liberate history and human rights from politics?

Richard Hovannisian
Holder, AEF Chair
Modern Armenian History
UCLA

"Do you think of yourself as an Armenian?
Or an American? Or hyphenated American?"
—D.M. Thomas

Chapter 1

IDENTITY AND HISTORY

WE BEGIN TO LEARN OUR CULTURE—THE WAYS OF OUR SOCIETY—JUST AFTER BIRTH. THIS PROCESS IS CALLED socialization, and it involves far more than schooling. It influences our values—what we consider right and wrong. Our religious beliefs are an integral part of our culture, as is our racial and ethnic heritage. Our culture shapes the way we work and play, and it makes a difference in the way we view ourselves and others. Psychologist Deborah Tannen warns of our tendency to generalize about the things we observe and the people we encounter. "Generalizations, while capturing similarities, obscure differences. Everyone is shaped by innumerable influences such as ethnicity, religion, race, age, profession, the geographical regions they and their relatives have lived in, and many other group identities—all mingled with personality and predilection."[1]

The readings in this chapter address questions about how people come to understand their place in the world. The questions are raised through the stories of individual Armenians. As you read their stories and hear their questions, you will come to see that many of their challenges are familiar to all of us. These readings ask: What factors influence how we see ourselves? How can we keep our individuality and still be part of a group? What role does group and family history play in shaping the way we see ourselves and the way others see us? And, finally, how do all of these facets of identity influence the choices that people make.

Project SAVE Armenian Photograph Archives, Inc., Courtesy of Jack Chiljian, boy on right.

An Armenian family, Ordu, Ottoman Empire, c. 1905.

Today most Armenians do not live in the Republic of Armenia. Indeed, they live in many countries and have deep ties to the countries where they live. Like a lot of us, many Armenians find themselves balancing their role in their new country with their historical and cultural roots. How far should they assimilate into their new countries? Does Armenian history and culture have something to offer Armenians as they go on with their lives now? When do historical and cultural memories create self-imposed limits on individuals?

This chapter also explores the way identity passes down from one generation to another. These issues are especially important for a group that lives with the memory of a genocide in which over a million and a half Armenians were systematically murdered between 1915 and 1923 in what is now Turkey. The deliberate historical revision, denial of the genocide, and the politicization of traumatic memory have consequences for the generations that live in the shadow of that history. Psychologist Ervin Staub, author of *The Roots of Evil*, observes that we can all learn about ourselves from the way Armenians have responded. He writes:

> *The intense need of the Armenians as individuals and as a community to have the genocide be acknowledged and known by the world teaches us something about ourselves as human beings. First, our identities are rooted not only in our group, but in the history of our group. For a complete identity, we must be integrated not only with our individual past, but also with our groups' past. Perhaps, this becomes especially important when our group is partly destroyed and dispersed; our families and ourselves have been deeply affected; and in a physical sense we have at best fragments of our group. Second, we have a profound need for our pain and suffering, especially when it is born of injustice, to be acknowledged, known and respected.*" [2]

Reading 1 — WHAT'S IN A NAME?

Individuals begin to understand their own identity—who they are—from their families, peers, traditions, values, history, and society in which they live. One of the first markers of that identity is a name. Names are often chosen very carefully to send a message to the child and the larger society about who a person is. For many national and ethnic groups, names convey an even deeper meaning, especially when members of those groups find themselves living outside their traditional homeland. Names can be a statement of identity, marker of membership, a sign of difference, or all of these.

Writers from Sandra Cisneros to Ralph Ellison have discussed the relationship between names and individual identity. It is a theme that has been picked up by many prominent Armenian writers as well, including Michael Arlen, Peter Balakian, Diana Der-Hovanessian, and William Saroyan.

In his memoir *Black Dog of Fate*, Peter Balakian uses the stories behind family names as a metaphor for the way history, family experiences, and individual identity become intertwined.

> *My grandmother's big brown eyes keep watching me intensely. I am Peter, Bedros in Armenian, named after her second husband, who went into a coma from a cerebral hemorrhage about the week I was con-*

> *ceived and who died without regaining consciousness about three months before I was born. I am the eldest grandchild east of Fresno, California, the first male [in] the next generation, a filial position that in our Near Eastern culture comes with patriarchal status. . . . I did not understand then what the presence of a new generation meant for a culture that had been nearly expunged from the planet only forty-five years earlier. . . .[3]*

Balakian's grandmother was a survivor of the Armenian Genocide. Balakian writes that "when I was with my grandmother I had access to some other world, some evocative place of dark and light, some kind of energy that ran like an invisible force from this old country called Armenia to my world in New Jersey."[4] After the death of Peter's grandmother the other world intruded into Peter's suburban American childhood through the rituals and stories of his family.

Peter Balakian with his grandmothers, June 1953. Nafina Aroosian, a survivor of the Armenian Genocide, is on the right.

Photo courtesy of Peter Balakian

As Balakian grew, exploration of his mother's name became an opening for him to learn about the collective history of the Armenian people.

Arax Aroosian. My mother's name. Unplaceable sounds to the American ear. A name that must have baffled teachers in Paterson in the 1930s when they stared at it on the top of the class list. Arax: a name of eastern Anatolia and the southern Caucasus, where the Araxes River flows from the Ararat plateau eastward and makes a border uniting Armenia, Turkey, and Iran. A name that means turbulence, synonymous with the river.

Aroosian, a name part Arabic and part Armenian, meaning "son of the bride," or more idiomatically, "son of beautiful ones." A name of southeastern Anatolia, north of Nineveh, where the Tigris hooks around the ancient stone-walled city of Diarbekir, a city the Hurrians, Urartians, Assyrians, Armenians, Persians, Greeks, Romans, Arabs, and Turks all controlled at one time or another. Diarbekir: a linguistic estuary where Armenian, Kurdish, Turkish, Arabic, and French mingled, forming a creole language that Armenians spoke. Dikranagerdsi Armenian, they called it, because they called their city by its Armenian name, Dikranagerd, the city of King Dikran, who was the most powerful king of the Armenian Empire at its height, circa 50 B.C. Diarbekir: a killing city where the Turkish government killed more than a hundred thousand Armenians in 1915....[5]

In Michael Arlen's *Passage to Ararat*, names create discomfort. Early in the book Arlen reflects on his father's name.

At the age of twenty-one he had changed his name from Dikran Kouyoumjian to Michael Arlen.

My mother (who was American and Greek) sometimes called my father Dikran in private, and this was the only way I knew as a child that he was something other than—or in addition to—English. "It's an Armenian name," she explained to me one long-ago afternoon. For a while, I thought this referred to the kind of name—a private name. I understood that some of my far-off my uncles were called Kouyoumjian—an odd and difficult name for a child to scrawl on a thank-you letter. But my father, while he was well disposed toward the uncles, evidently detached himself from the name.[6]

CONNECTIONS

↝ A journal is a way of documenting the process of one's thinking. For author Joan Didion and others, it is also a way of examining ideas. She explains: "I write entirely to find out what I'm thinking, what I'm looking at, what I see, and what it means." You may find it helpful to use a journal to explore the ideas raised in this resource book. Begin by writing about your own name. How did you get it? What does it connect you to?

❧ You may choose to write on the subject of your name—first name, last name, whole name, or nickname—for five minutes. This exercise may serve as an icebreaker in a class. Share your reflections in pairs before reporting back to the larger group. You may have partners share some of what they have learned about each other.

❧ What do names connect people with? Can those ties be severed when the name is changed?

❧ What are the connections between Peter Balakian and his family name?

❧ What might have influenced Michael Arlen's father to change his name?

In her novel *The House on Mango Street*, Sandra Cisneros' narrator, Esperanza, reflects on her name.

> *In English my name means hope. In Spanish it means too many letters. It means sadness, it means waiting. It is like the number nine. A muddy color. It is the Mexican records my father plays on Sunday mornings when he is shaving, songs like sobbing.*
>
> *It was my great-grandmother's name and now is mine. She was a horse woman too, born like me in the Chinese year of the horse—which is supposed to be bad luck if you're born female....*
>
> *At school they say my name funny as if the syllables were made out of tin and hurt the roof of your mouth. But in Spanish my name is made of a softer something, like silver, not quite as thick as sister's name—Magdalena—which is uglier than mine. Magdelena who at least can come home and become Nenny. But I am always Esperanza.*
>
> *I would like to baptize myself under a new name, a name more like the real me, the one nobody sees. Esperanza as Lisandra or Maritza or Zeze the X. Yes. Something like Zeze the X will do.*[7]

❧ What does Esperanza connect with her name?

❧ Why do you think she wants to change her name?

❧ What does her desire to change her name suggest about the relationship between names and identity?

❧ How does Esperanza's reflection connect with the stories shared by Peter Balakian and Michael Arlen?

⌣

Reading 2 — MULTIPLE IDENTITIES

Often people have many identities that are important to who they are as individuals. Many times those identities exist in the same person without creating conflict. For example a person may be an African-American woman, with one grandparent from Ecuador and another from Russia, and the daughter of parents who are both Christian—one Episcopalian and the other Catholic. For her, all these identities may live harmoniously, while in others they could provide a source of conflict.

Diana Der-Hovanessian is an Armenian-American writer born in the United States. Her grandparents came to the United States from Ottoman Armenia. In her poem "Two Voices," Diana Der-Hovanessian reflects on how her family history influences who she is as a person. The poem begins with a question from the British writer D.M. Thomas.

Project SAVE Armenian Photograph Archives, Inc., courtesy of George and Miriam Kachadorian Markarian.

Armenian immigrants celebrating Easter in Worcester, MA, U.S.A., 1925.

Two Voices

by Diana Der-Hovanessian

"Do you think of yourself as an Armenian?
Or an American? Or hyphenated American?"
—D.M. Thomas

In what language do I pray?

Do I meditate in language?

In what language am I trying
to speak when I wake from dreams?

Do I think of myself as an American,
or simply as a women when I wake?

Or do I think of the date and geography
I wake into, as a woman?

Do I think of myself in my clothes
getting wet walking in the rain?

Do I think velvet, or do I think skin?

Am I always conscious of genes and
heredity or merely how to cross my legs
at the ankle like a New England lady?

In a storm do I think of lightning
striking? Or white knives dipped
into my great aunt's sisters'
sisters' blood?

Do I think of my grandfather telling
about the election at the time
of Teddy Roosevelt's third party,

and riding with Woodrow Wilson
in a Main Street parade
in Worcester?

Or do I think of my grandmother
At Ellis Island,

or as an orphan in an Armenian village?

Or at a black stove in Worcester
baking blueberry pie for my grandfather
who preferred food he had grown
to like in lonely mill town
cafeterias while he studied
for night school?

Do I think of them as Armenian
or as tellers of the thousand and
one wonderful tales in two languages?

Do I think of myself as hyphenated?

No. Most of the time, even as you,
I forget labels.

Unless you cut me.

Then I look at the blood.
It speaks in Armenian.[8]

Courtesy of Richard Hovannisian

Richard Hovannisian on his family's farm.

Richard Hovannisian, Professor of Armenian and Near Eastern History at the University of California Los Angeles, grew up in a small Armenian community in the San Joaquin Valley of California. A dozen or so Armenian families lived in his rural town: "almost all farmers of small vineyards and nearly all from the same village in historic Armenia." Hovannisian recalls hearing Armenian women, survivors of the genocide, sharing stories of the horrors that they had witnessed. During his childhood, he was not aware of the impact these stories would have on his life. He tried to distance himself from the older generation. He remembers:

I was sure I was not a hyphenated American. In fact, like most of my generation, even though we were the children of survivors or of first generation immigrants, the tribulations of the older generation seemed to have little bearing on our lives. [The Armenian Genocide] was something that had occurred far away and a long time ago—all of ten or fifteen years.[9]

CONNECTIONS

Below is an identity chart for a high school student from the United States.

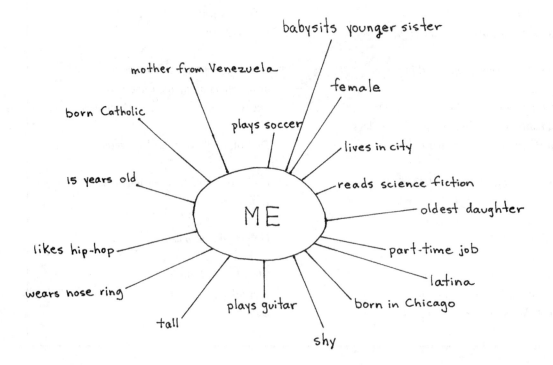

➤ Using this model, create an identity chart for Diana Der-Hovanessian. What labels does she use for herself? How do you decide which labels should be most prominent?

➤ Create an identity chart for yourself. Begin with words or phrases that describe the way you see yourself. Add those words and phrases to your chart. Compare your chart with those of your classmates. Which categories appeared on every chart? Which of them appeared on only a few charts? As you look at other charts, your perspective may change. You may wish to revise your chart and add new categories to those you have already included.

➤ This activity allows you to see the world through multiple perspectives. What labels would others attach to you? Do they see you as a leader or a follower? A conformist or a rebel? Are you a peacemaker or a bully. Are you an active participant or a bystander? How do society's labels influence the way you see yourself? The kinds of choices you make each day? Note the many identities that make up who you are. Consider which of them are most prominent in shaping your identity. Which identities might someone who does not know you recognize? Which would they fail to see?

➤ Diana Der-Hovanessian wrote "Two Voices" in response to a question: "Do you think of yourself as an Armenian? Or an American? Or hyphenated American?" How does she answer that question? Are there times when one aspect of your identity seems more important than others?

➤ How do children of immigrants negotiate their identity in a new culture? What pressures do they face that are unique? Which pressures are shared by their peers?

➤ Richard Hovannisian says that as a boy he was sure that he "was not a hyphenated American." What does he mean? What are the ways that people can honor their multiple identities? Why are some people threatened by the recognition of dual identities and multiple loyalties?

➤ In "Two Voices," Diana Der-Hovanessian writes that her blood speaks Armenian. She is not describing literal truth. She is using a metaphor to make a point. Scientists know identity and nationality are not literally carried in the blood, but the expression that "it's in my blood" remains part of everyday speech. If identity isn't literally carried in the blood, how is it passed from generation to generation?

Similar issues to those raised in "Two Voices" can be found in the Facing History and Ourselves study guide for the documentary *Becoming American: The Chinese Experience*. The guide is available at *www.facinghistory.org*, and the film is available from the Facing History and Ourselves resource library and *www.pbs.org*.

To extend a study of the relationship between the Individual and Society, see Chapter 1 of *Facing History and Ourselves: Holocaust and Human Behavior* as well as opening readings from all of the Facing History and Ourselves resource materials.

Reading 3 — AM I ARMENIAN?

What makes us part of a group? Biology? Language? Religion? Experience? Geography? And what holds those groups together over time? Most Armenians live in diaspora—scattered across the globe from the country of Armenia throughout the Middle East and the United States. Diana Der-Hovanessian's poem "Diaspora" captures the complex relationship between an Armenian-American and her "father's land."

Diaspora
by Diana Der-Hovanessian

I am the tourist
who looks just like
the native girl
who greets me, salt
and bread on her tray.

We have the same eyes,
the same smile and stride
but different tongues with which to say.

I am the stranger
in my father's land,
the traveler to the country
I can neither leave
nor stay,
a foreigner in the place,
where millenniums ago
my kind was bred.

I am no one
without these trees, these stones
and streets. But their shadows
have grown short and tall without my weight.

I am the tourist
from far away
where I left tables of plenty
thirsty and unfed.[10]

↩

Armenian Refugee, photograph by John Elder, c. 1917-1919.

Sara Cohan, a teacher, also struggled with her relationship to Armenia and Armenian identity. She writes: "I do not practice the religion, speak the language, I am not directly from Armenia, and I only take part in a few of the traditions."

While visiting an Armenian school in California, those issues came to a head when a student at the school asked: "How is it again that you are Armenian?" Cohan shared her reflections on the student's question:

She had not meant for her question to hurt or challenge me, but it did. To know and love Armenian foods like choereg, boreg, and dolma does not make me Armenian. Knowing simple catch phrases like "gameer maz" (red hair) or "Sode gus-ez?" (Would you like a soda?) does not make me Armenian. My family's experiences during the Armenian Genocide makes me Armenian.

Born and raised in the United States, I am an American, but I have always considered myself to be Armenian too. Being American is who I am and Armenian is who my family was. When I talk to friends about being Armenian I inevitably start with the Armenian Genocide, because that is where my family always begins the discussion of who we are. In another way, the Armenian Genocide is where my family's story ended since only a handful survived the genocide.

As an Armenian, I feel compelled to teach the history of the Genocide to whoever will listen because the story is not over. Without an apology and without reparations from the Turkish government, my ancestors died in vain.

Photo courtesy of Sara Cohan

I am proud of my grandfather because he survived a genocide and was successful in his life. He started a family and was a psychiatrist trained at the American University of Beirut. He eventually helped establish the school of psychiatry at the University of Tennessee. At the same time, I mourn the loss of a lineage—sixty-nine members of my family perished in the genocide and only seven lived. There are approximately 6.1 billion people in the world and approximately 8 million Armenians. Most are in Diaspora and disappearing quickly. What my ancestors have accomplished and endured is worthy of remembrance and respect. With so few Armenians left in the world each one needs to do as much as s/he can to teach others about Armenians and the Genocide.

Sara Cohan's family after the genocide.

Recently, I saw The Official Story, *a movie about the Disappeared in Argentina. In the beginning of the film the main character is teaching a history course in a high school. She tells the class: "No people can survive without memory. History is the memory of the people." When I heard those lines I finally knew how I could answer the young girl who asked how I was Armenian: I was born a descendant of Armenians and I am Armenian because my love for my grandfather has inspired me to learn about Armenian history and the history of the Genocide. I am Armenian because I will never forget my family's history and, as long as I remember, Armenians will survive.*

Thousands of Armenian survivors settled in communities in the United States that had been established in the late nineteenth and early twentieth centuries. Many of the survivors did not speak about their history, and many of the second generation did not make a concerted effort to learn about their history. In more recent generations, people like Sara Cohan have begun to explore their Armenian heritage. For many, one of the starting points for that exploration has become Peter Balakian's memoir *Black Dog of Fate*. Although Balakian learned about the genocide later in life, other rituals and traditions marked his Armenian identity, like baking Armenian treats with his grandmother while she shared mysterious stories from the old world. As a boy, Balakian recalls seeing his Jewish neighbors celebrating Jewish holidays and he recalls asking his mother why his family was not Jewish.

"Because we're Christians," she answered.

"Why are we Christians?"

"Our people decided to follow the teachings of Jesus." She paused. "There's a legend that Noah's ark landed on Mt. Ararat in Armenia. That makes Jews and Armenians cousins."

"What's Mt. Ararat?"

My mother exhaled as if she wished I would go away. "Mt. Ararat is our national symbol."

"The symbol of America?"

"No. Of Armenia."

"Where's Armenia?"

As long as I had known language the word Armenia had existed; it was synonymous with the rooms of my house. As assumption. Ar. Meen. Ya. Armenia. Like ma-ma, da-da. Like hurt and horse. Arm. You. Me. Eat. The word rolled to the back of my mouth and just as I almost swallowed it, I caught it back near the epiglottis and unrolled it, pushing it forward as my jaw dropped open to the Ya and the word spilled into the air. Armenia. It was such an unconscious part of my life that I had never even thought to ask: Where is it? What is it? [11]

CONNECTIONS

* What makes us part of a group? What holds groups together? How are religious and ethnic groups different from groups of friends or from colleagues at work?

* Most Armenians live in diaspora—spread across the world. How is it possible for a group to hold on to a cohesive group identity when they are so spread out? What tools might people use to maintain their culture?

* What is Diana Der-Hovanessian's relationship to her "father's land"? What words does she use to describe that relationship?

* Do you feel connected to any countries beyond the one in which you live? What is your relationship to that place? What words do you use to describe your connection?

* After reading the poem "Diaspora," you may choose to revise the identity chart you created for Diana Der-Hovanessian. Which words would you consider adding? Have the issues raised in her poem "Diaspora" influenced the ways you think about your own identity? You may choose to revise your own identity chart as you encounter new ideas from the readings or from discussions with your classmates.

* Create an identity chart for Sara Cohan. Compare her identity chart with the one you created for Diana Der-Hovanessian. How are they similar? Which differences do you find most striking?

* How can someone be part of a group without being actively involved in many of the customs that have traditionally been part of the group's identity? How would Sara Cohan answer that question?

* Peter Balakian says that Armenia was synonymous with the rooms of his house: "It was such an unconscious part of my life that I had never even thought to ask: Where is it? What is it?" How does an identity become unconscious? What sort of experiences bring questions of identity to the surface?

* At the Armenian school she visited, Cohan noticed that many of the students would "assign degrees of Armenianness to their peers." Why would kids do that? What does it suggest about their identity and the way they feel about themselves? To create a "we," or an "in" group, do groups also need to create a "they"?

Reading 4 — GENERATIONS

Families pass stories down from generation to generation. Often these stories become the lore around which a family shares their identity and values. For many children, the stories of their parents and grandparents have a profound effect on the way they understand their own role in society.

What happens when these family stories are about being victims of injustice? What happens, not only to the survivors, but also to their children, when the larger world has not acknowledged that injustice? Journalist J.D. Lasica spoke to several Armenian families living in Sacramento, California, about the legacy of the Armenian Genocide and its impact on their family's identity. In the first of two stories in this reading Lasica writes about a relationship between a mother and her son:

"Emmy" has never before told her story to an odar, the Armenian word for foreigner. There is a reason for this: She does not speak English.

Emmy—an English transliteration of the Arabic word for "mother"—is what everyone calls Haygouhi Shahinian.

At an even 5 feet tall, she is a slight, wiry woman of 86, with white hair and a high-pitched voice. Her son, George, translates, but she forges ahead with her story before he can get the words out.

"I remember when the troubles started," she begins. "I was in the first grade, in Tarsus. One day my grandmother came and pulled me out of school. She was crying. We rushed home, and my father and uncle were standing with a gun at the window, looking at all the commotion in the streets.

"Finally, our whole family ran off to the fields on the outskirts of town. The Allewi (a [Muslim] sect) farmers were helping Armenians to hide there. We hid in the fields for three days, but the Turkish government declared that anyone helping Armenians would be put to death. So the farmers began to turn the people in the fields over to the soldiers.

"The Turkish soldiers began rounding us up in groups for firing squads. They were getting ready to shoot the next group of us when suddenly I saw an officer on a white horse come galloping, shouting in Turkish, 'Do not cut (kill) the Armenians, they have been pardoned by the new government.' We were so happy we were going to live, we showered the officer with kisses. We showered his horse with kisses."

Emmy clasps her face, and she takes a deep breath. Her account, like the others', meshes with the historical literature: The [new] Ottoman government was overthrown briefly in April 1909; there were massacres in the Tarsus [Cilicia] region at that time.

Emmy returns to her story: It is six years later, and her family has moved to Adana, a nearby city.

"In 1915, the Turkish government ordered all Armenians in our village to be deported into the Syrian desert," she says. "The local mayor—he was Turk—tried to prevent [this], but he was told to follow orders. The gendarmes gathered us into a caravan, and we set off, a thousand of us. My parents bribed the officials to let us take two small mule-driven carts. Along the way, we had to bribe the guards for food and water.

"Halfway through our journey, at the town of Ghatma, we passed a death field. Bodies, death were everywhere." An earlier caravan had passed this way.

"After 18 days, we reached Aleppo (a city in what is now Syria). They let some of us go, but we had nothing. We were forced to live like paupers on the street. My father supported us by working for the town—he used his wagon to pick up corpses, stacking them in the cart and hauling them to the city dump."

When the massacres ended, the Armenians were not allowed to return to their homeland, so Emmy's family remained in Aleppo. Life was better after that.

She married and raised six children. The youngest, George, came to this country in 1959 to attend college before settling with his family in Carmichael [California]. Emmy followed in 1971.

George Shahinian is quiet for a long time. This is the first time he has heard his mother's story at length. Finally, he says quietly: "It was just a miracle that she escaped. For our whole family, there was a very thin thread between life and death."

Shahinian, 55, is a short, soft-spoken man who wears bifocals and a kind expression. He works as a mechanical engineer with the state Air Resources Board.

Shahinian worries that his three children will not fully appreciate what the Armenians endured. "It's important to remember who we are and where we came from," he says.

One way the Shahinians tried to pass along a sense of ethnic identity to their children was through language.

An Armenian family before the genocide, c. 1900.

Leon, at 22 the eldest, recalls: "Up until I was 4 or 5, we spoke only Armenian in the house. Then I went to kindergarten and picked up English after only a couple of weeks. Now, when I'm home, my parents still speak to me in Armenian, but I answer in English."

Shahinian still worries about his children's assimilation. "It's weakening our culture. We don't know how to stop it, and when it comes to our kids, I'm not sure, deep inside, we want to stop it."[12]

J.D. Lasica also interviewed two generations of Boyajians, who shared some of their stories about Armenian identity in the United States.

Joyce Poirot is the only offspring of Mesrop Boyajian, the boy who was sold into slavery for a silver coin.

Boyajian seldom talked about his experience, so it was not until adulthood that Poirot understood her father's place in the massacres. But she knew, from her early years in Detroit, that there was something about her heritage that set her apart.

"I knew it from the secret language we spoke at home and the way my grandmother dressed me," she says. "I knew it when I'd open my lunch box in kindergarten. Everybody else would have bologna on Wonder Bread. I'd open mine, and a couple of kuftas (meatballs) or lahmajoun (meat pies), smelling of garlic, would roll out."

Poirot, 51, rests on a sofa in her downtown condominium. She is a top academic administrator at the University of California, Davis, overseeing a statewide continuing-education program.

"My first awareness of Armenians being discriminated against came after our family moved to Fresno when I was 11," she says. "In Detroit, an Armenian was just another minority. But in Fresno, we were looked down upon.

"A few years later I came across a photograph of a sign in Fig Garden, an exclusive area of Fresno. It said, 'No Negroes, No Jews, No Mexicans, No Armenians.' And I thought, wow, this is for real."

As a young adult she became estranged from her culture because of the way in which women have been treated in traditional Armenian households. But Poirot has now made peace with her roots.

"About 10 years ago I began realizing there was a part of me I didn't know," she explains.

In 1983 she traveled to Yerevan, capital of Soviet Armenia. There she came upon the monument called Dzidzernagabert, or Fortress of [Swallows]. It is dedicated to the victims of the Armenian tragedy.

Poirot recalls: "The first time I came up to it, I was with my (now former) husband. I thought, 'This is no tourist site; this is something I want to be alone with.' Suddenly and unexpectedly I felt part of that distant experience.

"Later, when the sun was setting, I went back alone. I was just overcome, wracked with pain and grief and tears. I felt connected with it, with the martyrs, with my past. I felt there's no escaping it—it's in me. There's no more denying that I carry pieces of the trauma."

There is a long silence, and then: "I think I finally came to terms with it by accepting it."

Poirot's father, Mesrop Boyajian, ambles over to the television in his apartment, flicks it off, and settles into his favorite chair. "It's not a pleasant thing to talk about, being sold as a slave," he says, "so I very seldom talk about it."

Boyajian is 80 years old. He has smooth features, good, strong hands that once worked the vineyards, and a lilting, almost boyish voice. A patch of white hair shoots up from his head.

1915–1916, two orphaned Armenian boys, Ottoman Empire, in what is now Syria. Photograph by Armin T. Wegner.

Courtesy of the Armenian National Institute

Looking back on his stolen youth, he lets out a hollow sigh and says, "It feels like I've lost something. Something of myself."

Of course, things might have been worse, he points out. "Perhaps I was lucky to have been sold. Otherwise, who knows what would have happened? I understood later that most of those kids who were not sold died in the desert."

For Boyajian, freedom carried a $40 price tag. When he was 16, his brothers sent him the money to join them in the United States. Mesrop had no trouble getting permission to leave from his Syrian owners, who were grateful for 10 years of good work.

He entrusted the $40 with a Near East Relief missionary, who arranged for an Arab guide to smug-

gle him and 10 other Armenian children across the Turkish border to Aleppo, Syria. From there, he made his way to New York in 1925.

Boyajian spent 21 years in the U.S. Army, serving in World War II, when he won a Purple Heart, and in Korea. He lived for years in the Bay Area before settling in Sacramento.

"I have seen many many things in my time," Boyajian says philosophically. "Men are capable of great evil...."[13]

CONNECTIONS

Psychologist Ervin Staub, author of *The Roots of Evil*, has written about the impact of the genocide on Armenian identity. He observed:

The intense need of the Armenians as individuals and as a community to have the genocide be acknowledged and known by the world teaches us something about ourselves as human beings. First, our identities are rooted not only in our group, but in the history of our group. For a complete identity, we must be integrated not only with our individual past, but also with our group's past. Perhaps, this becomes especially important when our group is partly destroyed and dispersed; our families and ourselves have been deeply affected; and in a physical sense we have at best fragments of our group. Second, we have a profound need for our pain and suffering, especially when it is born of injustice, to be acknowledged, known and respected.[14]

☙ What happens when that history has not been acknowledged?

In a book that explores the relationship between family and identity, Elizabeth Stone writes:

We are shaped by our families' notions of our identities which exist as an idea beyond the reach of measurement. The image they mirror back to us exists earlier and more substantially than we ourselves do. And among the primary vehicles families use to mirror us to ourselves are the family stories we hear about ourselves. These stories ... are a record of our family's fantasies, often unconscious about who they hope we are or fear we are.[15]

☙ What parts of our identity are within "the reach of measurement"? What parts exist beyond its reach? What hopes and fears for the family and cultural identity emerge from the stories of the Boyajians and the Shahinians?

☙ How do the two families' experiences of survival affect the ways they think about Armenian identity? What aspects of Armenian identity seem most important to Joyce Poirot and George Shahinian?

↝ Why do you think Poirot's father, Mesrop Boyajian, has been reluctant to talk about his experiences during the genocide? How do you think the experience influenced the way he saw himself?

↝ As a follow up to this reading, interview your relatives about their identity and values. How have they come to understand their place in the world? What experiences and ideas have shaped their values?

↝ Many scholars have written about the pain caused by deniers who claim the genocide never happened. Professor Henry Theriault writes that for some survivors the psychological consequences of trauma can be mitigated over time, but denial blocks this, expanding the genocide's impact over time and increasing the original trauma. He argues: "Deniers thrust the genocide back onto its victims, so they must recall the violence done to and witnessed by them."[16] Several scholars note that trauma, when not responded to, can be passed down through families. What do you imagine would help to break the cycle?

↝ Haygouhi Shahinian and Mesrop Boyajian are not only survivors. They are refugees as well. They left their homeland and moved to the United States because of the oppression they faced in the Ottoman Empire. Are there refugee communities where you live? Who are they? What stories do they have to tell? What can you learn from their experiences?

↝

NOTES

1. Deborah Tannen, *You Just Don't Understand* (New York: Morrow, 1990), preface.
2. Ervin Staub, "The Genocide of the Armenians: Psychological and Cultural Roots and the Impact on Survivors," *Armenian Review*, 42 (Winter 1989), p. 55.
3. Peter Balakian, *Black Dog of Fate* (New York: Basic Books, 1997), p. 5.
4. Ibid., p. 17.
5. Ibid., p. 59.
6. Michael J. Arlen, *Passage to Ararat* (Saint Paul: Hungry Mind Press, 1996), pp. 3–4.
7. Sandra Cisneros, *The House on Mango Street* (New York: Vintage Contemporaries, 1991), pp. 10–11.
8. Diana Der-Hovanessian, "Two Voices," in *Selected Poems* (New York: Sheep Meadow Press, 1994), p. 23.
9. Richard Hovannisian speaking in Providence, Rhode Island, March 26, 2000.
10. Diana Der-Hovanessian, "Diaspora," in *Selected Poems* (New York: Sheep Meadow Press, 1994), p. 11.
11. Balakian, *Black Dog of Fate*, p. 40.
12. J.D. Lasica, "Emmy Shahinian," available at *http://www.well.com/user/jd/armenia2.html*.
13. J.D. Lasica, "The Boyajians," available at *http://www.well.com/user/jd/armenia3.html*.
14. Staub, "Genocide of the Armenians," p. 55.
15. Elizabeth Stone, *Black Sheep and Kissing Cousins* (New York: Times Books, 1988), p. 167.
16. Henry C. Theriault, "Denial and Free Speech: The Case of the Armenian Genocide," in *Looking Forward, Moving Backward: Confronting the Armenian Genocide*, Richard Hovannisian ed. (New Brunswick: Transaction Publications, 2003), pp. 231–262.

" There has been no war, no conflict between the two contending powers, but a pitiless tornado of bloody ruin....Has it come to this, that in the last days of the nineteenth century humanity has placed itself on trial? "
—U.S. Senator Shelby Collum

Chapter 2

WE AND THEY
Armenians in the Ottoman Empire

THROUGHOUT HISTORY MANY PEOPLE HAVE ESCAPED PERSECUTION AND VIOLENCE IN THEIR HOMELANDS and taken refuge in countries that have provided them an opportunity to start again. This book is about the twentieth-century genocide of the Armenians. In every history, some stories are particular, while others connect universally. The first chapter of this resource book examined the power of historical memory to shape identity. It looked at how Armenians today are influenced by stories of the Armenian past and the impact those stories have on their identity. Most of those stories were told by families who settled in the United States as refugees. This chapter begins a case study of the choices that ultimately resulted in the genocide of the Armenians in the Ottoman Empire and forced those families from their homes. As we tell this story our focus will be on the responses by individuals, groups, and nations—inside and outside of the Ottoman Empire—to the treatment of Armenians before and during the genocide. The readings focus on the roots of violence, the roles of leaders, the power of stereotyping, and the creation of the "other." It is important to study the steps that led to violence. If we can recognize how a conflict escalates, perhaps we can prevent future genocides.

The case of the Armenians under Ottoman rule offers insight into the problems faced by advocates for humanitarian causes. These problems become especially grave when there are no common rules for the

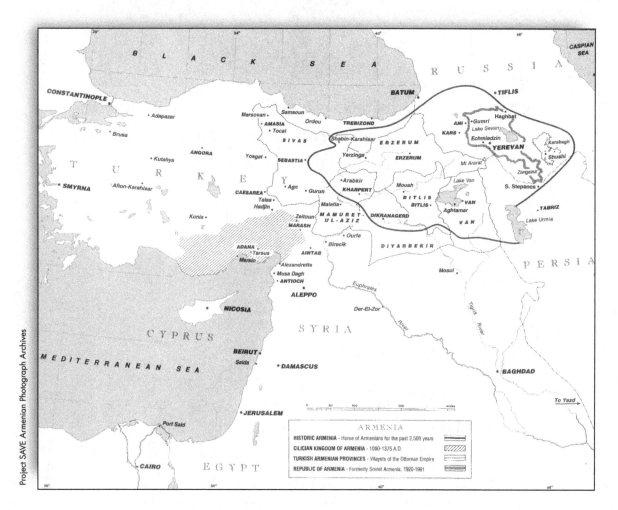

HISTORIC ARMENIA

This map of historic Armenia shows the general area that Armenia once encompassed, notable in comparison to the much smaller area delineated as the Republic of Armenia at the end of World War I.

protection of human rights. Many people wanted to protect the Armenians by including them in what Helen Fein calls "the Universe of Obligation"[17]—a circle of individuals and groups toward whom obligations are owed, to whom rules apply, and whose injuries call for amends. Without an international system for the protection of human rights, advocates of the Armenians met stiff resistance and, in the face of unfulfilled promises, left the Armenians even more vulnerable.

The Armenians are an ancient people that have lived on much of the same land for more than two thousand years. For some of that time, they ruled their own kingdom. During long periods of Armenian history, however, they have been a subject population, ruled by others. By the sixteenth century the Armenians were subjects in the Ottoman Empire. The Ottoman sultan ruled not only as a monarch but also assumed the title of Caliph—the official leader of the Islamic faithful. Ottoman law conformed in many ways with Islamic law and was overseen by the Sheikh-ul-Islam (a religious leader who was appointed by the sultan). Christians and Jews, including Armenians, Bulgarians, Croatians, Greeks, Romanians, Serbs, and others, were classified as *dhimmi* (protected subject non-Muslims). The dhimmi were granted considerable religious freedom, but they were not subject to Islamic law and therefore were without equal legal standing. Codes also prohibited non-Muslims from certain professions—including service in the Ottoman army—and subjected them to additional taxes. Despite their second-class status, as long as the empire prospered the Armenians fared reasonably well.

During the nineteenth century, the Ottoman Empire's fortunes declined. The economy stagnated, and corruption was rampant. In addition, the empire was in debt to the European powers, especially France, England, and Belgium. Life for Armenians and other non-Muslims became progressively more difficult. Burdened by increasing taxation and without legal means to protect themselves or their families from exploitation, the subject populations looked for a way to improve their conditions.

Nationalism—the belief in a collective identity and destiny determined by membership in an ethnic, linguistic, or religious group—influenced the various groups of the empire. While the Greeks and others sought to break from the empire, Armenians were not concentrated in a single area that could easily become an independent state. Instead, they placed their hopes on promised reforms of the Ottoman administration. While waiting for the reforms to materialize, Armenians organized in a movement for civil rights. The sultan, however, responded to Armenian protests with repression and massacre. Some Armenian leaders now believed that help had to come from the outside.

There was a precedent for intervention on the behalf of Ottoman minorities. After the Greek revolution of 1821, the Great Powers—England, France, and Russia—became increasingly involved in Ottoman affairs. Describing the conditions of the Empire to a British envoy, Czar Nicholas I of Russia explained: "What we have on our hands is a sick man—a very sick man." What to do with the sick man became the obsession of European journalists and diplomats. Sometimes the European powers supported the independence struggles of Ottoman subjects as opportunities to achieve their own strategic interests under the guise of "humanitarian intervention." At the same time, the growth of the media and a burgeoning concern for human rights made it possible for ordinary people, thousands of miles from the Ottoman Empire, to read about the suffering of the Armenians. In the United States, a movement for Armenian relief began in Christian churches but soon spread to communities at large and eventually to Congress.

By the late nineteenth century Armenian activists worked cooperatively with Turkish groups who were also advocating change. One of those groups, the Young Turks, a revolutionary organization promising equality for all, forced the sultan to enforce the Ottoman constitution and submit to constitutional rule in 1908.

This chapter traces that history by addressing several guiding questions.

◆ How do groups, nations, and empires define their "universe of obligation"?

◆ Who is responsible for protecting the vulnerable from being mistreated inside a sovereign state?

◆ When does humanitarian intervention make a difference on behalf of the vulnerable? What kinds of intervention leave the vulnerable population even more exposed?

◆ What is the difference between resisting oppression, advocating change, and revolution?

◆ What tensions emerge in the transition from a traditional society to a constitutional state?

From the private collection of Berj Fenerci

This postcard depicts Armenian women at work knitting socks in Ada-Pazar, Ottoman Empire. It was sent to the Armenian Church of Gedikpasha.

Reading 1 — THE OTTOMAN ARMENIANS

In the nineteenth century, Armenians were one national group within the vast Ottoman Empire. Over time, borders had changed and a portion of the traditional Armenian homeland had become part of the neighboring Russian Empire. Ottoman Armenians, like the rest of the population, were divided into millets, semi-autonomous communities organized by religion. Leaders of the millet ran most of the administration of the group including education and tax collection. While the sultan oversaw the Muslim millet—including Turks, Arabs, and Kurds—Christian patriarchs ran the Greek and Armenian millets, and the grand rabbi headed the Jewish millet. The leaders of the millets were held accountable for the behavior of the members of the group.

Under this system, Christians and Jews in the Ottoman Empire were second-class citizens.

Richard Hovannisian, the principal author of the 1988 California model curriculum for teaching about human rights explains: "Despite these disabilities, most Armenians lived in relative peace so long as the Ottoman Empire was strong and expanding." He continues:

> But as the empire's administrative, fiscal, and military structure crumbled under the weight of internal corruption and external challenges in the eighteenth and nineteenth centuries, oppression and intolerance increased. The breakdown of order was accelerated by Ottoman inability to modernize and compete with the West.
>
> The decay of the Ottoman Empire was paralleled by cultural and political revival among many of the subject peoples. The national liberation struggles, supported at times by one or another European power, resulted in the Turkish loss of Greece and most of the Balkan provinces in the nineteenth century and aggravated the Eastern Question; that is, what was to happen to the enervated empire and its constituent peoples. A growing number of Ottoman liberals came to believe that the empire's survival depended on effective administration reforms. These men were movers behind several significant reform measures promulgated between 1839 and 1876. Yet time and again the advocates of reform became disillusioned in the face of the entrenched, vested interests that stubbornly resisted change.
>
> Of the various subject peoples, the Armenians perhaps sought the least. Unlike the Balkan Christians or the Arabs, they were dispersed throughout the empire and no longer constituted an absolute majority in much of their historic homelands. Hence, most Armenian leaders did not think in terms of independence. Expressing loyalty to the sultan and disavowing any separatist aspirations, they petitioned for the protection of their people and property from corrupt officials and marauding bands. The Armenians had passed through a long period of cultural revival. Thousands of youngsters enrolled in elementary and secondary schools, and hundreds of students traveled to Europe for higher education. Many returned home imbued with ideas of the Enlightenment and the French Revolution to engage in teaching, journalism, and literary criticism. As it happened, however, this Armenian self-discovery was paralleled by height-

ened administrative corruption and exploitation. It was this dual development, the conscious demand for enlightened government and security of life on the one hand and the growing repression and insecurity on the other, that gave rise to the Armenian Question as a part of the larger Eastern Question.[18]

Even though conditions for Armenians continued to deteriorate, many Muslims felt that the sultan's reforms went too far. In *The Genesis of Young Ottoman Thought*, Serif Mardin writes that with reform came a backlash. After the 1856 law of nationalities was introduced: "Many [Muslims] began to grumble: 'Today we lost our sacred national rights which our ancestors gained with their blood. While the Islamic nation used to be the ruling nation, it is now bereft of this sacred right. This is a day of tears and mourning for the [Muslim] brethren.'"[19]

CONNECTIONS

✤ Many Europeans called the Ottoman Empire the "sick man of Europe." What makes a country sick?

✤ What minimum protections do individuals and groups need for safety and security?

✤ In the Ottoman Empire, religious affiliation determined the rules of membership in the larger society. In your community, what factors influence participation in the larger society?

✤ The Armenians, as Christians, were promised tolerance as "people of the book" under the Islamic law of the Ottoman Empire. Create a working definition of the word "tolerance"? What are the strengths of the idea of tolerance? What are the limitations of the idea?

✤ Richard Hovannisian notes, "as the empire's administrative, fiscal, and military structure crumbled under the weight of internal corruption and external challenges in the eighteenth and nineteenth centuries, oppression and intolerance increased." What is the relationship between the health of a society and its treatment of minorities?

✤ Psychologist Ervin Staub studies genocide and the prevention of collective violence. He notes that economic problems and widespread violence threaten individuals on a personal level. Staub suggests those forces influence the way people view the "other." How did the Ottoman "universe of obligation" change as the economic situation became worse? How do you explain the changes?

From the private collection of Berj Fenerci

Brousse. Intérieur de la Filature à Soie

This postcard is of a silk factory in Brossa that belonged to the Bay brothers, who were Armenian, 1890.

William Ramsay, a British ethnographer, described the impact of prejudice and discrimination on the Armenians in graphic terms:

> *Turkish rule . . . meant unutterable contempt. . . . The Armenians (and the Greek) were dogs and pigs . . . to be spat upon, if their shadow darkened a Turk, to be outraged, to be mats on which he wiped the mud from his feet. Conceive the inevitable results of centuries of slavery, of subjection to insult and scorn, centuries in which nothing that belonged to the Armenian, neither his property, his house, his life, his person, nor his family, was sacred or safe from violence—capricious, unprovoked violence—to resist which by violence meant death! I do not mean that every Armenian suffered so; but that every one lived in conscious danger from any chance disturbance or riot.[20]*

ᐦ What tools do people need to survive when living in "constant danger"?

ᐦ The authors of the California curriculum note a period of "Armenian self-discovery" during a time of increased discrimination. What is the relationship between ethnic and national awareness and discrimination? Under what conditions do individuals stress the importance of their group identity?

Successful movements for national liberation within the Ottoman Empire led to a huge loss of territory. *The American Heritage Dictionary of the English Language* defines nationalism as follows:

> 1. *Devotion to the interests or culture of one's nation.*
> 2. *The belief that nations will benefit from acting independently rather than collectively, emphasizing national rather than international goals.*
> 3. *Aspirations for national independence in a country under foreign domination.*[21]

ᐦ Why do you think some people view nationalism as a positive ideal while others believe it is dangerous? Should every national group have the right to form its own country? What problems might be resolved? What new challenges would you anticipate?

ᐦ Considering the recent loss of Greece and much of the Balkans, why would many Ottoman leaders believe that "Armenian self-discovery" was a threat? Why might many Armenians have considered "self-discovery" necessary for survival?

ᐦ When Ottoman rulers promised equal rights to the all nationalities of the empire, many Muslims interpreted these measures as a loss of their own status. How do people behave when they feel that their status is threatened? Why do you think many Muslims would have interpreted equal protection for all as a loss of their own rights?

Reading 2 — IRON LADLES FOR LIBERTY STEW

Throughout the nineteenth century, the Ottoman Empire fought several wars over territory. In 1877, Russia and the Ottoman Empire fought in the Balkans and in the traditional Armenian provinces of the empire. As the war went on, Armenians, who were legally forbidden from serving in the Ottoman military, faced a dilemma. Should they support the Russians, Christians, who promised the Armenians would be treated fairly under the Czar's rule, or should they remain loyal to the empire that treated them as second-class citizens? In a pastoral letter, the Armenian Patriarch—the official leader of the Armenian millet—called on his people to pray for the victory of the empire. Despite the loyalty of Armenians, Kurds (a Muslim nationality that lived in the Ottoman Empire), fighting as irregular soldiers, looted and burned several Armenian villages. In the aftermath, many Armenians greeted Russian troops, led by Russian Armenians, as liberators.

In January 1878, the Ottoman government asked Russia for an end to fighting, and peace negotiations began. Negotiations soon collapsed, and the Russian army moved towards the Ottoman capital. Their actions set off alarms through the capitals of Europe, and the British government sent a squadron to prevent the Russians from taking Constantinople [Istanbul]. At a meeting in San Stefano, on the outskirts of the Ottoman capital, a second attempt was made to come to terms for a lasting peace. The resulting treaty granted independence to Serbia, Montenegro, and Romania, and autonomy to Bulgaria. It also awarded Russia several districts in the Caucasus with large Armenian populations and warned that Russian troops would not leave the western Armenian districts until reforms were enacted to ensure the security of the Armenian population.

Archbishop Mkrtich Khrimian.

Courtesy of Azed Ozzie Aslanian, Antronig Shahinian, and Harry Dickran

Russian gains were too much for the European powers. They coerced Russia into renegotiating the treaty in Berlin during July, 1878. To the disappointment of the Armenian delegation, led by Armenian Archbishop Mkrtich Khrimian, Russia was pressured into withdrawing its troops from the Armenian provinces and the Armenians were once again offered promises of reform without a means to guarantee their enforcement.

Upon returning from the Berlin negotiations, Archbishop Khrimian shared his disappointment in a sermon at the Armenian cathedral in Constantinople.

You know that according to the decision of Patriarch Nerses and the National Assembly we went as delegates to Berlin in order to represent the Armenian Case to the

Great Powers attending the Congress. We had great hopes that the Congress would grant peace to the world and freedom to the small and oppressed nations—among them our own. The Congress convened and the statesmen of the Great Powers assembled around a diplomatic table covered with green cloth while the delegates of the small and oppressed nations were waiting outside the Congress. In the middle of the Congress on the table covered with a green cloth was placed a big cauldron of Liberty Stew (Harriseh) from which big and small nations and states were to receive their share. Some of the participants were pulling towards the East, others were pulling towards the West and after a long argument they began to call in order one by one the delegates of the small nations. First the Bulgarian walked in followed by the Serb and Gharadaghian [Montenegrans]; the rattling and clinking of the sabres dangling from their sides attracted the attention of those present. After much talking these three delegates drew their sabers and using them as iron ladles dipped them in the cauldron of the Liberty Stew, took their portion and departed proud and dauntless. It was now the turn of the Armenian delegate. I drew near with the paper petition given to me by the National Assembly imploring them to fill my plate with Liberty Stew, too. The officials standing around the cauldron at the time asked me: "Where is your iron ladle? It is true that the Liberty Stew is being distributed here but one who doesn't have an iron ladle can't approach it." Hearken this if in the near future should the Liberty Stew again be distributed at that time, don't come without a ladle, you will go back empty-handed.

Ah! Dear Armenian people, could I have dipped my Paper Ladle in the cauldron it would sog and remain there! Where guns talk and sabers shine, what significance do appeals and petitions have?

… I had been given a piece of paper, not a saber, and for that reason we were deprived of Liberty Stew. In spite of all, in view of the future, going to the Congress of Berlin was not useless.

People of Armenia, of course you will understand what the gun could have done and can do. Therefore, dear and blessed Armenians, upon returning to your fatherland, each of you take a gun as a gift to your friends and relatives. Again and again, arm yourselves! People, place the hope for your liberation on yourselves. Use your intellect and muscle. Man must toil himself in order to be saved. . . .[22]

Not all Armenians were as pessimistic as Archbishop Khrimian. The Armenian Patriarch Nerses Varzhapetian remained hopeful that the sultan would implement reforms that would provide meaningful change in the life of Armenians living within the empire.

CONNECTIONS

↝ Khrimian was disappointed by the terms of the Treaty of Berlin. What is a treaty? How is a treaty created? How is it enforced?

꙯ List the metaphors that Khrimian used in his speech. How do you interpret their meaning? What does Khrimian mean by iron ladles and the paper ladle? How were the nations with iron ladles different from the Armenian nation?

꙯ According to Khrimian, how did the European diplomats define their "universe of obligation"? What recourse do victims of oppression have for violations of their safety?

꙯ What is the difference between a reformer and a revolutionary? Based on your understanding of those terms, how would you describe Khrimian? How do you think the Ottoman government would have understood Khrimian's call?

꙯ What was the major conclusion that Khrimian made about the outcome of the Congress of Berlin? Why does he say that the attendance of Armenians was not completely useless?

꙯ What advantages do you see in following Khrimian's path for change? What are the disadvantages?

Members of the Armenian Revolutionary Federation (c. 1912-1913) that was created in 1890 in a desire to advance Armenian civil rights.

Project SAVE Armenian Photograph Archives, Inc., Courtesy of Rose Babigian Koobatian.

Reading 3 — ORGANIZING FOR CHANGE

From 1878 until 1881, the European powers issued collective warnings reminding the sultan and the Ottoman government of their obligations under the Treaty of Berlin. Despite the protests, conditions for Armenians in the empire did not improve. Armenians on the frontier were still subject to violent raids from local tribes. The Christians were still second-class subjects, victims of elevated taxation and unable to seek legal recourse in the courts. Inspired by Khrimian's example as well as by efforts of Christian groups in the Balkans to organize, some Armenians now believed that change had to come from within.

In the book, *The Burning Tigris: The Armenian Genocide and America's Response*, Scholar Peter Balakian writes about the founding of Armenian political parties and their strategies to bring reform to the Ottoman government.

In Turkish Armenia, the rising tide of progressive ideas about liberty, human rights, and equality came both from the Armenian intellectuals in Russia and from a long-standing intellectual relationship with Europe and its Enlightenment. Western ideas had come to Armenians either in the course of travel or study in Europe, if their families were well-to-do, or because they had been educated at one of the many American Protestant schools in Anatolia, where they were instilled with the egalitarian ideas of the American Revolution.

But the formation of three political parties gave voice to Armenian aspirations in ways that were unprecedented for them and their Turkish rulers. The fall of 1885 saw the founding of the Armenakan Party in Van--that Armenian cultural center near the Russian border. It was a secret society and literally had its first meetings underground in a burrow used for pressing grapes. The party espoused Armenian self-defense in the face of violence and it affirmed Armenia's right to self-rule, trusting that the Powers would finally come to Armenia's aid. More vociferous and centralized was the Hunchak Party, which was founded in 1887 by a group of Russian Armenians in Geneva. A socialist party with a strong Marxist orientation, they sought change and emancipation for Armenia through a socialist program, and they believed that a new and independent Armenia would initiate a worldwide socialist revolution.

By the summer of 1890 Dashnakstutiun (Armenian Revolutionary Federation) was founded in Tiflis. Dedicated to a revolutionary struggle for Armenian advancement and freedom, the party evolved into a more nationalist platform that involved a commitment to engage in armed struggle in the face of wholesale violence and oppression, and before long would become the best known and most controversial of the these.

As the political parties evolved so did civic protest. And by the summer of 1890 in Erzeroum about 200 Armenians met in the cathedral church yard to draw up a petition to protest the conditions under which Armenians were living throughout the Empire. But, as the rally began the police interceded, and before long an Ottoman battalion was dispatched to Erzurum. Before it was over, the Armenian quarter was attacked and looted, and there were more than a dozen dead and 250 wounded. A month later in Constantinople, Armenians demonstrated outside their cathedral in the Kum Kapu section of the city, and again violence broke out between the police, some soldiers and the Armenian demonstrators. Of the fracas that followed, the British Ambassador, Sir William White, noted what seemed to him the historical importance of the occasion by referring to it as "the first occasion since the conquest of Constantinople by the Turks on which Christians have dared resist soldiers in Stamboul."

By 1893, Armenian activists were placing yaftas—placards—on the public walls of certain towns in western and central Anatolia. The placards were addressed to Muslims around the world asking them to stand up to the sultan, an incompetent oppressor. Instead of instigating Muslim rebellion, however, the plan, which had come from Hunchak cells throughout Anatolia, instigated a mass of arbitrary arrests and torture across the empire. Nonetheless, by the early nineties the Armenians were making themselves heard, which further enraged the already paranoid sultan.[23]

Repression was not limited to the Armenians alone. Balakian describes the sultan's attempt to stamp out all reform.

He declared numerous words and subjects taboo and illegal. Beyond his strict censorship of all words and references to Armenia, he ordered a ban on any form of expression that referred to regicide or the murders of heads of state. The name of the deposed Sultan Murad V was banned; and the king and queen of Serbia were reported to have died of indigestion; Empress Elizabeth of Austria was said to have died of pneumonia, French President Carnot of apoplexy, and President McKinley of anthrax. So far did his paranoia carry him that he ordered his censors to expunge all references to H_2O from science textbooks because he feared the symbol would be read as meaning "Hamid the second is nothing."

The French writer Paul Fesch in 1907 summed up the state of the press under the sultan: "For thirty years the press has ceased to exist in Turkey. There are indeed newspapers, many of them even, but the scissors of the censorship cut them in so emasculating a manner that they no longer have any potency. If I dare, I would call them gelded newspapers—or rather, to keep the local colors, eunuchs." Correspondingly, intellectual freedom and book publishing were also under strict censorship.

It is not surprising, then, that Armenian political activism was met with rage by the sultan. Anyone suspected of sedition—which meant a genuine part of the population, in a society which was enveloped in the sultan's network of espionage and surveillance—was arrested, tortured, killed or exiled. It was in this climate that a group of liberal Turkish intellectuals…created a movement that demanded reform and constitutional government. As it grew in power, Abdul Hamid did what he could to tighten the muzzle on all political opposition. But the empire-wide corruption and the sul-

tan's own paranoia had corroded even the military, so that what was supposed to be the army of the sultan's protection became the seat of discontent and the seed ground for the Young Turk movement.[24]

CONNECTIONS

* Between 1878 and 1881 the European powers warned the sultan that there would be consequences for the treatment of minorities in the Ottoman Empire. Despite those warnings, conditions for the Armenians did not improve. What lessons might the sultan have taken away? What lessons do you think the Armenians learned?

* Peter Balakian characterizes the Armenian protests in this reading as acts of *civil disobedience*. In the mid 1800s American writer Henry David Thoreau popularized the concept of civil disobedience. Since that time, it has been invoked by such notable activists as Mahatma Gandhi and Dr. Martin Luther King, Jr. What does the term *civil disobedience* mean? What attributes would you use to characterize actions taken by those engaged in civil disobedience?

* Armenian civic protest and civil disobedience were repressed by the Ottoman government. In the United States the First Amendment is meant to protect the rights of individuals and groups to protest, petition, associate, and voice outrage. Why are those protections necessary in a democracy?

* Armenians engaged in civil disobedience were often met with collective punishment—looting and massacre. What did the sultan's forces hope would happen as a result of those measures?

Scholar Vartan Gregorian explains that there are many factors that contributed to the decline of the Ottoman Empire. Among several other factors, he highlights the challenges in creating a collective identity. Gregorian notes:

* *Among Ottoman rulers, there also developed a sense of complacency and a belief in the infallibility of Ottoman institutions and the inferiority of the "infidels."*

* *The failure of the empire to integrate various nations, peoples and regions into a cohesive whole. As a result, the empire remained a collection of different ethnic and religious populations (millets), such as Greek Orthodox, Armenian and Jewish, as well as semiautonomous regions (Arabia, Lebanon, North Africa and the like) without a common, unifying identity or unity of purpose.*

* *Perhaps most important of all, the rise of 19th-century nationalism in all the regions of the Ottoman empire, involving Christians at first and then, later, even Muslim peoples within the empire, such as Arabs and Turks.*[25]

❧ Who decides the rules of membership in a society? How can nations and empires create a cohesive identity? What obstacles get in the way? How can those obstacles be overcome?

❧ What do you think the sultan feared would happen if the Armenians were to publicly air their grievances?

❧ Paul Fesch observed the intense censorship under the rule of Sultan Abdul Hamid II. He wrote:

> *For thirty years the press has ceased to exist in Turkey. There are indeed newspapers, many of them even, but the scissors of the censorship cut them in so emasculating a manner that they no longer have any potency.*

❧ What is the purpose of the press? How does censorship deprive the press of its potency? Why is censorship such a powerful tool in resisting social change?

Reading 4 — HUMANITY ON TRIAL

The tensions between the Ottoman government and the Armenians erupted in 1894 after the Hunchak party in Sassun encouraged ordinary Armenians—farmers, peasants, and merchants, frustrated by their second-class status as symbolized by double taxation—to withhold their taxes. Ottoman troops were sent in to stop the protest. Instead of restoring the peace, the soldiers began massacres that would spread throughout the Turkish Armenian provinces during the winter of 1895-1896. The semi-regular *Hamidye* regiments of Kurdish and Circassian horseman carried out the campaign. In all nearly 200,000 Armenian were killed in the massacres. Reports of the massacre were smuggled out of Turkey and later collected as part of an official investigation conducted by the British, French, and Russian governments. The first public mention of the massacre to an outside source came on September 26, 1894. In published accounts of the massacres, names were withheld or replaced with initials in an effort to prevent retribution:

> *Troops have been massed in the region of the large plain near us. Sickness broke out among them, which took off two or three victims every few days. It was a good excuse for establishing quarantine around, with its income from bribes, charges, and the inevitable rise in the price of already dear grain. I suspect that one reason for placing a quarantine was to hinder the information as to what all those troops were about in that region....The sickening details are beginning to come in . . . it has been the innocent who have been the greatest sufferers. Forty-eight villages are said to have been wholly blotted out.*

By late October more details of the massacres were known.

> *We have word from Bitlis that the destruction of life in Sassoun, south of Moosh, was even greater than supposed. The brief note that reached us says: "Twenty more villages annihilated in Sassoun. Six thousand men, women, and children massacred by troops and [Kurds]. The awful story is just beginning to be known here, though the massacre took place early in September. The Turks have used infinite plans to prevent news leaking, even going to the length of sending back from Trebizond many hundreds from the Moosh region who had come this way on business." The massacre was ordered from Constantinople in the sense that some [Kurds] having robbed Armenian villages of flocks, the Armenians pursued and tried to recover their property, and a fight ensued in which a dozen [Kurds] were killed. The slain were semi-official robbers, "i.e. enrolled as troops and armed as such, but not under control." The authorities then telegraphed to Constantinople that Armenians had "killed some of the Sultan's troops" and they did it; only, not finding any rebellion, they cleared the country so that none should occur in the future.[26]*

It was common for Ottoman officials to describe the massacres of the Armenians as a justified response to armed rebellion. Despite those claims, British historian Lord Kinross observed that each massacre followed a similar pattern.

First into town came Turkish troops, for the purposes of massacre; then came the Kurdish irregulars and tribesmen for the purposes of plunder. Finally came the holocaust, by fire and destruction, which spread, with the pursuit of fugitives and mopping-up operations, throughout the lands and villages of the surrounding provinces. This murderous winter of 1895 saw the decimation of much of the Armenian population and the devastation of their property in more than twenty districts in eastern Turkey. Often the massacres were timed for a Friday, when the Muslims were in their mosques and the myth was spread by the authorities that the Armenians conspired to slaughter them at prayer. [27]

U.S. President Grover Cleveland

Ottoman soldiers recorded their participation in the massacres in letters they sent home. These letters offer a glimpse of the way Armenians had become dehumanized in the eyes of the soldiers. One soldier wrote:

My brother, if you want news from here we have killed 1,200 Armenians, all of them as food for the dogs . . . Mother, I am safe and sound. Father, 20 days ago we made war on the Armenian unbelievers. Through God's grace no harm befell us. . . . There is a rumor that our battalion will kill all the Armenians there. Besides, 511 Armenians were wounded, one or two perish every day. [28]

Reports of the massacres horrified members of the United States Congress. In December 1895, Senator Wilkinson Call, a Democrat from Florida, proposed a resolution calling for the creation of an independent Armenian state protected by the "civilized" nations of the world. Although the resolution proved too radical for the Committee on Foreign Affairs, the Committee did support the resolution of Senator Shelby Collum of Illinois condemning the massacres. Senator Collum urged President Grover Cleveland to take a stand:

Destruction and rapine have been and now are the orders obeyed in the beautiful valleys and on the rugged hills of Armenia. There has been no war, no conflict between the two contending powers, but a merciless, pitiless tornado of bloody ruin. . . .

Has it come to this, that in the last days of the nineteenth century humanity itself is placed on trial? [29]

U.S. Senator Wilkinson Call

Although Congress passed Collum's resolution, President Cleveland refused to support the measure, fearing the military and economic repercussions such an action would have on relations between the Ottoman Empire and the United States. Without U.S. support, the European and Russian governments continued to pressure the sultan to implement the reforms promised in The Treaty of Berlin. While diplomats talked, massacres of Ottoman Armenians continued intermittently until January 1896.

CONNECTIONS

- Turkish officials commonly characterized protests by Armenians and other minority groups within the Ottoman Empire as rebellion. The government spread false rumors to confuse the facts and justify slaughter. Without an independent press, official fabrications often went unchallenged. It is often said that a lie repeated over and over again becomes the truth. How does that happen? How do you think those distortions influenced the way Turks thought about Armenians?

- Lord Kinross writes: "Often the massacres were timed for a Friday, when the Muslims were in their mosques and the myth was spread by the authorities that the Armenians conspired to slaughter them at prayer." What is the danger when religious differences are exploited to reinforce a "we" and "they"? How do you learn about people who practice other religions? What can be done to build trust across religious divisions?

- Richard Hovannisian believes the Ottoman massacres were "the way traditional regimes respond to calls for change and equality." Why would traditional regimes respond to calls for change with slaughter? How is a democracy supposed to respond to dissent? What protections are there for those that advocate for change in your community? School? Country?

- In a letter to his family, an Ottoman soldier writes: "We have killed 1,200 Armenians, all of them as food for the dogs. . . Father, 20 days ago we made war on the Armenian unbelievers." How do explain his attitude toward the victims? How do individuals and groups become dehumanized?

- In the 1890s the massacres of Armenians were often described as a *holocaust*, literally a destruction by fire. At the time, the word holocaust did not have the same associations and meaning that it has throughout much of the world today. Today, the word *Holocaust*, with a capital H, is most frequently used to describe the Nazis' attempt to destroy all of European Jewry during the 1930s and 1940s. At times there has been intense debate about whether it is appropriate to use the word *Holocaust* to describe other events. For example, some people refer to the Armenian Genocide as the Armenian Holocaust. Why does the language matter?

- How is it possible for a group to become so dehumanized that the local population would allow them to be massacred in broad daylight? What are the small steps that lead to dehumanization? *After the First*, a video resource available in the Facing History and Ourselves library, explores some of the ways individuals may become accustomed to violence.

❧ The reading describes the struggle of politicians in the United States to find an appropriate response to the massacres of Armenians. Samantha Power, a scholar of U.S. foreign policy, describes those options as a "tool box." What tools are turned to most frequently? Think creatively. What other tools are available to those who believe that governments should intervene to protect human rights?

⤚

Reading 5 — THE SULTAN RESPONDS

In Europe, the popular press reported stories of the Armenian massacres. Newspapers featured cartoons of the "Bloody Sultan," a name coined by British Prime Minister William Gladstone. The press called upon the "civilized" world to do something to stop the bloodshed. Descriptions of "Turkish tyranny" and "outrages" against Christians written by Christian missionaries excited concern for the Armenians while reinforcing anti-Muslim stereotypes. After Sir Philip Currie, the British ambassador to the Ottoman Empire, rebuked Sultan Abdul Hamid II for the Armenian massacres, the sultan felt compelled to defend his position. This is his response:

> *His Majesty states that he is well aware of your Excellency's friendly disposition towards himself and the Empire, and he does not for a moment imagine that in bringing these matters to his notice Your Excellency wishes to raise the Armenian Question.*

> *His Majesty continues by stating that just as in other countries there are Nihilists, Socialists, and Anarchists, endeavoring to obtain from the government concessions and privileges which it is impossible to grant them, and just in the same manner steps had to be taken against them, so it is with the Armenians who, for their own purposes, invent these stories against the Government, and finding that they receive encouragement from British officials, are emboldened to proceed to open acts of rebellion, which the government is perfectly justified in suppressing by every means in its power.*

> *His Majesty says that your Excellency will remember that the Bulgarians concocted the same stories against the government and proceeded just as the Armenians do, and that the British government extended a certain protection to the Bulgarians, who have now been formed into separate provinces. This cannot possibly, however, happen in the case of the Armenians. The Armenian population is spread over a large extent of the country and no place are they the majority. Their expectations, therefore, can never be realized, and all the exaggerated stories of oppression and persecution, got up with the object of exciting European sympathy to enable them to obtain an impossible end, should not be relied upon.*

> *Naturally the Ottoman government was bound to take strong measures to put down sedition, and when the people were found with arms in their hands resisting the authorities, it was only natural that the government should mete*

Sultan Abdul Hamid II

Courtesy of Clip Art. Some images © 2003-2004 www.clipart.com

out to them summary punishment. Only a short time ago, in Italy, the Italians put down disorder with a strong hand. England herself had in India, resorted to the strongest measures to stamp out rebellion, and even in Egypt, England had put down disorder with a high hand. His Imperial Majesty treated the Armenians with justice and moderation, and as long as they behaved properly, all toleration would be shown to them, but he had given orders that when they took to revolt or to brigandage the authorities were to deal with the Armenians as they deal with the authorities.

His Majesty had read the account which your Excellency had given to him with horror and sorrow. His Majesty had had no knowledge of these facts, and yesterday morning, when he read the report, he immediately instructed the Minister of the Interior to make inquiries and cause a telegram to be sent to Zeki Pasha, Commandant of the Fourth Corps d'Armee, instructing him to report at once.[30]

Despite European pressure to implement long-promised reforms for the Armenians, the sultan resisted. Without any signs of progress the Armenians grew increasingly frustrated.

CONNECTIONS

➤ The sultan explains: "His Imperial Majesty treated the Armenians with justice and moderation, and as long as they behaved properly, all toleration would be shown to them, but he had given orders that when they took to revolt . . . the authorities were to deal with the Armenians as they deal with the authorities." Scholar Henry Theriault argues that "the Sultan's characterization of what the Armenians were asking for—'concessions and privileges'—suggests that the Sultan was explicitly aware that they were reformers, not revolutionaries in the true sense. Indeed, at the time and after, Armenian political activity strove toward full integration of Armenians into an egalitarian Ottoman state, not the destruction of the state or its government." Why is the distinction between revolution and reform important? Regardless of the motivation of the protesters, would massacre ever be a legitimate response? Why would the sultan suppress movements for change with radical violence?

➤ The sultan suggests that "the Ottoman Government was bound to put down sedition." What is sedition? U.S. President Thomas Jefferson once wrote that "a little rebellion now and then is a good thing . . . it is a medicine necessary for the sound health of a government."[31] How would you describe the Armenians' actions? Were they acts of rebellion? Are there times when rebellion is justified?

➤ Why do you think the sultan goes to great lengths to point out the policy of the British government in Egypt and India? Do the comparisons with European colonialism influence the way you think about the massacres?

➤ Often efforts to draw attention to the plight of the Armenians reinforced cultural stereotypes about

Muslims. Is it possible to call attention to injustice without further reinforcing attitudes of "we" and "they"? How can advocates for victims distinguish between the perpetrators, their supporters, and cultural attitudes about the victims, without depicting the conflict as a clash of civilizations?

Reading 6 — SEEKING CIVIL RIGHTS

While massacres of Armenians continued throughout the Ottoman Empire, Armenian leaders worked to find a strategy that finally would bring about the protections they had sought for so long. Although other minorities in the Ottoman Empire were able to break free into protected provinces or even separate countries, Armenians were scattered throughout the empire. Hopes for safety and security did not rest as much on independence as they did on real changes in the way they were governed. The two largest Armenian political parties—the Hunchaks and the Armenian Revolutionary Federation—planned direct action in an attempt to educate the world about their situation.

On October 1, 1895, 2,000 Armenians gathered in the Ottoman capital to demand civil rights. Peter Balakian describes how a non-violent protest turned into a slaughter.

> *As the sultan stalled on the new demands for reform in the Armenian provinces, the frustration among Armenians grew. By the summer of 1895, the Hunchak Party was planning a demonstration in the capital. The mass rally took place at noon on October 1, 1895, as nearly 2,000 Armenians gathered in the Kum Kapu section near the Armenian patriarchate to march to the Sublime Porte. Their goal was to deliver a petition, a "Protest-Demand" which decried the Sasun massacre, the condition of Armenians throughout the empire, and the inaction of the central government.*

Courtesy of Clip Art. Some images © 2003-2004 www.clipart.com

Palace of the Ottoman Sublime Port, Constantinople.

The petition was—especially given its time and place—an extraordinary statement about civil rights. In clear language the Armenians protested "the systematic persecution to which our people has been subjected, especially during the last few years, a persecution which the Sublime Porte has made a principle of government with the one object of causing Armenians to disappear from their own country." They protested the "state of siege" under which Armenians were forced to live and the recent massacres at Sasun. Peace and security were essential, the text went on, "to a nation which desires to reach by fair means a position of comparative prosperity, which it has certainly a right to aspire to, and to reach the level of progress and civilization towards which other peoples are advanc-

ing." The list of Armenian demands was broad and basic: fair taxation; guarantees of freedom of conscience; the right of public meetings; equality before the law; protection of life, property, and honor (and this meant the protection of women). The petition also demanded the cessation of mass political arrests and the brutal torture that most often followed them, as well as the right to bear arms for self-defense. The Armenian authors of the petition underscored that the Armenians had waited patiently for the reforms promised them in the Treaty of Berlin in 1878. As one historian put it, it was "the first time in Ottoman history that a non-Muslim, subject minority had dared to confront the central authorities in the very capital of the empire."

As the rally commenced there was tension all over the city. The Sublime Porte was surrounded by cavalry and police, as the huge crowd made its way into the center of the city and approached the Porte. Copies of the Protest-Demand had already been delivered to various embassies. As the Hunchak leaders were about to deliver the petition at the Porte, they were stopped by Maj. Servet Bey, the adjutant to the minister of police, who ordered them to disband. As the soldiers and the police let loose on the protestors, about twenty people were bludgeoned to death and hundreds were wounded. Major Servet was killed, fights broke out and shots were fired, and a massacre began in the clear daylight on the streets of the capital. Foreigners and European diplomats looked on in horror....

During the first week of October, massacres continued throughout Constantinople day and night. Horrified by what they were witnessing, the foreign diplomats sent a collective message to the Porte asking for an end to the massacres. British ambassador Philip Currie telegraphed the grand vizier [the chief minister of the Ottoman government] to tell him that conditions were deteriorating by the day and that Armenians were being massacred in the city and throughout the suburbs. As the number of dead piled up on the streets and the hospitals filled with wounded, 2,400 Armenians stayed locked up inside their churches throughout the many sections of the city. Finally, on October 10, with assurances from all six foreign embassies, they agreed to come out into the open air. But by then the Constantinople massacre had set off a new wave of violence against Armenians throughout the empire.[32]

CONNECTIONS

❧ What demands did the Hunchaks make in their petition? What arguments did they make to support their positions?

❧ Balakian writes that the Hunchak petition was, "given its time and place—an extraordinary statement about civil rights." What are civil rights? Where do civil rights come from? How are they protected? What is the difference between a civil right and a human right?

❧ Throughout the nineteenth century, Armenians tried many strategies to bring about change in the

Ottoman Empire. Some worked within the system, while others organized into political parties and suggested alternatives. Still others looked for help from abroad. Despite promises, significant change never came. What obstacles did Armenians confront as they sought safety and security? What other strategies were still available to Armenians?

Reading 7 — HUMANITARIAN INTERVENTION

By the mid 1890s the "Armenian Crisis" received prominent coverage in the popular press of the United States. The *New York Times, Boston Globe,* and *San Francisco Examiner* featured stories on the situation nearly every week. At the same time, activists around the country began to raise money for food and clothes for distribution through networks set up by Christian missionaries in Ottoman Armenia. Although the missionaries played a prominent role, the movement was not limited by religion or politics. In the United States, Christians, Jews, liberals and conservatives, took up the issue of Armenian relief.[33]

Activists lobbied Clara Barton, the American founder of the Red Cross, a national symbol of humanitarian activism, to take up the cause. Impressed by extensive relief efforts in New York and Boston, Barton, who had become a household name for her work during the American Civil War, soon agreed. The 75-year-old humanitarian decided that it was time to take her work to Ottoman Armenia. She explained her decision by saying that "'immediate action was urged by the American people. Human beings starving could not be

reached, hundreds of towns and villages had not been heard from since the fire and swords went over them." Barton argued that her intervention was justified on the basis that Turkey was one of the signers of the Red Cross Treaty of Geneva, and consequentially it had to be familiar with its humanitarian objectives.

Balakian believes that American intervention on the behalf of the Ottoman Armenians had a profound impact on the way Americans viewed their responsibility to those that lived beyond their borders.

Although the United States sent money... to aid Greece during the Greek War of Independence in 1824-25, and Americans aided Ireland during the potato famine of the 1840s, the movement for humanitarian intervention for the Armenians in Turkey in 1896 commenced what I believe can be called the modern era of American international human rights relief.... In many ways Barton's mission anticipated the kind of work the Peace Corps would do in the second half of the twentieth century. Barton's voyage to Turkey was also another part, and a bright one, of America's growing global involvement during the decade that would bring the

Clara Barton

United States a new international identity....

In many ways, American women played a crucial role in the movement for Armenian relief, and their work helped to give shape to a new vision of what might be called global sisterhood. As survivor accounts and eyewitness reports came to public knowledge through the press, the magnitude of sexual violence committed against Armenian women—rape and sexual torture, abduction, slavery, and imprisonment in harems—appeared to be unprecedented in modern Western history, and it affected Americans deeply.[34]

The activism of American women did not take place in a vacuum. The treatment of minorities in the Ottoman Empire galvanized a growing international movement for humanitarian intervention—a belief that states, not just individuals and groups, have a responsibility to take action, using diplomacy or force, to prevent or end the abuse of human rights in a separate sovereign nation. Human rights expert Paul Gordon Lauren writes that efforts to intervene in the name of persecuted Ottoman minorities during the nineteenth century "contributed heavily to the growing theory of humanitarian intervention and its slow but steady acceptance as an increasingly important component of international law." In practice, Lauren explains, those efforts raised many questions about the tension between human rights, politics, and national sovereignty—questions that are still with us.

Humanitarian intervention both in theory and practice also helped to identify serious and troubling problems created when trying to transform visions of international human rights into reality. Even at this early stage, for example, it became evident that humanitarian intervention in the name of "humanity" might well be genuinely beneficent and justified, but at the same time always carried the dangerous potential of providing a convenient pretext for coercion or a guise for masking more suspicious motives of national self-interest and aggrandizement. Similarly, difficulties arose as to precisely what nations or group of nations could legitimately or precisely define the "laws of humanity," "the conscience of mankind," and the meaning of "human rights" for the world as a whole while still avoiding accusations of having arbitrary standards that applied to some but not all. The Great Powers who demonstrated such eagerness to protect the rights of the persecuted in the Ottoman Empire, for example, also happened to be the same ones known to persecute and discriminate against indigenous peoples within their own overseas empires. In addition, whereas carefully negotiated and solemn treaty provisions concerning human rights indicated a strength of desire, the lack of enforcement provisions revealed a lack of will.... Humanitarian intervention always carried the risk that it could provoke even worse reactions against the very people that it wanted to protect. Even more serious in terms of international relations, such intervention could create the risk of a dangerous precedent that might be turned against those who employed it and thus threaten their own independence, domestic jurisdiction, territorial integrity, and national sovereignty. Each of these difficult problems would continue to confront those who struggled to advance international human rights for many years to come.[35]

CONNECTIONS

- Balakian writes: "Looking back at the twentieth century, it seems clear that no international human rights movement ever obsessed or galvanized the United States as did the effort to save the Armenians." As you read about the treatment of Armenians in the Ottoman Empire, what grabs your attention? What does it take for another group of people to become part of your "universe of obligation"? How do you express your concern?

- Paul Gordon Lauren highlights a series of dilemmas for those acting in the name of "humanity." He notes, "it became evident that humanitarian intervention in the name of 'humanity' might well be genuinely beneficent and justified, but at the same time always carried the dangerous potential of providing a convenient pretext for coercion or a guise for masking more suspicious motives of national self-interest and aggrandizement. Similarly, difficulties arose as to precisely what nations or group of nations could legitimately or precisely define the 'laws of humanity,' 'the conscience of mankind,' and the meaning of 'human rights' for the world as a whole while still avoiding accusations of having arbitrary standards that applied to some but not all." How can those dilemmas be resolved? Do the tensions need to resolved before any action is taken?

- Does the international community have a moral duty to intervene when human rights are being violated? If so, what standards should be used to determine when to act? How should nations determine when to respond diplomatically and when to use force?

- What human rights stories are in the news today? What obstacles need to be negotiated as individuals, groups, and nations respond?

- Lauren warns that intervention may provoke unexpected consequences: "Humanitarian intervention always carried the risk that it could provoke even worse reactions against the very people that it wanted to protect." How can those that plan humanitarian actions minimize the risk of a backlash?

Reading 8 ⌣ SHOWDOWN AT BANK OTTOMAN

In August of 1896 leaders of the Armenian Revolutionary Federation decided they needed help from the European powers to stop the anti-Armenian massacres. Attempts to organize nonviolent protests often ended with the sultan's forces brutally breaking up the protests. In the aftermath, protesters were blamed for their own fate, and often the Armenian community was collectively held responsible. A small group of desperate Armenian leaders felt that it was time to try something else. Nearly two dozen members of the Armenian Revolutionary Federation plotted to take over Bank Ottoman, a European-controlled bank in Constantinople, the capital of the Ottoman Empire. Before they took over the bank, the organizers of the operation, Armen Garo, Papken Siuni, and Haig Tiryakian, issued several public declarations outlining their objectives. The plotters made it clear that they did not want to harm anyone or even to rob the bank. One manifesto was addressed to the Turkish public at large.

> *For centuries our forbears have been living with you in peace and harmony . . . but recently your government, conceived in crimes, began to sow discords among us in order to strangle us and you with greater ease. You, people, did not understand this diabolical scheme of politics and, soaking yourselves in the blood of our brothers, you became an accomplice in the perpetration of the heinous crime. Nevertheless, know well that our fight is not against you, but your government, against which your own best sons are fighting also.[36]*

The plotters also addressed a letter to the European powers. The attitude of the Europeans, the letter claimed, tolerated "Turkish tyranny...Sultan Hamit's murderous vengeance. Europe has beheld this crime and kept silence. . . . The time of diplomatic play is passed. The blood shed by our 100,000 martyrs gives us the right to demand liberty."[37] Another letter explained "it is the criminal indifference of humanity which has pushed us to this extreme."[38]

Courtesy of the Library of Congress

Bank Ottoman, Constantinople.

After a shootout leaving both Armenians and bank guards dead and wounded, over a dozen Armenian revolutionaries stormed the bank. Armen Garo, one of the leaders of the operation, later wrote that his fellow Armenians were so inexperienced in handling weapons that several of them blew themselves up while trying to evade gunfire. Once the bank was secure, he went to the second floor to talk to the bank personnel. Armen Garo recalled:

> In my hoarse voice, I began to explain to them that they did not need to fear us, that we were Armenian revolutionaries who had occupied the bank to compel the European ambassadors to intervene in order to end the massacre of Armenians. I even reminded them: "Do you hear that howling outside? The Turkish mob has resumed the massacre of Armenians. . . ." In very courteous language, I explained to them what our aim was. I told them, unless we received guarantees that no more Armenians would be killed and the promised reforms would be enacted, we were not getting out of the bank. Should they try from outside to recapture the building by force, we would resist to the last bullet and the last bomb, and in the end blow up the building not to surrender ourselves. Therefore, it would be in their interest as well to bring about the European intervention as soon as possible, before our ammunition was exhausted.
>
> They all started to look at each other and then at me with terrified eyes. Their elemental terror of a short while ago was followed by a new one, more definite, and all together began asking how they could help us to bring about the European intervention as soon as possible.[39]

The Armenian revolutionaries spelled out their demands in a message to the ambassadors of the European powers.

> We are in control of the Bank Ottoman and we will not leave until the following conditions are met:
>
> 1. To stop immediately the massacre now on in Constantinople;
>
> 2. To stop the armed attack on the bank, otherwise we shall blow up the building when our ammunition is exhausted;
>
> 3. To give written guarantees concerning the enactment of Armenian reforms with the amendment suggested by the Central Committee of the A.R.F. [Armenian Revolutionary Federation] in a special communication to you;
>
> 4. To set free all Armenian revolutionaries detained because of current events;
>
> In the contrary situation, we shall be forced to blow up the building with everyone inside.[40]

To prevent further violence, the European ambassadors negotiated a deal. The sultan promised to end the massacres, and the Armenian revolutionaries agreed to leave the building and go into exile. The European powers pledged to press the Ottoman government for reforms to ensure the Armenians would be protected. Although the Armenians boarded a ship to France without further incident, neither of the sultan's promises were kept. Instead, 6,000 more Armenians were massacred in the streets of the capital shortly afterward.

CONNECTIONS

❧ Leaders of the Armenian Revolutionary Federation decided they needed help from the European powers to stop the anti-Armenian massacres. Attempts to organize nonviolent protests often ended with the sultan's forces brutally breaking up the protests. In the aftermath, protesters were blamed for their own fate, and often the Armenian community was collectively held responsible. What options did leaders of the Armenian community have as they worked for change? Earlier attempts by Armenians to advocate for their rights did not elicit the responses they desired. Armenians were still treated as second-class citizens. What happens to groups and individuals when they feel they are not safe and are not able to protect themselves and their families?

❧ Protests are often staged as attempts to educate the public by drawing attention to a situation. Whom were the Armenian revolutionaries trying to educate? What lessons did they try to teach with their public declarations? What lesson did they teach when they took over the bank?

❧ What is terrorism? What is the difference between terrorism and civil disobedience? What factors influence your understanding of the distinctions between the terms?

❧ Some publicists and many European diplomats denounced the seizure of the Bank Ottoman as a foolish act of terrorism. Others, however, commended the Armenian revolutionaries for their bravery. One British historian wrote that "as young men of ideals inexperienced in the wiles of political agitation, they had failed to benefit their friends and had played into the hands of the enemy." Reflect on this statement. What do you make of the actions taken by the Armenian revolutionaries at Bank Ottoman? How did their actions both help and hurt the Armenian cause?

↵

Reading 9 ⏤ THE RISE OF THE YOUNG TURKS

By the 1890s it was not just minorities within the Ottoman Empire who were calling for change and in some cases revolution. Christians, Muslims, and Jews were now joined by Turks and even members of the nobility—including the sultan's nephew, Prince Sabaheddin. At his home in Paris, the prince hosted a wide range of Ottoman dissidents in February of 1902 as the Congress of Ottoman Liberals. At the conference, 47 delegates, representing Turkish, Arab, Greek, Kurdish, Armenian, and Jewish groups, formed an alliance against the sultan. Together the groups called for equal rights for all Ottoman citizens, self-administration for minorities, and restoration of the suspended Ottoman constitution.

Despite their broad agreements, there were still tensions between the factions. Among the points of conflict was an intense debate about outside intervention. Many Armenians favored a resolution calling for European protection of all ethnic and national groups within the empire. Ahmed Riza, one of the leaders of the Young Turks—a coalition of Turkish groups that proposed transforming the empire into a representative constitutional government—believed that the Armenians and other minorities deserved equal rights and fair treatment, but he chafed at the suggestion that help from outside was necessary. According to Riza and others, many of the problems they were facing were partially the results of foreign intervention. Yet some Armenians worried that without help from the outside, they would be left with empty promises.

In 1907 the prince, with the support of the Armenian Revolutionary Federation, organized the second Congress of Ottoman Liberals. At the meeting representatives called for immediate overthrow of the sultan.

While the prince was organizing dissident groups in exile, military forces representing the Committee of Union and Progress (a branch of the Young Turk movement) found themselves on the brink of being exposed by the sultan's forces. Not knowing what else to do, they went public. The committee representatives demanded restoration of the Ottoman constitution and marched toward the capital. As they traveled from town to town, the mutiny picked up public support. Without sufficient troops to put down the uprising, the sultan gave in to the demands of the Committee of Union and Progress on July 24, 1908. The Young Turk revolution was greeted with broad support. Newspapers reported scenes of Christians, Jews, and Muslims embracing in the streets.

Upon taking power, the Young Turks issued a proclamation outlining their plan to reform the Ottoman Empire.

> *Provided that the number of senators does not exceed one-third the number of deputies, the Senate will be named as follows: one-third by the sultan and two-thirds by the nation, and the term of senators will be of limited duration.*
>
> *It will be demanded that all Ottoman subjects having completed their twentieth year, regardless of whether they possess property or fortune,*

A crowd of Armenians celebrating the Young Turk Revolution in 1908.

From the private collection of Berj Fenerci

shall have the right to vote. Those who have lost their civil rights will naturally be deprived of this right.

It will be demanded that the right freely to constitute political groups be inserted in a precise fashion in the constitutional charter, in order that article 1 of the Constitution of 1293 A.H. (Anno Hegira, 1876 C.E.) be respected.

The Turkish tongue will remain the official state language. Official correspondence and discussion will take place in Turkish.

Every citizen will enjoy complete liberty and equality, regardless of nationality or religion, and be submitted to the same obligations. All Ottomans, being equal before the law as regards rights and duties relative to the State, are eligible for government posts, according to their individual capacity and their education. Non-Muslims will be equally liable to the military law.

The free exercise of the religious privileges which have been accorded to different nationalities will remain intact.

Provided that the property rights of landholders are not infringed upon (for such rights must be respected and must remain intact, according to law), it will be proposed that peasants be permitted to acquire land, and they will be accorded means to borrow money at a moderate rate.

Education will be free. Every Ottoman citizen, within the limits of the prescriptions of the Constitution, may operate a private school in accordance with the special laws.

All schools will operate under the surveillance of the state. In order to obtain for Ottoman citizens an education of a homogenous and uniform character, the official schools will be open, their instruction will be free, and all nationalities will be admitted. Instruction in Turkish will be obligatory in public schools. In official schools, public instruction will be free. Secondary and higher education will be given in the public and official schools indicated above; it will use the Turkish tongue. Schools of commerce, agriculture, and industry will be opened with the goal of developing the resources of the country.[41]

CONNECTIONS

↪ The Young Turk proclamation describes rights that were to be given to citizens of the Ottoman Empire. What is a citizen? What is the difference between being a citizen of a country and being a resident of a country? What responsibilities come with citizenship?

↪ After reading the Young Turk proclamation for the Ottoman Empire, which platforms stand out? Why? Compare your selections with those of your classmates.

↪ How do the Young Turks' proposals address the challenges facing the empire? Which platforms might have created discomfort with their partners from the Congress of Ottoman Liberals? How do you anticipate supporters of the sultan would perceive these changes?

◆ Research the constitutions of emerging democracies. How do they try to protect individual freedoms while creating or maintaining a national identity?

Facing History and Ourselves online module *The Weimar Republic: The Fragility of Democracy* and Chapter 3 of *Facing History and Ourselves: Holocaust and Human Behavior* explore the challenges Germany faced in building democracy after World War I.

NOTES

17. Helen Fein, *Accounting for Genocide* (New York: Free Press, 1979), p. 4.
18. Model Curriculum for Teaching About Human Rights and Genocide, Reprinted by permission, California Department of Education, P.O. Box 271, Sacramento, CA 95812. Also available at *http://www.armenian-genocide.org/curricula/model_curric.htm.*
19. Quoted in Vahakn Dadrian, *Warrant for Genocide* (New Brunswick, NJ: Transaction Publishers, 1999), p. 20.
20. Dadrian, *Warrant for Genocide*, pp. 25–26.
21. *The American Heritage Dictionary* (Boston: Houghton Mifflin, 2000).
22. Prelacy of the Armenian Apostolic Church of America, *Hayrig: A Celebration of His Life and Vision on the Eightieth Anniversary of His Death, 1907–1987* (New York: Prelacy of the Armenian Apostolic Church of America, 1987).
23. Peter Balakian, *The Buring Tigris: The Armenian Genocide and America's Response* (New York: HarperCollins, 2003), pp. 44–45.
24. Ibid., p. 49.
25. Vartan Gregorian, "Islam: A Mosaic, Not a Monolith," in *Report of the President* (New York: Carnegie Corporation of New York, Annual Report, 2001), pp. 19–20.
26. Frederick Davis Greene, *The Armenian Massacres and Turkish Tyranny* (Philadelphia: American Oxford, 1896; reprint, Astoria, NY: J.C. and A.L. Fawcett, Inc. Publishers, 1990), pp. 10, 12–13.
27. Lord Kinross, *The Ottoman Centuries* (New York: Morrow, 1977), pp. 559–560.
28. Vahakn N. Dadrian, *The History of the Armenian Genocide* (Providence, RI: Berghahn Books, 1996), p. 159.
29. For a full copy of the Congressional Resolution, see *The Statutes at Large of the United States of America, from December, 1895, to March, 1897, and Recent Treaties, Conventions, and Executive Proclamations, with an Appendix containing the concurrent resolutions of the two houses of Congress*, Vol. XXIX (Washington, DC: Government Printing Office, 1897), as cited in *The Armenian Genocide and America's Outcry: A Compilation of U.S. Documents 1890–1923* (Washington, D.C.: Armenian Assembly of America, 1985).
30. Robert Melson, *Revolution and Genocide: On the Origins of the Armenian Genocide and the Holocaust* (Chicago: University of Chicago Press, 1992), pp. 59–60.
31. Thomas Jefferson, "Letter to James Madison" [Paris, January 30, 1787], in Merill D. Peterson ed. *The Portable Thomas Jefferson* (New York: Penguin), pp. 416–417.
32. Balakian, *The Burning Tigris*, pp. 57–59.
33. Ibid., pp. 63–80.
34. Ibid., pp. 63–65.
35. Paul Gordon Lauren, *The Evolution of International Human Rights: Visions Seen* (Philadelphia: University of Pennsylvania Press, 1998), pp. 69–70.
36. Vahakn Dadrian, *History of the Armenian Genocide*, p. 139.
37. Ibid.
38. Ibid., p. 140.
39. Simon Vratzian, ed., *Bank Ottoman: The Memoirs of Armen Garo*, trans. Haig T. Partizian (Detroit: Armen Topouzian, 1990), pp. 119–122.
40. Ibid., 122.
41. "The Young Turks," trans. A. Sarrou, in Rondo Cameron, ed., *Civilization since Waterloo* (Paris, 1912), pp. 40–42; and *http://www.fordham.edu/halsall/mod/1908youngturk.html.*

*" Religion has a place for a conscience,
which racist ideologies do not."*
—Christopher Walker

Chapter 3

THE YOUNG TURKS IN POWER

THIS CHAPTER LOOKS AT THE CHOICES MADE IN THE OTTOMAN EMPIRE BETWEEN 1908 AND 1914 THAT would eventually result in genocide. No historical event is inevitable. Individuals and groups operate within a particular historical moment, and the choices they make ultimately define the age.

In 1908, the Young Turk revolution brought great hope for many people living in the Ottoman Empire. The reintroduction of the constitution, with its promises of equal rights, seemed to offer opportunities to people who had been left behind in the old system. The Young Turk vision of a strong central government promised an alternative to the corruption and disorder of the sultan's regime. Many hoped the violence that had come to characterize the sultan's reign would now end.

For the Armenians, the constitution and its guaranteed equality seemed to offer many of the reforms they had long desired. But there were still unresolved tensions. What role would Muslims have in this new order? Were they going to quietly accept the loss of their special status in this new regime? What would happen to supporters of the sultan? What about the members of groups that suffered under the old regime? Could they trust the Young Turks? Who would enforce the changes they promised?

There were tensions within the Young Turk movement as well. Between 1908 and 1913, the diversity of opinion within the Young Turk movement became clear. Although one branch of the movement worked with Armenians and others, another branch of the party, favoring Turkish nationalism, began to gain influence. Others within the movement were less consumed by ideology than with the practical concerns of holding on to power. Internal unrest and further loss of territory aggravated the divide.

In 1913, Mehmed Talaat, Ahmed Djemal, and Ismail Enver organized a military coup and formed a coalition of ultranationalists who believed that the only way to hold on to the empire was to embrace a radical ideology of ethnic resettlement and deportation. The Turkish nationalists gained strength when Germany, and the Ottoman Empire entered into a military alliance just before World War I. Old stereotypes about Armenian disloyalty were combined with religiously inspired ideas of the "other" and spread by the government to further a sense of "us" and "them."

Photo courtesy of the Morgenthau Collection

Young Turk leaders Talaat and Enver reviewing the troops.

Reading 1 — BLOODY NEWS FROM ADANA

For the Ottomans and their new leaders, 1908 brought disappointment. Austria-Hungary annexed the territories of Bosnia and Herzegovina. Bulgaria declared independence from the empire, and the island of Crete broke away to become part of Greece. In the chaos, Turks loyal to the sultan attempted a counter-coup to restore him in April 1909. Although supporters of the sultan grew bitter as the empire lost land to former subjects, Armenians within the Ottoman Empire had rarely enjoyed so much freedom.

A postcard of the Armenian Quarter in Adana after the 1909 massacre.

From the private collection of Berj Fenerci

In the province of Adana, in the region of Cilicia near the Mediterranean Sea, tensions between Turks and Armenians exploded as Turks still loyal to the sultan watched Armenians celebrate their new opportunities. Historian Richard Hovannisian traces how those tensions expressed themselves in massacre.

After the Young Turk revolution, many Armenians were emboldened to believe that they could now enjoy freedom of speech and assembly. The audacious prelate [religious leader] of Adana, Bishop Mushegh, expounded in nationalistic rhetoric, proclaiming that the centuries of Armenian servitude had passed and that it was now the right and duty of his people to learn to defend themselves, their families, and their communities. For Muslims, however, the new era of constitutional government undermined their traditional relationship with Armenians and threatened their legal and customary superiority. At the same time that Abdul Hamid's partisans in Constantinople initiated a countercoup to restore the authority of the sultan, conservatives of similar sentiments lashed out at the Armenians of Adana. A skirmish between Armenians and Turks on April 13 set off a riot that resulted in the pillaging of the bazaars and attacks upon the Armenian quarters. The violence also spread to nearby villages. When the authorities finally intervened two days later, more than 2,000 Armenians lay dead. An uneasy ten-day lull was broken on April 25 with an inferno. Army regulars who had just arrived in the city now joined the mobs. Fires set in the Armenian quarters spread rapidly in all directions. Armenian Protestants and Catholics, who had generally remained aloof from nationalistic movements, were not spared as the massacre and plunder fanned out over the width and breadth of Cilicia. . . . Hakob Papikian, member of a parliamentary commission of investigation, reported that there had been 21,000 victims, of whom, 19,479 were Armenian, 850 Syrian, 422 Chaldean, and 250 Greek. Thousands of widows and orphans now stood as a grim reminder of the first massacre of the Young Turk era. Several Turks and Armenians were hanged in Adana for provoking the violence, but the most responsible persons, including the governor and commandant, got off with no real punishment.[42]

Adom Yarjanian, an Armenian poet who went by the pen name Siamanto, wrote a series of poems known as *Bloody News from My Friend* about the massacres and their aftermath. Siamanto's poem "Grief" reflects the Armenian sense of isolation and despair in the wake of the massacres.

Grief
by Siamanto

You, stranger soul mate
Who leaves behind the road of joy,
listen to me.
I know your innocent feet are still wet with blood.
Foreign hands have come and yanked out
the sublime rose of freedom
which finally bloomed from the pains of your race.

Let its divine scent intoxicate everyone,
Let everyone—those far away, your neighbor, the ungrateful,
come and burn incense
before the goddess of Justice
that you carved from the stone with your hammer.
Proud sowers, let others reap with your scythes
the wheat that ripens in the gold earth you ploughed.
Because if you are chased down by raw Evil,
don't forget that you are
to bring forth the fruitful Good.

Walk down the avenues of merriment
and don't let the happy ones see in your eyes
that image of corpse and ash.
Spare the passerby, whether a good man or a criminal,
because Armenian pain
rises up in the eye's visage.
As you walk through the crossroad of merriment
don't let a speck of gladness or a tear
stain grief's majesty.
Because for the vanquished, tears are cowardly
and for the victors, the smile is frivolous, a wrinkle.

Armenian woman, with veils darkening you like death.

You, young man with native anguish
running down your face,
walk down roads without rage of hate
and exclaim: what a bright day,
what a sarcastic grave digger…
What a mob, what dances, what joy
and what feasts everywhere…
our red shrouds are victory flags.
the bones of your pure brothers are flutes…
with them others are making strange music.
But don't shudder, unknown sister
or brother of fate.
As you study the stars,
take heart, go on.
The law of life stays the same
human beings can't understand each other.

And this evening before the sunset
all of you will go back to your houses,
whether they are mud or marble,
and calmly close the treacherous
Shutters of your windows.
shut them from the wicked Capital,
shut them to the face of humanity,
and to the face of your God…,
Even the lamp on your table
will be extinguished
by your soul's one clear whisper.[43]

In the aftermath of the massacre, the Armenian Revolutionary Federation and the Young Turk Committee of Union and Progress released a joint statement promising to continue to work together to guarantee the full realization of the Ottoman constitution, suppress reactionary movements, and work to counter the myth that Armenians desired independence from the Ottoman Empire.

CONNECTIONS

❧ The Armenians in Adana and other places in Cilicia fell victim to the rage of those who were angered by the changes taking place in the Ottoman Empire. What changes do you think they found so threatening? Why did that anger express itself in violence against the Armenians?

❧ Despite the revolution, some Young Turks joined the mob as they targeted Armenians and others. How do you interpret their participation in the violence?

❧ One strategy for analyzing poetry is to break the larger piece down into smaller sections and focus on those before moving on to try to understand the whole piece. Start with a close read of one stanza and then try to convey the mood and message in your own words.

❧ As you read "Grief," identify key words, images, or phrases. What do they mean? What does Siamanto hope to convey? What message does he have for the reader?

❧ What does Siamanto mean when he says: "The law of life stays the same. Human beings can't understand each other." How does his message resonate with what you have studied in this unit? What role can education play in helping people bridge differences?

❧ A British warship was in the area of the massacres and aware of the conditions. The commander of the ship applied to the Turkish governor of the district for permission to land and offer relief, but his request was refused. After being refused, the ship left the area. Why do you think the governor refused the commander's request? Why do you think the commander complied? Consider the political, diplomatic, and military issues that would have influenced his decision.

Reading 2 — IDEOLOGY

After the massacres in Adana and other places in Cilicia the Young Turks government declared a state of siege and limited some of the rights that had been newly granted to citizens of the empire.

British historian Christopher Walker describes the search for an ideology that the Young Turks could use to unify the fraying empire.

The options had emerged as Ottomanism, Islam or Turkism. Ottomanism meant strengthening the institutions of the existing empire and making them available for all its citizens, irrespective of ethnic origin. It gained a brief vogue, but never had much of a chance when compared with the other more exciting ideologies. Islam meant deepening relations between all Muslim peoples and nations within the empire and throughout the world, and perhaps creating a political unit out of the faith. There was a problem here too. It raised the possibility of a confrontation with the Christian powers, unknown since the Crusades. Moreover, the empire to the east of the Ottoman Empire, that of Iran, although Muslim was shi'i, would never accept the authority of the Sunni Ottomans. And anyway many of the Young Turks, and certainly those who organized the revolution of 1908, were atheists and positivists. Islam to them was little more than a vehicle through which they might mobilize the masses.

There remained Turkism: Turkish nationalism based on the Turkish race. This was an idea that developed and gained popularity among Turkish thinkers from the 1890s. It grew from ideas expounded by Europeans who were friendly to the Turks and who perhaps also sought to weaken imperial Russia. The idea that the Turks were not just the ruling elite in a declining empire, but had a vast kinship, based on race and the Turkic languages, stretching from the Balkans to Siberia, was attractive, something to revive them after the hangover of democracy. Turkism soon became the central ideology of the Young Turks. It gave them a clear new vision of their position, following the ending of the old hierarchies that had occurred with the 1908 revolution. Within a few years it had been accepted by most leaders of the Committee of Union and Progress as a central ideology.

The Armenians failed to grasp the nature of Turkism. They continued to see themselves primarily as Christians. If the Young Turks had adopted Islam as the guiding ideology, they would have understood the nature of the situation. Religion was an integral part to being an Ottoman Armenian, so a nonreligious ideology was hard to comprehend. They found it almost impossible to see what it meant to be up against a nonreligious, race-based ideology.

The chief Turkist ideologist was Ziya Gokalp, who was born in Diarbekir, a Kurdish city, in 1875; the Kurdish locality may have encouraged him to stress his Turkishness more forcefully as an identity. The subtext to his ideas makes it clear just what a threat Turkism was to Armenians....He held that the country of the Turks was not Turkey, or even Turkestan; it was a broad and everlasting coun-

Courtesy of Martin Gilbert, from *The First World War: A Complete History*, revised edition (Henry Holt: New York, 2003)

THE OTTOMAN EMPIRE BEFORE WORLD WAR I

Before World War I, the Ottoman Empire was a vast territory, including the countries we now call Turkey, Syria, Jordan, Lebanon, Israel, Palestine, Kuwait, and parts of Saudi Arabia and Iraq.

try, Turan. One of his slogans was. . . . "All of the Turks are one army." This was a fearful threat to any nation in the way of such a grand union of Turkic peoples, but it was a threat that found little resonance with the Armenians, even though their homeland was most at risk from the "one army." They continued to believe that their woes came from Islam, from the Muslim nature of the Ottoman Empire, and from local tyrannical Muslims.

It should be pointed out that Islam has in fact a definite . . . place for Christian peoples ("people of the book") which race based Turkism does not. . . . Religion has a place for a conscience, which racist ideologies do not.[44]

CONNECTIONS

❧ What is the purpose of an ideology? How does ideology influence action? What transforms something from an idea into an action?

❧ Christopher Walker describes three potential ideologies for the Young Turk leaders: Ottomanism, Islam, or Turkism. How would you describe the differences in the ideologies? Why did the differences matter?

❧ How does Walker describe the appeal of Turkism to the Young Turks?

❧ Why do some people find racist ideas attractive? When are people most vulnerable to believing racist ideologies? In hard economic times? After negative experiences with differences? When fear of the "other" is especially strong? How was racism manifest in other parts of the world at the turn of the twentieth century?

❧ Why do you think the ideas of Turkism had such resonance among the Young Turk leaders?

❧ Walker writes: "The Armenians failed to grasp the nature of Turkism. They continued to see themselves primarily as Christians. If the Young Turks had adopted Islam as the guiding ideology, they would have understood the nature of the situation. Religion was an integral part to being an Ottoman Armenian, so a nonreligious ideology was hard to comprehend. They found it almost impossible to see what it meant to be up against a nonreligious, race based ideology." Under religious law, Armenians, as Christians, were not afforded the same opportunities and protections as Muslims. The spread of Turkism brought new challenges for the Armenians. What differences do you notice between the two visions?

❧ Racism and pseudo-scientific racist thinking known as eugenics were becoming increasingly influential among educated Americans and Europeans throughout the late nineteenth and early twentieth century. Eugenic ideals exerted a powerful influence over individuals as well as public policy in the United States and Europe and in the ways leaders in those countries related to people from across the world. Some Ottoman and Armenian scholars suggest that the ideology of Turkism was another expression of that pernicious form of racist thinking. To learn more about the influence of scientific racism in the American and European context, refer to *Facing History and Ourselves: Race and Membership in American History.*

⸺

Reading 3 ⌐ IDEOLOGY IN ACTION

French scholars Gerard Chaliand and Yves Ternon write that in the Ottoman Empire, at the beginning of the twentieth century, "there was a latent feeling of humiliation born of the weakening of the empire that had once been feared."[45] The problem was exacerbated in the spring of 1912 when the Balkan League was formed with Russian help. Serbia, Bulgaria, Greece, and Montenegro, all former subjects of the Ottoman Empire, united with the goal of taking the Ottoman territory of Macedonia. At the same time, Ottoman forces were already fighting a war with Italy over Tripoli [Libya], a Muslim territory in North Africa. On October 8, Montenegro declared war on the Ottoman Empire. It was joined by the rest of its allies from the Balkan League ten days later. During the war, Armenian Christian soldiers fought along-side Muslims in defense of the Ottoman Empire for the first time. Their cooperation wasn't enough; the forces of its former subjects routed the Ottoman army. An armistice was signed on December 3, 1912, but before the peace agreements were completed a coup toppled the Ottoman government. Minister of War Enver, Minister of the Interior Talaat, and Military Governor of Constantinople Djemal created a new government of extreme Turkish nationalists.

An Armenian, name not known, serving in the Turkish Army, c. 1912.

Project SAVE Armenian Photograph Archives, Inc.,
Courtesy of Anahid Nakashian Tashjian

Even before the coup Turkish nationalists were gaining power. During the war nationalists organized a boycott of Greek Ottoman shops. Before long targets of the boycott included Armenians and other non-Muslim businesses. Tekinalp, an architect of Pan-Turkist ideology, boasted that the boycotts "caused the ruin of hundreds of small Greek and Armenian tradesman." Furthermore, he argued:

> *The systematic and rigorous boycott is now at an end, but the spirit it created in the people still persists. There are Turks who will not set foot in foreign shops unless they are certain that the same articles cannot be purchased under the same conditions in the shops of men of their own race, or at least of their own religion. The feeling of brotherhood has taken firm root in the hearts of the people all over the empire.*[46]

Following the coup, the U.S. Ambassador to Turkey, Henry Morgenthau, chronicled Talaat, Enver, and Djemal's implementation of Pan-Turkish policy in the remaining territories of the empire.

> *In place of a democratic constitutional state they resurrected the idea of Pan-Turkism; in place of*

equal treatment of all Ottomans, they decided to establish a country exclusively for Turks. . . . Their determination to uproot [Christian schools], or at least to transform them into Turkish institutions, was merely another detail in the same racial progress. Similarly they attempted to make all foreign business houses employ only Turkish labor, insisting that they should discharge their Greek, Armenian, and Jewish clerks, stenographers, workmen, and other employees. They ordered all foreign houses to keep their books in Turkish; they wanted to furnish employment for Turks, and enable them to acquire modern business methods. The Ottoman government even refused to have dealings with the representative of the largest Austrian munition maker unless he admitted a Turk as a partner. They developed a mania for suppressing all languages except Turkish. For decades French had been the accepted language of foreigners in Constantinople; most street signs were printed in both French and Turkish. One morning the astonished foreign residents discovered that all the French signs had been removed and that the names of streets, the directions on street cars, and other public notices, appeared only in . . . Turkish characters, which very few of them understood. Great confusion resulted from this change, but the ruling powers refused to restore the detested foreign language.[47]

CONNECTIONS

Project SAVE Armenian Photograph Archives, Inc., Courtesy Hagop Atamian.

Teacher, priest (bearded), and students of the National Apostolic Church School. Tulgadin village, Kharpert, Historic Armenia, Ottoman Empire, c. 1902.

☙ In their book on the Armenian Genocide, Gerard Chaliand and Yves Ternon write that at the beginning of the twentieth century in the Ottoman Empire, "there was a latent feeling of humiliation born of the weakening of the empire that had once been feared." Imagine the impact that the loss of a war to former subjects would have on the empire. Why do you think Turkish nationalist ideas found support in this environment?

☙ Psychologist James Gilligan, author of *Violence: Reflections on a National Epidemic* states: "I have yet to see a serious act of violence that was not provoked by the experience of feeling shamed and humiliated, disrespected and ridiculed, and that did not represent the attempt to prevent or undo this 'loss of face'—no matter how severe the punishment, even if it includes death." What do his comments suggest about the relationship between self-esteem and violence? How do Gilligan's comments relate to the observation made by Chaliand and Ternon?

❧ How did the boycott of Greek and Armenian businesses bring Turks together? In what ways did it divide the nation? How did it prepare the country for dehumanizing a group of people? What lasting effects from the boycott does Tekinalp describe? Create a list of possible reasons why an ordinary Turk might have participated in the boycott.

❧ Morgenthau writes that the Young Turks' determination to "uproot" Christian schools "was merely another detail" of their desire for "racial progress." Why have some Turks viewed the elimination of Christian schools as a sign of "racial progress"? What was meant by "racial progress" at the turn of the twentieth century?

To learn more about the history of the idea of race and its impact on public policy see Facing History and Ourselves' resource book *Facing History and Ourselves: Race and Membership in American History*.

An editorial in the Turkish journal Hilal in 1916 reflects the psychological effects of Turkism on a people that previously felt shamed and humiliated.

> *The Turkish People, while it saw its own individuality develop, became conscious of its rights. It suddenly became evident to it that it was the only master in its own house and that nobody should exploit it or displace it in any field. The foreigners were in its eyes nothing but guests, who were entitled to its respect, but whose duty it was to become worthy of the hospitality they were enjoying. . . .*
>
> *Thanks to their schools foreigners were able to exercise great moral influence over the young men of the country and they were virtually in charge of the spiritual and intellectual guidance of our country. By closing them the Government has put an end to a situation as humiliating as it was dangerous, a situation which, unfortunately, had already lasted too long. Other measures of a political and economic nature were taken to complete a work which might be called the taking possession of the country by its own sons, who had too long been deprived of their rights.*
>
> *Thanks to this awakening, a little late but still in time, and thanks especially to this activity, Turkey has today become a "Fatherland," like Sweden, Spain, or Switzerland. Our country is no longer an estate or fief for anybody; it is the country of a people which has just been recalled to life, and which aspires, in its independence and liberty, to happiness and glory.*[48]

❧ How do the editors suggest Pan-Turkish ideology changed the ways in which the Turkish people thought about their place in the world?

Reading 4 — NEIGHBOR TURNS AGAINST NEIGHBOR

Relationships between Turks and non-Muslim minorities deteriorated as Pan-Turkish ideas became law. Armenians, who had always held an inferior position in the Ottoman Empire, were increasingly labeled gavours or "infidels." Veron Dumehjian, an Armenian girl who grew up at the turn of the twentieth century in the Ottoman Empire, remembers how she disgraced her family when she cut her hair in bangs to look like the Turkish mayor's daughter, Lehman.

> *"You should be ashamed of yourself," Auntie said. "Only Turkish girls wear their hair in bangs. You have brought disgrace upon your family."*

As Veron grew older she recognized that the differences between being Turkish and Armenian had taken on a new meaning.

> *I had never thought about time or change. But slowly changes began to occur. Our lives went on as before, but now our days, which had always seemed to be lit by the sun, were being shadowed by a dark cloud.*

> *For the first time I began to sense the seriousness of our problems with the Turks. I had always known that they were not our friends, even though there were some with whom we were friendly, but now it seemed, in truth, that they were our enemies. We were Christians, and they were [Muslims], but it was not this alone that separated us: we were also different in language, race and custom. We did live on the same soil, but I was told that soil could be owned and that the present owner of this soil, which we had always called home, was Turkey.*

> *Grandma had hinted in the past that there might be trouble between the Armenians and the Turks, but now it was being talked about more openly—not only by her, but by everyone in our quarter. I was told that the Turks had massacred several hundred thousand Armenians a few years before, in 1895, and then again in Adana, in 1909, when I was two years old. And now there were rumors that there would be more massacres. I wasn't sure what all this meant, but I could see that the elders were worried. This made me worried, too, and I began to talk about my fears with the older children. No one could understand what was happening, but I could see that they were uneasy, too. This made me aware for the first time that our fears were not imagined, not childish, but real and deep rooted.*

Veron Dumehjian

I began to hear whisperings—at home and at Grandma's, especially at night, when my parents thought we were asleep. But more than their whisperings, it was the way they looked, the way they talked and moved about, that made me know something was wrong. I began to hear words like "deportations," "massacres," "annihilation." I didn't like the sounds of the words, but mostly I didn't like the looks on their faces when they said these words.

It was around this time that the Turkish army drafted my uncles Apraham and Hagop. When I asked Grandma about this, she said something about the World War.[49]

In August 1914, the inner circle of the Young Turk leaders signed a secret alliance with Germany. Even before the war, those leaders had already put forth proposals to the German ambassador outlining their war aims. Historian Christopher Walker notes that the Ottoman dictators hoped the war would give them an opportunity to "establish a link with the Muslim peoples of Russia." Creation of the link would require finding a solution to the "Armenian Question," because Armenians were concentrated on both sides of the Russian border. When the Ottoman Empire entered the war at the end of October 1914, the government issued a proclamation declaring intent to extend its borders and unite "all branches of our race."[50] Quickly rumors began to spread about the safety of Christians within the Ottoman Empire.

An article in the January 11, 1915, *New York Times* brought the con-

Articles from the New York Times reporting on the vulnerability of the Christian population in the Ottoman Empire from January, 1915.

From Kloian, Armenian Genocide: News Accounts

The New York Times

January 11, 1915.

(2;2)

SAYS TURKS ADVISE CHRISTIANS TO FLEE

Fear of General Massacre in Constantinople if Allied Fleet Passes Dardanelles.

Special Cable to THE NEW YORK TIMES.
ATHENS, Jan. 8. (Dispatch to The London Daily Telegraph.)—A man arriving from Constantinople who is in a position to know the facts has given me a mass of information concerning the present condition of affairs in the Turkish capital. He says the Turkish Government has no fear of an international revolution, and that the measures taken against the enemies of the Young Turk Committee are so drastic that no concerted movement on their part is possible.

The whole attention and anxiety of the Government is concentrated on the possible forcing of the Dardanelles by the allied fleet. It seems also that this fear is shared by their German mentors, for Baron von Wangenheim, the German Ambassador, has warned the Minister of a Balkan State in Constantinople that in the event of the allied fleet's forcing the straits, the Turks will vent their wrath by a massacre of the Christian population. In Constantinople no endeavor is any longer made by the Ministers to hide their feelings toward their Christian subjects.

To the Greek Patriarchate, who was sent to Talaat Pasha to remonstrate against the excesses committed by the organs of his Ministry, he unequivocally replied that there was no ...

January 13, 1915

CHRISTIANS IN GREA[T]

Talaat Bey Declares Tha[t] Room Only for Turks i[n]

Special Cable to THE NEW YO[RK]
ATHENS, Jan. 12, (Dispat[ch to]
London Morning Post.)—It i[s]
in well-informed circles that [...]
for the present have aband[oned]
advance against Egypt.

In Constantinople anxiety [over]
the possible forcing of the Da[rdanelles]
continues.

It is evident that the situa[tion of]
Christians is extremely precari[ous]
in the large cities, and Talaat [...]
Minister of the Interior, has s[o]
the Councillor of the Greek Patr[iarchate]
that in Turkey henceforth there [is]
room only for Turks. While [...]
profuse in assurances to the Gre[ek Min-]
ister regarding the cessation o[f]
Greek persecutions, no real an[...]
tion of the situation is perceptibl[e.]
The Turks are again fortifyi[ng]
Tchatalja lines.

cerns of the empire's Christians to the world's attention. Titled "Turks Advise Christians to Flee," the article reported that Mehmet Talaat, now the Minister of the Interior, had told the Greek Patriarch that there was no room for Christians living in Turkey. The story read:

> A man arriving from Constantinople who is in a position to know the facts has given me a mass of information concerning the present condition of affairs in the Turkish capital. He says the Turkish government has no fear of an international revolution, and that the measures taken against the enemies of the Young Turk Committee are so drastic that no concerted movement on their part is possible.

> The whole attention and anxiety of the Government is concentrated on the possible forcing of the Dardanelles [the straits connecting the Aegean and Black Seas] by the allied fleet. It seems also that this fear is shared by their German mentors, for Baron von Wangenheim, the German ambassador, has warned the Minister of a Balkan State in Constantinople that in the event of the allied fleet's forcing the straits, the Turks will vent their wrath by a massacre of the Christian population. In Constantinople no endeavor is any longer made by the Ministers to hide their feelings toward their Christian subjects.

> To the Greek Patriarchate [Patriarch], who was sent to Talaat Pasha to remonstrate against the excesses committed by the organs of his Ministry, he unequivocally replied that there was no room for Christians in Turkey and that the best the Patriarchate could do for his flock would be to advise them to clear out of the country and make room for the [Muslim] refugees.[51]

CONNECTIONS

❧ Veron came to understand that, "we" were the Armenians, and the "they" were the Turks. How did she learn those differences? How did you learn about which differences mattered? The lyrics to one of the songs from the musical *South Pacific* suggests: "You've got to be taught to hate and fear. You've got to be taught from year to year. It's got to be drummed into your sweet little ear. You've got to be carefully taught, you've got to be carefully taught." Where does hatred come from? Is it true that you have to be taught to hate?

❧ Under what conditions do differences between people and groups become obstacles to empathy? Under what conditions do those differences lead to violence?

❧ How did the Ottoman leaders view their "universe of obligation" in October of 1914? How had it changed since the Young Turk revolution in 1908?

❧ What did the *New York Times* article suggest was going to happen? What choices were available to people who read the article in January 1915? What choices were available to world leaders? What options were available to Christians living in the Ottoman Empire? Which options seem most likely to have made a difference?

❧ Armenian survivor Abraham Hartunian tells a story to illustrate the increasing fear and mistrust between Turkish officials and ordinary Armenians:

> [O]ne day, as I was conversing with a Turkish official, he said to me, "My friend, there is no hope. No longer can the Turk and the Armenian live together. Whenever you find the opportunity, you will annihilate us; and whenever we find the opportunity, we will annihilate you. Now the opportunity is ours and we will do everything to harm you. The wise course for you will be, when the time comes, to leave this country and never to return."[52]

❧ Even though the Armenians had no army of their own, the Turkish official expressed fear that the Armenians would try to annihilate the Turks at any opportunity. How does prejudice distort the way people see the world? What is the danger when people no longer believe that a conflict can be resolved peacefully?

⤚

Reading 5 — PLANNING MASS MURDER

As the situation for Armenians in the Ottoman Empire deteriorated, Talaat and other Turkish leaders warned the Armenians not to turn to the European powers for help. In February 1914, however, after intense negotiation European leaders and the Young Turk government agreed that two foreign inspector generals would be allowed to monitor the treatment of Armenians in the empire.

Despite the Armenians' growing frustration with the Young Turk government, thousands of Armenian soldiers entered the armed forces to fight to defend their country after the outbreak of World War I. Russian efforts to expand into Ottoman Armenian provinces had little success. Ottoman Armenians pledged loyalty to the empire.

In December 1914 or January 1915, a small group of Young Turk leaders met secretly to discuss the fate of the Armenians and other minorities living within their dwindling empire. Their attitudes have been recorded in several documents that now reside in national archives and research libraries around the world. Plans were circulated to very few people to prevent leaks. Most of those documents were immediately destroyed. With the documents that remain, the information on one document often has to be understood in relation to another and then a case has to be pieced together in relationship with the physical evidence and the stories of survivors, perpetrators, and bystanders.

Many historians of the Armenian Genocide have been struck by a document that appears to outline the original plans for the mass murder of the Armenians. The document was acquired early in 1919 with several other incriminating documents by British officials. A cover note from one of the officials explains the context in which the document was found:

> *Just before Christmas, I was approached confidentially by someone who stated that there was still in the Direction of Public Security, Constantinople, an official who has been in the Minister of the Interior's Department during the whole of the war, and who had charge of the archives relating to the secret measures and orders issued by the Minister of the Interior as a result of the decisions taken by the Committee of Union and Progress. He said that just before the Armistice, officials had been going to the archives department at night and making a clean sweep of most of the documents, but that the original draft of the orders relating to the Armenian massacres had been saved and could probably be procured by us through him on payment of Ltq. £10,000 paper money. He pledged me to secrecy if I went any further in the matter.*
>
> *In the course of the next few weeks, I followed the matter up. The man who stole or rescued this draft copy is today an official in the Direction of Public Security. I persuaded him without any great difficulty that it would be in his own interests to let us have the documents without payment, and that if in the future he gets into trouble, we would protect him.*

There are four documents in this dossier. The first is what is called the "Ten Commandments" and is by far the most interesting. It is unsigned and is the rough draft, but the handwriting is said to be that of Essad Bey, who was at the time one of the confidential secretaries keeping secret archives in the Ministry of the Interior. . . . My informant states that at the meeting when this draft was drawn up, there were present Talaat Pasha, Dr. Beheddin, Shakir, Dr. Nazim, Ismail Jambolet (the Young Turk central committee) and Colonel Sefi, sub-Director of the Political Section at the Ministry of War; its date is given as December or January 1914 or 1915.

My informant declares that messengers were sent to the different [governors] in the provinces with instructions to read these orders to them and then return the originals which were to be destroyed. Analysis of the documents the "Ten Commandments" numbers 3 and 4 shows that in order to economize their forces, the Turks distinguished between places where they could rely on the population to go ahead with the massacres almost unaided, and other localities where they felt it required the presence of the military in case the population did not show sufficient zeal.

THE 10 COMMANDMENTS OF THE COMITÉ UNION AND PROGRES.

(1). Profiting by Arts: 3 and 4 of [the Committee of Union and Progress], close all Armenian Societies, and arrest all who worked against Government at any time among them and send them into the provinces such as Baghdad or Mosul, and wipe them out either on the road or there.

(2). Collect arms.

(3). Excite [Muslim] opinion by suitable and special means...

(4). Leave all executive to the people in the provinces such as Erzeroum, Van, Mumuret ul Aziz, and Bitlis, and use Military disciplinary forces (i.e. Gendarmerie) ostensibly to stop massacres, while on the contrary in places as Adana, Sivas, Broussa, Ismidt and Smyrna actively help the [Muslims] with military force.

(5). Apply measures to exterminate all males under 50, priests

A postcard showing the Armenian population on the streets of Erzeroum.

From the private collection of Berj Fenerci

and teachers, leave girls and children to be Islamized.

(6). Carry away the families of all who succeed in escaping and apply measures to cut them off from all connection with their native place.

(7). On the ground that Armenian officials may be spies, expel and drive them out absolutely from every Government department or post.

(8). Kill off in an appropriate manner all Armenians in the Army—this to be left to the military to do.

(9). All action to begin everywhere simultaneously, and thus leave no time for preparation of defensive measures.

(10). Pay attention to the strictly confidential nature of these instructions, which may not go beyond two or three persons.

N.b. Above is verbatim translation—date December 1914 or January 1915.[53]

CONNECTIONS

❧ Historian Helen Fein describes four "preconditions, intervening factors, and causes that lead toward genocide." She suggests that these follow one another in order.

1. The victims have previously been defined outside the universe of obligation of the dominant group.

2. The rank of the state has been reduced by defeat in war or internal strife. (This is a predisposing condition toward a political or cultural crisis of national identity in which the third step becomes more likely to occur.)

3. An elite that adopts a new political formula to justify the nation's position and idealizes the rights of the dominant group.

4. The calculus of exterminating the victim group—a group excluded from the moral universe of obligation—changes as the perpetrators become part of a coalition at war against antagonists who have previously protested the persecution of the victim. Under these conditions the crime planned becomes less visible, and they no longer fear pressure from the antagonists.[54]

❧ How many of these conditions were met by the winter of 1914–1915? Like Helen Fein, Israel Charny, editor of the *Encyclopedia of Genocide*, has worked to understand conditions that increase the likelihood of genocide. Among them, he notes that perpetrators often feel that "retaliation for genocidal acts" by neutral nations is unlikely. What actions can be taken by neutral nations to prevent genocide before it actually begins? How would you respond to the concern of critics of international intervention who argue that proof of the perpetrators' intent is needed before any preemptive measures are taken? How does the work of Fein and Charny attempt to answer those critics?

- Point 3 of the "10 Commandments" document describes the need to "excite" public opinion against the Armenians. How can leaders "excite" opinion and turn one group of people against another?

- Point 5 of the document describes the goals to "exterminate all males under 50, priests and teachers, leave girls and children to be Islamized." Why would they treat men and women differently? What would be the fate of those who were "Islamized" or converted?

- It is likely that the meeting described by the British official took place secretly during one of the meetings of the inner circle of the Committee of Union and Progress's party meetings. Scholar Vahakn Dadrian describes these meetings:

> The picture that emerges from these party congresses is the dual track performance of Ittihad [Committee of Union and Progress]. On one hand there is the formulation of a platform outlining a party program that is intended strictly for public consumption. On the other hand, there is the clandestine mapping of a sketchy plan that is ominous and undoubtedly sinister in nature, and is, therefore kept secret from the public, even from the regular organs of the party leadership and naturally from rank and file.

Why would the leaders require such secrecy? What do you think they feared if their plans were made public?

- This document included in translation in this reading is a primary source. What techniques have you used for analyzing primary sources? What do you learn by analyzing this document? What questions does it raise?

- Deniers of the Armenian Genocide have often worked to discredit much of the primary source evidence of the genocide—telegrams sent by the perpetrators, copies of orders, as well as this document—by claiming they are forged or mistranslated or incomplete. Although the veracity of the documents have been authenticated by countless historians, deniers continue their efforts. Why would deniers focus on documents such as this one? What does the document tell us about the genocide?

Reading 6 — DICTATING RELIGION

In the early days of World War I, the Young Turk leaders stepped up efforts to define the enemy. Recognizing the power of religious authority, Enver Pasha, the minister of war, declared that the Young Turks hoped to "make [Qur'an] serve Turan [the name for the mythical pan-Turkish homeland]."[55] In *The Armenian Genocide: News Accounts from the American Press: 1915-1922*, Jack Zakarian explains how the Young Turk leaders manipulated religious authority to suit their needs.

The Ottoman Empire was the center of the Islamic world, and the Sheikh-ul-Islam was the chief religious authority for all Muslims. The Sheikh was usually appointed by the Sultan, but the CUP [the Committee of Union and Progress] chose their own candidate, Mustafa Hayri Bey, who was not from the religious elite and who had served in other political offices, unlike previous Sheikhs. The Sheikh was compelled by the CUP dictators and the German government to issue a "Jihad", or a declaration of Holy War, on November 23, 1914. Ignoring the fact that Germany and Austria were Christian allies of Turkey, the Jihad appealed to all Muslims to fight a holy war against "the unbelievers". . . . The Jihad never had the influence over the masses that the CUP dictators hoped for; nonetheless, the Jihad created an atmosphere of distrust and incited wrath toward Christian minorities in the Ottoman lands, and it later facilitated the government's program of Genocide against the Armenians.[56]

Morgenthau

The Sultan Mohammed V going to Friday prayers.

Vahakn Dadrian studies the role of religion in the treatment of Christian minorities in the Ottoman Empire. After reviewing documents and testimony, Dadrian concludes, "organizing agitation against the Armenians in wartime Turkey, especially in the mosques during Friday prayers, was an integral part of the scheme of genocide." He explains:

> This was a continuation of the legacy of massacres which were perpetrated during the reign of Sultan Abdul Hamid. Nearly every episode of massacre in the provinces then was launched from mosques on Fridays, following inflammatory harangues by appointed agitators inciting the faithful. Such agitation gained a powerful impetus with the declaration of holy war in 1914. Non-Muslim subjects of the empire, especially Christians, were utterly vulnerable. In the case of the Armenians, this vulnerability was carefully exploited by the Ittihadist leaders who proceeded to cultivate and disseminate rumors about Armenian sedition, acts of sabotage, espionage, and rebelliousness.[57]

Fa'iz El-Ghusein, a Muslim Bedouin from Damascus who witnessed the mistreatment of the Armenians in the name of Islam, expressed horror about how his faith was being used to justify the brutality:

> Is it right that these imposters, who pretend to be the supports of Islam and the Khilafat[community of the Muslim faithful], the protectors of the [Muslims], should transgress the command of God, transgress the [Qur'an], the Traditions of the Prophet, and humanity! Truly, they have committed an act at which Islam is revolted, as well as all [Muslims] and all the peoples of the earth, be they [Muslims], Christians, Jews, or idolaters.[58]

In September 1915, after a summer of systematic deportation and mass murder, the Sheikh-ul-Islam, resigned his position in the cabinet in protest of the "extermination of the Christian element."[59]

CONNECTIONS

✦ What are the dangers when religion becomes an instrument of the state?

✦ What authority is given to a cause when it is given religious blessing?

✦ Under what conditions does hateful language lead to mass violence? How does the fear and uncertainty of wartime influence the way people think about the "other"?

✦ In the United States there is a constitutional separation of religion and state. Why do you think the framers of the U.S. Constitution found that separation important for the strength of democracy? Are there ways that religion can strengthen democracy while still respecting pluralism and religious differences?

~ Many people are confused by the word jihad. Although the term has been used to describe holy war, the Arabic word jihad translates into English as "struggle." Most Islamic religious scholarship suggests that only under certain circumstances can the term be applied to military conflicts, similar to the idea of "just war," which is shared by many religious traditions.[60] Why does the difference matter?

NOTES

42. Richard Hovannisian, "The Armenian Question in the Ottoman Empire, 1876–1914," in Richard G. Hovannisian ed. *The Armenian People: From Ancient to Modern Times*, Vol. 2 (New York: St. Martin's Press, 1997), pp. 230–231.

43. Siamanto, *Bloody News from My Friend: Poems by Siamanto*. trans. Peter Balakian and Nevart Yaghlian (Detroit: Wayne State University Press, 1996), pp. 37–39.

44. Christopher J. Walker, "World War I and the Armenian Genocide," in Richard G.Hovannisian ed. *The Armenian People: From Ancient to Modern Times*, vol. 2 (New York: St. Martin's Press, 1997), pp. 241–243.

45. Gerard Chaliand and Yves Ternon, *The Armenians: From Genocide to Resistance* (London and Totowa, NJ: Zed Books, 1984).

46. Stephan H. Astourian, "Modern Turkish Identity and the Armenian Genocide," in Richard Hovannisian ed. *Remembrance and Denial: The Case of the Armenian Genocide* (Detroit: Wayne State University Press, 1999), p. 37.

47. Henry Morgenthau, Sr., *Ambassador Morgenthau's Story* (Plandome, NY: New Age Publishers, 1975), pp. 283–285.

48. Viscount Bryce, *The Treatment of Armenians in the Ottoman Empire 1915–1916* (London: H. M. S.O., 1916), Annex A.

49. David Kherdian, *The Road from Home* (New York: Greenwillow Books, 1979), pp. 29–30.

50. Christopher J. Walker, "World War I and the Armenian Genocide," in Richard G. Hovannisian ed. *The Armenian People: From Ancient to Modern Times*, vol. 2, (New York: St. Martin's Press: 1997), p. 244.

51. Richard Kloian, ed., *The Armenian Genocide: News Accounts from the American Press: 1915–1922* (Richmond, CA: Anto Publishing, 1988), p. 3.

52. Abraham Hartunian, *Neither to Laugh Nor to Weep: A Memoir of the Armenian Genocide*, 2nd ed., trans. Vartan Hartunian (Cambridge, MA: American Heritage Press, 1986) p. xixi.

53. Great Britain, Pubic Record Office: FO 371/4172/1270/folios 385-386,#388.

54. Adapted from Helen Fein, *Accounting for Genocide: Victims—and Survivors—of the Holocaust* (New York: The Free Press, 1979), p. 9.

55. Quoted in Florence Mazian, *Why Genocide?: The Armenian and Jewish Experiences in Perspective* (Ames: Iowa State University Press, 1990), p. 69.

56. Kloian, *Armenian Genocide: News Accounts*, p. [xiii.]

57. Vahakn N. Dadrian, "The Secret Young-Turk Ittihadist Conference and the Decision for the World War I Genocide of the Armenians," *Holocaust and Genocide Studies*, 7 (Fall 1993), pp. 186–187.

58. *Armenian Genocide: News Accounts*, p. 158.

59. *New York Times*, September 14, 1915, (reprinted in *Armenian Genocide: News Accounts*, p. 29).

60. Islamic Supreme Council, "What Jihad Is," available at *http://www.islamicsupremecouncil.org/bin/site/wrappers/default.asp?pane_2=content-legal-jihad_is_isnot*

*"The Armenians, living in Turkey, will be destroyed to the last.
The government has been given ample authority. As to the organization of
the mass murder, the government will provide the necessary explanations."*
—Behaeddin Shakir, a member of the Central Committee
of the Committee of Union and Progress

Chapter 4

GENOCIDE

SCHOLAR ROBERT MELSON WRITES THAT ALTHOUGH THE ARMENIAN GENOCIDE WAS CARRIED OUT DURING World War I, it was not an action of military necessity.

> *The genocide of the Armenians should be understood not as a response to "Armenian provocations" but as a stage in the Turks' revolution, which as a reaction to the continuing disintegration of the empire settled on a narrow nationalism and excluded Armenians from the moral universe of the state. Once the Ottoman Empire joined the Central Powers [Austria-Hungary and Germany] against Russia, the CUP could use the excuse of military necessity to destroy the Armenians. As many historians have noted, the Turkish revolution initiated by the CUP was successful in creating a new Turkey, but it also came close to destroying an ancient people in the process.[61]*

In 1915, there was no word to accurately describe what the Turks were doing to the Armenians. Raphael Lemkin did not coin the term "genocide" until Nazi brutality in Europe brought mass murder closer to the heart of the Western world. In the Ottoman Empire, journalists, diplomats, and other witnesses struggled to find language to convey the depth and the enormity of the anti-Armenian measures. Accounts refer to "horrors," "barbarity," "massacres," "murder," "deportations," or "ravages," but no word captures the scale of the violence. American Ambassador Henry Morgenthau, after reading report after report from his consuls in the provinces, proclaimed that Turkish plans amounted to "race murder." On July 10, 1915, he cabled Washington:

> *Persecution of Armenians assuming unprecedented proportions. Reports from widely scattered districts indicate systematic attempt to uproot peaceful Armenian populations and through arbitrary arrests, terrible tortures, whole-sale expulsions and deportations from one end of the empire to the other accompanied by frequent instances of rape, pillage, and murder, turning into massacre, to bring destruction and destitution on them. These measures are not in response to popular or fanatical demand but are purely arbitrary and directed from Constantinople in the name of military necessity, often in districts where no military operations are likely to take place.*[62]

The perpetrators also looked for language. They looked for language to cover up the nature of the crime and for ways to distort language to blame the victims for their own misfortune. Armenian resistance to deportation and murder was called "revolt" or "rebellion." Armenians, once called "the loyal millet," were now accused of joining the enemy. The government claimed that Armenian deportations were necessary for the "security of our country" and the "welfare of the Armenians."

Even without contemporary language, people knew what they saw. On May 24, 1915, the Allied nations of Great Britain, France, and Russia warned the Young Turk leaders that their "crimes against humanity and civilization" would not go unpunished. Somebody had to be held accountable. The genocide was the result of choices made by individuals and groups acting in the name of the Ottoman government. The readings in this chapter focus on the results of those choices.

If reading this history makes you feel powerless, and without a sense that people could stop the horror, then consider the importance of recognizing when there were opportunities to alter the course of history.

Reading 1 — EVACUATION, DEPORTATION, AND DEATH

In April 1984, The Permanent Peoples' Tribunal—a public tribunal that hears cases of human rights abuses and tries them according to international law—held a session considering the facts of the Armenian Genocide. After hearing arguments, the international panel of jurors, which included three Nobel prize winners and other prominent figures from around the world, ruled that the Turkish government was responsible for the crime of genocide against the Armenians. A section of their report details the genocidal process.

Beginning in January 1915, Armenian soldiers [serving in the Ottoman army] and gendarmes were disarmed, regrouped in work brigades of 500 to 1,000 men, put to work on road maintenance or as porters, then taken by stages to remote areas and executed. It was not until April that the implementation of a plan began, with successive phases carried out in a disciplined sequence. The signal was first given for

Project SAVE Armenian Photograph Archives, courtesy of Garbis Kazanjian, River Vale, New Jersey, and Alice Jernazian Haig, Dana Point, California, daughter of Rev. Ephraim R. Jemazian.

Survivors of the genocide hold a burial service for the Ourfa Armenian victims whose bones were found strewn around the monastery yard. At the top, the words of Armenian poet Krikor Zohrab in translation say, "We are gone now, but the nation has 400,000 orphans. Save them."

deportation to begin in Zeytun [Zeitun] in early April, in an area of no immediate strategic importance. It was not until later that deportation measures were extended to the border provinces.

The pretext used to make the deportation a general measure was supplied by the resistance of the Armenians of Van. The vali [governor]of Van, Jevdet, sacked outlying Armenian villages and the Van Armenians organized the self-defense of the city. They were saved by a Russian breakthrough spear-headed by the Armenian volunteers from the Caucasus. After taking Van on May 18th, the Russians continued to press forward but were halted in late June by a Turkish counter-offensive. The Armenians of the vilayet [region] of Van were thus able to retreat and escape extermination.

When the news of the Van revolt reached Constantinople, the Union and Progress (Ittihad) Committee seized the opportunity. Some 650 personalities, writers, poets, lawyers, doctors, priests and politicians were imprisoned on April 24th and 25th, 1915, then deported and murdered in the succeeding months. Thus was carried out what was practically the thorough and deliberate elimination of almost the entire Armenian intelligentsia of the time.

From April 24 onwards, and following a precise timetable, the government issued orders to deport the Armenians from the eastern vilayets. Since Van was occupied by the Russian army, the measures applied only to the six vilayets of Trebizond (Trabzon), Erzerum, Bitlis, Diarbekir, Kharput, and Sivas. The execution of the plan was entrusted to a "special organization" (SO), made up of common criminals and convicts trained and equipped by the Union and Progress Committee. This semi-official organization, led by Behaeddin Shakir, was under the sole authority of the Ittihad central committee. Constantinople issued directives to the valis, kaymakans [district governors], as well as local SO men, who had discretionary powers to have moved or dismissed any uncooperative gendarme or official. The methods used, the order in which towns were evacuated, and the routes chosen for the columns of deportees all confirm the existence of a centralized point of command controlling the unfolding of the program. Deportation orders were announced publicly or posted in each city and township. Families were allowed two days to collect a few personal belongings; their property was confiscated or quickly sold off. The first move was generally the arrest of notables, members of Armenian political parties, priests, and young men, who were forced to sign fabricated confessions then discreetly eliminated in small

From the private collection of Berj Fenerci

Special organization gangs known as "chetes" or "shotas."

groups. The convoys of deportees were made up of old people, women, and children. In the more remote villages, families were slaughtered and their homes burned or occupied. On the Black Sea coast and along the Tigris near Diarbekir boats were heaped with victims and sunk. From May to July 1915, the eastern provinces were sacked and looted by Turkish soldiers and gendarmes, SO gangs ("chetes"), etc. This robbery, looting, torture, and murder were tolerated or encouraged while any offer of protection to the Armenians was severely punished by the Turkish authorities.

It was not possible to keep the operation secret. Alerted by missionaries and consuls, the Entente [Allied] Powers enjoined the Turkish government, from May 24, to put an end to the massacres, for which they held members of the government personally responsible. Turkey made the deportation official by issuing a decree, claiming treason, sabotage, and terrorist acts on the part of the Armenians as a pretext.

Deportation was in fact only a disguised form of extermination. The strongest were eliminated before departure. Hunger, thirst, and slaughter decimated the convoys' numbers. Thousands of bodies piled up along the roads. Corpses hung from trees and telegraph poles; mutilated bodies floated down rivers or were washed up on the banks. Of the seven eastern vilayets' original population of 1,200,000 Armenians, approximately 300,000 were able to take advantage of the Russian occupation to reach the Caucasus; the remainder were murdered where they were or deported, the women and children (about 200,000 in number) kidnapped. Not more than 50,000 survivors reached the point of convergence of the convoys of deportees in Aleppo.

At the end of July 1915, the government began to deport the Armenians of Anatolia and Cilicia, transferring the population from regions which were far distant from the front and where the presence of Armenians could not be regarded as a threat to the Turkish army. The deportees were driven south in columns which were decimated en route. From Aleppo, survivors were sent on toward the deserts of Syria in the south and of Mesopotamia in the southeast. In Syria, reassembly camps were set up at Hama, Homs, and near Damascus. These camps accommodated about 120,000 refugees, the majority of whom survived the war and were repatriated to Cilicia in 1919. Along the Euphrates, on the other hand, the Armenians were driven ever onward toward Deir-el-Zor; approximately 200,000 reached their destination. Between March and August 1916, orders came from Constantinople to liquidate the last survivors remaining in the camps along the railway and the banks of the Euphrates.

There were nevertheless still some Armenians remaining in Turkey. A few Armenian families in the provinces, Protestants and Catholics for the most part, had been saved from death by the American missions and the Apostolic Nuncio. In some cases, Armenians had been spared as a result of resolute intervention by Turkish officials, or had been hidden by Kurdish or Turkish friends. The [majority of the] Armenians of Constantinople and Smyrna also escaped deportation. Lastly, there were cases of resistance (Urfa, Shabin-Karahisar, Musa-Dagh). In all, including those who took refuge in Russia, the number of survivors at the end of 1916 can be estimated at 600,000 out of an estimated total population in 1914 of 1,800,000, according to A. Toynbee.

In Eastern Anatolia, the entire Armenian population had disappeared. A few survivors of the slaughter took refuge in Syria and Lebanon, while others reached Russian Armenia.[63]

CONNECTIONS

❧ Why was the Committee of Union and Progress able to use the story of Armenian resistance at Van as an excuse to begin widespread deportation and mass murder? What is a pretext? How is a pretext used to cover the truth?

❧ The report notes that: "The execution of the plan [of genocide] was entrusted to a 'special organization', made up of common criminals and convicts trained and equipped by the Union and Progress Committee [the Young Turks]." How did the use of a "special organization" create a cover for the government's plans?

❧ In 1915 German officer Liman Von Sanders rejected a deportation order for the Armenians and Greeks of Smyrna and the central government backed off. What questions does the story raise for you?

❧ The genocide unfolded in several stages. List the turning points in the process that led to mass murder?

❧ The treatment of the Armenians in the Ottoman Empire had been of international concern long before the deportations began. Given that attention, how is it possible that no country intervened and that the genocide was not prevented?

❧ Reread the description of the genocide. What choices had to be made to make the genocide possible? Who made those choices? When was prevention possible?

❧ Based on the description of the genocide, is it possible that people did not know what was happening to the Armenians? If people knew, how do you explain why more people did not try to stop the deportations and massacres? What options were available to leaders, to ordinary people, and to other governments?

╼

To view an interactive map of the Armenian Genocide including the principal routes of deportation, massacre sites, and concentration camps, visit *www.armenian-genocide.org*. A chronology of the genocide is also available on the same website.

Reading 2 — UNDER THE COVER OF WAR

Historians Deborah Dwork and Robert Jan van Pelt note: "The genocide of the Armenians was made possible by two events: the final collapse of the Ottoman Empire in the first decade of the twentieth century and the advent of total war in the second."[64] During the early months of World War I, Young Turk leaders continued to target the Christian population of the empire—Armenians, Greeks, and Assyrians. Behaeddin Shakir, a member of the central committee within the Committee of Union and Progress, outlined a rationale and structure for the forthcoming genocide in March of 1915.[65] He claimed that the Armenian Revolutionary Federation was preparing an attack and that the Armenians stood in the way of the central committee's "patriotic efforts." Shakir wrote:

> *Unable to forget the humiliations and the bitterness of the past, and filled with an urge for vengeance, the Cemiyet [central committee of the Committee of Union and Progress], full of hope for the future has reached a decision. The Armenians, living in Turkey, will be destroyed to the last. The government has been given ample authority. As to the organization of the mass murder, the government will provide the necessary explanations to the governors, and to the army commanders. All the delegates of the Ittihad ve Terakki in their own regions will be in charge of this task.*[66]

Throughout the late winter and spring, follow-up telegrams were sent to local officials with rationalizations for the deportation and murder of the Armenians. Arrests of Armenian leaders began in several regions as well as mass deportations of the Armenians from Zeitun and Erzerum. In late May, a law legalizing the deportations was enacted without debate in the Ottoman Parliament. By June, notices were hung in villages and towns throughout the empire meant to justify the government's plans to ordinary people.

> *Our Armenian fellow countrymen, who form one of the Ottoman racial elements, having taken up with a lot of false ideas of a nature to disturb the public order, as the result of foreign instigations for many years past, and because of the fact that they have brought about bloody happenings and have attempted to destroy the peace and security of the Ottoman state, of their fellow countrymen, as well as their own safety and interests, and, moreover, as the Armenian societies have now dared to join themselves to the enemy of their existence, our Government is compelled to adopt extraordinary measures and sacrifices, both for the preservation of the order and security of the country, and for the continuation of their existence and for the welfare of the Armenian societies. Therefore, as a measure to be applied until the conclusion of the war, the Armenians have to be sent away to places which have been prepared in the interior vilayets [provinces], and a literal obedience to the following orders, in a categorical manner, is accordingly enjoined upon all Ottomans:*
>
> *1. With the exception of the sick, all Armenians are obliged to leave, within five days from the date of this proclamation, and by villages or quarters, under the escort of the gendarmery [police force].*

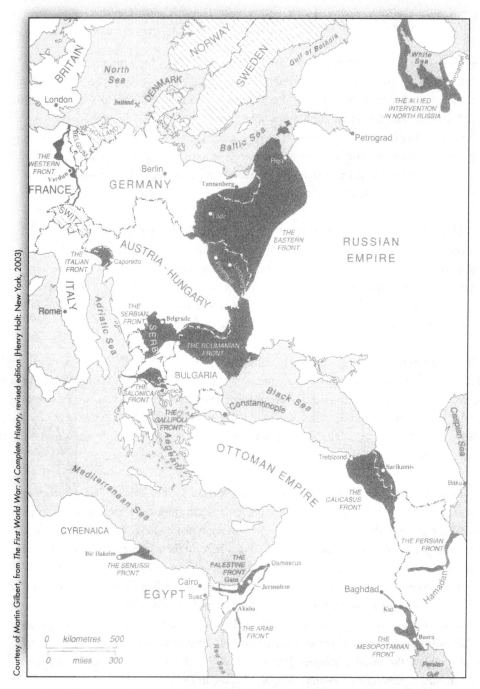

Courtesy of Martin Gilbert, from *The First World War: A Complete History*, revised edition (Henry Holt: New York, 2003)

THE WAR FRONTS OF WORLD WAR I

With World War I being fought on numerous fronts, the Young Turk government found in the war a nationalist rationale—and shield—for their deportations of the Armenians.

2. *Although they are free to carry with them on their journey the articles of their movable property which they desire, they are forbidden to sell their landed and their extra effects, or to leave them here and there with other people. Because their exile is only temporary, their landed property will be taken care of under the supervision of the Government, and stored in closed and protected buildings. Any one who sells or attempts to take care of his movable effects or landed property in a manner contrary to this order shall be sent before the Court Martial. They are only free to sell to the Government, of their own accord, those articles which may answer the needs of the army.*

3. *To assure their comfort during the journey, hans [inns] and suitable buildings have been prepared, and everything has been done for their safe arrival at their places of temporary residence, without their being subjected to any kind of attack or affronts.*

4. *The guards will use their weapons against those who make any attempts to attack or affront the life, honor, and property of one or of a number of Armenians, and such persons as are taken alive will be sent to the Court Martial and executed. This measure being the regrettable result of the Armenians having been led in error, it does not concern in any way the other races, and these other elements will in no way or manner whatsoever intervene in this question.*

5. *Since the Armenians are obliged to submit to this decision of the Government, if some of them attempt to use arms against the soldiers or gendarmes, arms shall be employed only against those who use force, and they shall be captured dead or alive. In like manner, those who, in opposition to the Government's decision, refrain from leaving, or hide themselves here and there, if they are sheltered or are given food and assistance, the persons who thus shelter them or aid them shall be sent before the Court Martial for execution.*

6. *As the Armenians are not allowed to carry any firearms or cutting weapons, they shall deliver to the authorities every sort of arms, revolvers, daggers, bombs, etc, which they have concealed in their places of residence or elsewhere. A lot of weapons and other things have been reported to the Government, and if their owners allow themselves to be misled, and the weapons are afterwards found by the Government, they will be under heavy responsibility and receive severe punishment.*

7. *The escorts of soldiers and gendarmes are required and*

© Armenian National Institute, Inc., courtesy of Sybil Stevens (daughter of Armin T. Wegner). Wegner Collection, Deutches Literaturarchiv, Marbach & United States Holocaust Memorial Museum.

An Armenian mother and child, fleeing from death. This photograph was taken by Armin T. Wegner, an eyewitness to the Armenian Genocide.

are authorized to use their weapons against and to kill persons who shall try to attack or damage Armenians in villages, in city quarters, or on the roads for the purpose of robbery or other injury.

8. Those who owe money to the Ottoman Bank may deposit in its warehouses goods up to the amount of their indebtedness. Only in case the Government should have need thereof in the future are the military authorities authorized to buy the said goods by paying the price therefor. In the case of debts to other people it is permitted to leave goods in accordance with this condition, but the Government must ascertain the genuine character of the debt, and for this purpose the certified books of the merchant form the strongest proof.

9. Large and small animals which it is impossible to carry along the way shall be bought in the name of the army.

10. On the road the vilayet, leva, kaza and nahieh [province, county, district, village and cluster] officials shall render possible assistance to the Armenians.

25 June 1915 [67]

Witnesses recorded the atrocities of the deportations. Deportations to the desert meant death, either by starvation or through the butchery of special battalions created by emptying the jails of former prisoners and impoverished Kurdish tribesmen. Kurds and other Muslims became the beneficiaries of Armenian property when a second law, the Law of Expropriation and Confiscation became national policy.

CONNECTIONS

◆ Deborah Dwork and Robert Jan van Pelt note: "The genocide of the Armenians was made possible by two events: the final collapse of the Ottoman Empire in the first decade of the twentieth century and the advent of total war in the second."[68] What is total war? Why would the staggering brutality of World War I make the Armenian Genocide possible?

◆ What did the Young Turks hope to teach ordinary people about the Armenians through their public notices? What words and phrases stand out? How did they hope the notices would influence the way people think about the deportations of Armenians? How might an Armenian individual or an Armenian group respond to the decree?

◆ How do you explain the differences in tone and content between the two government statements about the Armenians? Who is the intended audience for each?

• By the time the deportation order was posted thousands of Armenian leaders from across the empire had been separated from their families and murdered. How does this order try to explain those executions?

• Just before the United States entered World War I, President Woodrow Wilson told a friend: "Once [I] lead this people into war and they'll forget there ever was such a thing as tolerance . . . a nation cannot put its strength into a war and keep its head level; it has never been done." What makes it difficult to keep a nation's "head level" during war? How might the outbreak of the war have influenced ordinary people's responses to the deportations?

• Compare the language of the order with the reading "Describing the Genocide" as well as other survivor and witness accounts. How is language used to cover what really happened?

• How do the messages in this order compare with the myths and rumors that had been spread through the Young Turks' propaganda?

• Look carefully at the photograph of the Armenian mother and child on page 89. What can you learn about their situation by studying the image? What questions are you left with? Armin Wegner, the photographer who took the picture, wrote a longer caption for the photograph which he called "Mother and Child." His caption reads:

> *Fleeing from death. An Armenian mother on the heights of the Taurus Mountains. Her husband has been killed or slaughtered, thrown into prison or driven to forced labour. On her back she carries all that she owns, i.e. what she could take with her, a blanket for sleeping or to use as a tent to protect against the sun, some wooden sticks, and then, on top of everything else, her baby. How much longer can she carry this weight?* [69]

How do Wegner's comments influence the way you respond to the photograph? What context does he add that you could not learn from looking at the photograph on your own?

Reading 3 — THE ROUND UPS BEGIN

While the ministry of war coordinated propaganda, Talaat, the minister of the interior, coordinated the mass murder of the Armenians. In January 1915, Talaat warned the Greek Patriarch that there was no room for Christians in Turkey and their supporters should advise them to clear out. Orders announcing the Committee of Union and Progress's plans for deportation began to circulate in late February 1915. By March, Armenian men in the Turkish army were being disarmed, placed in labor battalions, and killed.[70] Quietly, deportation had already begun in several communities. Armenian resistance was labeled sedition and used as propaganda to justify the murder and deportation of ordinary Armenian men, women, and children. By April, Armenian schools were closed. Later that month, on the night of April 23 and all through April 24, Armenian leaders and intellectuals in Constantinople were arrested and led outside of the city, where they were subjected to torture and many were executed.

One of the survivors, the priest (later to become Bishop) Krikoris Balakian recalls how he and others were resting after Easter celebrations while a secret project was being carried out near the central police station.

> *Blood-colored buses were already transporting groups of Armenians who had just been arrested from the near and far suburbs and neighborhoods to the central prison. Chief of Police, Betri, had sent official letters weeks earlier in sealed boxes to all the Guard offices with orders to open them on the same day and to carry out the assignments with precision and in secret.*

> *The letters contained the blacklist of Armenians to be arrested—a list which had been compiled with the help of Armenian traitors, and in particular by Artin Mkrtchian, as well as the neighborhood Ittehatist [Young Turk] clubs. Those listed for death were the Armenians who had played vital roles as social reformers or non-partisans, and were deemed to be able to incite revolution or resistance.[71]*

[Balakian and eight friends were arrested and put in the central prison.]

> *Every few hours until morning, newly arrested Armenians were brought to the prison. Behind the fences of the prison, there was a strange hustle and bustle to the growing crowd of prisoners. Like some dream it seemed as if on one night, all prominent Armenians of the capital—assembly men, representatives, progressive thinkers, reporters, teachers, doctors, pharmacists, dentists, merchants, and bankers—had made an appointment in those dim cells of the prison. More than a few people were still wearing their pajamas, robes, and slippers, and it made the whole scene seem even more dreamlike.*

> *On the Sunday the prisoners were subjected to searches and were crowded on buses under police escort and taken in the direction of the sea shore near Sirkedji. The buses then entered the area of the Saray-Bournou orchards where in the 1890s hundreds of young ... Armenian intellectuals had been*

killed. From there they were crowded on a steam ship under armed army and police officials as well as army spies.

For a moment we were so shaken, we were convinced that we were being taken out to the Sea of Marmara to be drowned. Many of the men were crying, many were remembering their loved ones, as we sailed toward the open sea. In a few months, many of us would regret that we had not thrown ourselves into the sea that night. Because death by sea would have been kinder than the torture the Turks did to us with axes and hatchets in the places they would later take us.[72]

Armenians being marched to prison in nearby Mezireh under the guard of armed Turkish soldiers, Kharpert, Historic Armenia, Ottoman Empire, 1915.

Project SAVE Armenian Photograph Archives, Courtesy of anonymous donor

CONNECTIONS

✢ Why do you think the Young Turk government singled out intellectuals and professionals for arrest and deportation?

✢ What choices were available to Balakian and other leaders of the Armenian community? If they had chosen to resist, what do you think would the consequences for the rest of the Armenian community have been?

✢ Balakian uses the phrase "Armenian traitors" to describe the Armenians who cooperated with the Young Turks. What options were available to Armenians who were asked to cooperate with Young Turk authorities? Were they traitors, collaborators, or just trying to survive?

Reading 4 — THE GERMAN CONNECTION

Before becoming part of the triumvirate that seized power in Turkey at the beginning of 1913, Enver, the Ottoman minister of war, served as a military attaché to Berlin. During his four-year commission Enver developed a close relationship with German Kaiser Wilhelm II.[73] After the coup of 1913 that brought Enver to power, German-Ottoman military cooperation became national policy.

In December 1913, a German mission arrived in Turkey with the task of reorganizing the Ottoman army. Officers of the German military mission assumed responsibility for the command of the Turkish army under the leadership of Enver. The German-Turkish relationship was strengthened after the agreement of a military alliance between Germany and the Ottoman Empire in August 1914.

In notes written after a meeting with Young Turk leaders, Max Scheubner-Richter, a German vice consul and commander of a joint German-Turkish special guerrilla force, described plans to "destroy" the Armenians of the Ottoman Empire.

Courtesy of the Morgenthau Collection

Kaiser Wilhelm II, of Germany wearing a Turkish Fez

The first item on this agenda concerns the liquidation of the Armenians. Ittihad will dangle before the Allies a specter of an alleged revolution prepared by the Armenian Dashnak party. Moreover, local incidents of social unrest and acts of Armenian self-defense will deliberately be provoked and inflated and will be used as pretexts to effect the deportations. Once en route, however, the convoys will be attacked and exterminated by Kurdish and Turkish brigands, and in part by gendarmes, who will be instigated for that purpose by Ittihad.[74]

From their unique position as overseers of the Ottoman army, German soldiers watched as the genocide was carried out. The highest-ranking member of Germany's military mission to Turkey, General Bronsart von Schellendorf, directly issued orders for the round up and deportation of Armenians. Another high-ranking German officer, Lieutenant Colonel Boettrich, the military chief overseeing the construction of the Baghdad Railway, produced orders to deport the Armenian laborers, workmen, technicians, engineers, and administrators who were working on the railroad.[75] When Franz Gunther, deputy director of the

Anatolian Railway, learned about Boettrich's orders, he warned:

> *Our enemies will some day pay a good price to obtain possession of this document . . . they will be able to prove that the Germans have not only done nothing to prevent the Armenian persecutions but they even issued certain orders to this effect, as the [Turkish] Military Commander has ecstatically pointed out.*[76]

Enver Pasha

In a study of German participation in the Armenian Genocide, Vahakn Dadrian notes: "Whereas some German operatives went out of their way to avoid being drawn into acts that would have been tantamount to complicity, others willingly allowed the Turks to coopt them.... What is most noteworthy in this connection is the additional fact that the Germans belonging to the latter category had more power."[77]

On October 8, 1915, four members of the German missionaries staff to Turkey appealed to the German Minister of Foreign Affairs to intercede with their ally on behalf of the Armenians.

> *We think it our duty to draw the attention of the Ministry of Foreign Affairs to the fact that our school work will be deprived, for the future, of its moral basis and will lose all authority in the eyes of the natives, if it is really beyond the power of the German Government to mitigate the brutality of the treatment which the exiled women and children of the massacred Armenians are receiving.*
>
> *In face of the scenes of horror which are being unfolded daily before our eyes in the neighborhood of our school, our educational activity becomes a mockery of humanity. How can we make our pupils listen to the Tales of the Seven Dwarfs, how can we teach them conjugations and declensions, when, in the compounds next door to our school, death is carrying off their starving compatriots—when there are girls and women and children, practically naked, some lying on the ground, others stretched between the dead or the coffins made ready for them beforehand, and breathing their last breath!*
>
> *Out of 2,000 to 3,000 peasant women from the Armenian Plateau who were brought here in good health, only forty or fifty skeletons are left. The prettier ones are the victims of their gaolers' [jailers'] lust; the plain ones succumb to blows, hunger and thirst (they lie by the water's edge, but are not allowed to quench their thirst). The Europeans are forbidden to distribute bread to the starving.*

Every day more than a hundred corpses are carried out of Aleppo.

All this happens under the eyes of high Turkish officials. There are forty or fifty emaciated phantoms crowded into the compound opposite our school. They are women out of their mind; they have forgotten how to eat; when one offers them bread, they throw it aside with indifference. They only groan and wait for death.

"See," say the natives, "Taâlim el Alman (the teaching of the Germans)."

The German scutcheon [a shield with a coat of arms] is in danger of being smirched forever in the memory of the Near Eastern peoples. There are natives of Aleppo, more enlightened than the rest, who say: "The Germans do not want these horrors. Perhaps the German nation does not know about them. If it did, how could the German Press, which is attached to the truth, talk about the humanity of the treatment accorded to the Armenians who are guilty of High Treason? Perhaps, too, the German Government has its hands tied by some contract defining the powers of the [German and Turkish] State; in regard to one another's affairs?"

No, when it is a question of giving over thousands of women and children to death by starvation, the words "Opportunism" and "definition of powers" lose their meaning. Every civilized human being is "empowered" in this case to interfere, and it is his bounden duty to do so. Our prestige in the East is the thing at stake. There are even Turks and Arabs who have remained human, and who shake their heads in sorrow when they see, in the exile convoys that pass through the town, how the brutal soldiers shower blows on women with child who can march no farther.

We may expect further and still more dreadful hecatombs after the order published by Djemal Pasha. (The engineers of the Baghdad Railway are forbidden, by this order, to photograph the Armenian convoys; any plates they have already used for this must be given up within twenty-four hours, under penalty of prosecution before the Council of War.) It is a proof that the responsible authorities fear the light, but have no intention of putting an end to scenes which are a disgrace to humanity.

. . .We know that the Ministry of Foreign Affairs has already, from other sources, received detailed descriptions of what is happening here. But as no change has occurred in the system of the deportations, we feel ourselves under a double obligation to make this report, all the more because the fact of our living abroad enables us to see more clearly the immense danger by which the German name is threatened here.[78]

Despite the pleas of the mission's staff and many ordinary German citizens who witnessed the treatment of Christian minorities in the Ottoman Empire, the German government chose not to intervene.

CONNECTIONS

- Vahakn Dadrian believes that German officials were "indirect accessories to crimes perpetrated by the [Turkish] Special Organization functionaries whose overall goal they endorsed, financed to some extent, and shepherded." Dadrian uses legal language to describe the German officials' participation in the genocide. How would you describe the relationship in moral terms?

- How do the German missionaries express their outrage? What arguments do they make to convince the German foreign minister to intervene? What words or phrases from the letter stand out? What rules are needed so that individuals can know they are protected as they voice dissent?

- In the letter the German missionaries ask: "How can we make our pupils listen to the Tales of the Seven Dwarfs, how can we teach them conjugations and declensions, when, in the compounds next door to our school, death is carrying off their starving compatriots?" How would you answer their question?

- After the war, General von Schellendorf compared the Armenians and the Jews living in his country, Germany. In language laden with stereotypes, Bronsart von Schellendorf explains:

  > ...the Armenian is just like the Jew, a parasite outside of the confines of his homeland, sucking the marrow of the people of the host country. Year after year they abandon their native land—just like the Polish Jews who migrate to Germany—to engage in usurious activities. Hence, the hatred which, in a medieval form, has unleashed itself against them as an unpleasant people, entailing their murder. [79]

What stereotypes are reflected in his comparisons? Whom does he blame for the mistreatment of Armenians and Jews?

Between 1904 and 1907, German troops killed between 65,000 and 80,000 of the Herero people who inhabited present-day Namibia in Southwest Africa, then a German colony. Some scholars suggest that Germany's colonial experience, and its experiences during World War I and the Armenian Genocide served as models for the Nazi Holocaust. To research the relationship between the treatment of colonized Africans and genocide, see the book *Exterminate All the Brutes: One Man's Odyssey into the Heart of Darkness and the Origins of European Genocide* by Sven Lindqvist.

Reading 5 ⌐ FOLLOWING ORDERS

Lieutenant Said Ahmed Mukhtar al-Ba'aj, an Ottoman officer, was one of four Arab Muslim soldiers who defected to the Russian Army. The Russians turned the men over to the British, who interviewed them. In December 1916, the officer testified about his role in the deportation of Armenians from Trebizond and Erzerum.

An order came from Constantinople that Armenians inhabiting the frontier towns and villages be deported to the interior. It was said then that this was only a precautional measure. I saw at that time large convoys of Armenians go through Erzeroum. They were mostly old men, women and children. Some of the able-bodied men had been recruited in the Turkish Army and many had fled to Russia. The massacres had not begun yet. In May 1915 I was transferred to Trebizond. In July an order came to deport to the interior all the Armenians in the Vilayet of Trebizond. Being a member of the Court Martial I knew that deportations meant massacres....

Besides the deportation order. . . an Imperial "Iradeh" was issued ordering that all deserters when caught, should be shot without trial. The secret order read "Armenians" in lieu of "deserters." The Sultan's "Iradeh" was accompanied by a "fatwa" [Muslim legal opinion] from Sheikh-ul-Islam stating that the Armenians had shed [Muslim] blood and their killing was lawful. Then the deportations started. The children were kept back at first. The Government opened up a school for the grown up children and the American Consul of Trebizond instituted an asylum for the infants. When the first batches of Armenians arrived at Gumush-Khana all able-bodied men were sorted out with the excuse that they were going to be given work. The women and children were sent ahead under escort with the assurance by the Turkish authorities that their final destination was Mosul and that no harm will befall them. The men kept behind were taken out of town in batches of 15 and 20, lined up on the edge of ditches prepared beforehand, shot and thrown into the ditches. Hundreds of men were shot every day in a similar manner. The women and children were attacked on their way by the ("Shotas") the armed bands organised by the Turkish government who attacked them and seized a certain number. After plundering and committing the most dastardly outrages on the women and children they massacred them in cold blood. These attacks were a daily occurrence until every woman and child had been got rid of. The military escorts had strict orders not to interfere with the "Shotas."

He continues:

In July 1915 I was ordered to accompany a convoy of deported Armenians. It was the last batch from Trebizond. There were in the convoy 120 men, 700 children and about 400 women. From Trebizond I took them to Ghumush-Khana. Here the 120 men were taken away, and, as I was informed later, they were all killed. At Ghumush-Khana I was ordered to take the women and children to Erzinjian. On the way I saw thousands of bodies of Armenians unburied. Several bands of "Shotas" met us on the way and wanted me to hand over to them women and children. But I persistently refused. I did leave on the way about 300 children with [Muslim] families who were willing to take care of them and educate them. The "Mutessarrif" of Erzinjian ordered me to proceed with the convoy to Kamack [Kemakh]. At the latter place the authorities refused to take charge of the women and children. I fell ill and wanted to go back, but I was told that as long as the Armenians in my charge were alive I would be sent from one place to the other. However I managed to include my batch with the deport-ed Armenians that had come from Erzeroum. In charge of the latter was a colleague of mine Mohamed Effendi from the Gendarmerie. He told me afterwards that after leaving Kamach they came to a valley where the Euphrates ran. A band of Shotas sprang out and stopped the convoy. They ordered the escort to keep away and then shot every one of the Armenians and threw them in the river.

At Trebizond the [Muslims] were warned that if they sheltered Armenians they would be liable to the death penalty.

Government officials at Trebizond picked up some of the prettiest Armenian women of the best fam-ilies. After committing the worst outrages on them they had them killed.

Cases of rape of women and girls even publicly are numerous. They were systematically murdered after the outrage.

Courtesy of the Armenian National Institute

Family of deportees on the road in the Ottoman Empire, 1915. Armin Wegner, the photographer, described what he saw: "Armenian deportees—women, children and elderly men. Woman in foreground is carrying a child in her arms, shielding it from the sun with a shawl; man on left is carrying bedding; no other belongings or food noticeable among effects being carried. All are walking in the sun on an unpaved road with no means of shelter from the elements." [80]

The Armenians deported from Erzeroum started with their cattle and whatever possessions they could carry. When they reached Erzinjian they became suspicious seeing that all the Armenians had already been deported. The Vali of Erzeroum allayed their fears and assured them most solemnly that no harm would befall them. He told them that the first convoy should leave for Kamach, the others remaining at Erzeroum until they received word from their friends informing of their safe arrival to destination. And so it happened. Word came that the first batch had arrived safely at Kamach, which was true enough. But the men were kept at Kamach and shot, and the women were massacred by the Shotas after leaving that town.[81]

Not everybody went along. Upon taking command of the Third Army in February 1916 General Vehib learned that the unit had killed 2,000 Armenian soldiers. After a complete investigation he court-martialed two men in charge, both of whom had followed the directive to "kill all Armenians in the armed forces." They were convicted and hanged.[82]

CONNECTIONS

↝ How does Lieutenant Said Ahmed Mukhtar al-Ba'aj describe his role in the deportations? What orders did he receive? What did he know about the deportations before he received his orders? How would you describe his role in the genocide?

↝ The *American Heritage Dictionary* defines *perpetrators* as people responsible for committing a crime. Was al-Ba'aj a perpetrator? What choices were available to al-Ba'aj?

↝ In his account, where do you find examples of obedience to authority? Do you also see examples of resistance?

↝ The government's order for deportation was followed by a religious opinion that came from the Sheikh-ul-Islam—the religious leader appointed by the Young Turk dictatorship. What is the difference between the way people respond to political leaders as compared to religious figures?

Many psychologists have studied the way human beings respond to the roles they are given. Among the most famous experiments are Stanley Milgram's work on "Obedience to Authority" and Philip Zimbardo's prison experiment investigating "what happens when you put good people in an evil place?" Zimbardo's prison experiment is documented on line. Visit his web site at *http://www.zimbardo.com*. Videos of both experiments are available from the Facing History and Ourselves resource library. A Reading describing the experiments can be found on page 210 of *Facing History and Ourselves: Holocaust and Human Behavior.*

Reading 6 — WOMEN AND THE DEPORTATIONS

The deportation of Armenians from villages across the Ottoman Empire followed the same pattern. Families were given a few days to collect their belongings. Their property was sold off or given to the local population. Men were rounded up and killed. Convoys of the elderly, women, and children were sent on the road and subject to robbery, looting, and murder at the hands of the special operations units and local tribesmen.

Children were often separated from their parents, some were forcibly converted to Islam and joined Muslim families, and others were killed. A number of women were given a chance to convert and compelled to join Muslim families; countless women were raped. Their stories, often recounted by witnesses, or recorded on scraps of paper, were given to sympathetic strangers who in turn passed on the papers to journalists or those working for American relief groups. An Armenian woman from Bitlis told a witness about the brutality she and other Armenian women faced during the deportations. The witness recorded her story.

All the old women and the weak who were unable to walk were killed. There were about one hundred Kurdish guards over us, and our lives depended on their pleasure. It was a very common thing for

Project SAVE Armenian Photograph Archives, courtesy of Elizabeth Boyajian Roberts.

Armenian survivors from Kharpert on a forced march to Baghdad in 1916, pictured here on the banks of the Euphrates River at Der-Zor, Syria.

them to rape our girls in our presence. Very often they violated eight-or ten-year-old girls, and as a consequence many would be unable to walk, and were shot.

Our company moved on slowly, leaving heaps of corpses behind. Most of us were almost naked. When we passed by a village, all the Kurdish men and women would come and rob us as they pleased. When a Kurd fancied a girl, nothing would prevent him from taking her. The babies of those who were carried away were killed in our presence.

They gave us bread once every other day, though many did not get even that. When all our provisions were gone, we gathered wheat from the fields and ate it. Many a mother lost her mind and dropped her baby by the wayside.

Some succeeded in running away, and hid themselves in the fields among the wheat until it was dark. Those who were acquainted with the mountains of that region would thus escape and go back to seek their dear ones. Some went to Sassoun, hearing that it had not yet fallen, others were drowned in the Mourad [Lower Euphrates] River. I did not attempt to run away, as I had witnessed with my own eyes the assassination of my dear ones. I had a few piastres left, and hoped to live a few days longer.

We heard on our way from the Kurds that Kurdish Chettis (bands of robbers) had collected all the inhabitants of Kurdmeidan and Sheklilan, about 500 women and children, and burnt them by the order of Rashid Effendi, the head of the Chettis.

When we reached the Khozmo Pass, our guards changed their southerly direction and turned west, in the direction of the Euphrates. When we reached the boundary of the Ginj district our guards were changed, the new ones being more brutal. By this time our number was diminished by half. When we reached the boundary of Djabaghchour we passed through a narrow valley; here our guards ordered us to sit down by the river and take a rest. We were very thankful for this respite and ran towards the river to get a drink of water.

After half-an-hour we saw a crowd of Kurds coming towards us from Djabaghchour. They surrounded us and ordered us to cross the river, and many obeyed. The report of the guns drowned the sounds of wailing and crying. In that panic I took my little boy on my back and jumped into the river. I was a good swimmer and succeeded in reaching the opposite shore of the Euphrates with my precious bundle unnoticed, and hid myself behind some undergrowth.

By nightfall no one remained alive from our party.[83]

Two days after giving her account of the deportation the woman's son died of starvation. She was later tracked down and killed.

CONNECTIONS

How do you respond to such unspeakable horror? How do you understand the brutality this woman faced if you have never experienced it? What do you know after hearing stories like this that you would not know otherwise?

Much of this book has emphasized choice and decision-making. But in accounts like the one in this reading, the victims are faced with what Professor Lawrence Langer refers to as "choiceless choices." In *Versions of Survival*, a book about survivors of the Holocaust, Langer describes these as decisions made in the "absence of humanly significant alternatives—that is, alternatives enabling an individual to make a decision, act on it, and accept the consequences—all within a framework that supports personal integrity and self-esteem." What distinguishes a "choiceless choice" from other decisions? Why does Langer believe that normal standards for judging behavior will not apply to all the "choices" of victims?

Donald Miller and Lorna Touryan Miller have studied the testimony of women who survived the deportations. They believe the conditions of the deportations had tragic consequences for Armenian parents and required Armenian mothers to make unthinkable choices. They frame some of those choices:

1. Whose life is of more value? My own or those of my children?

2. If I cannot care for all of my children, which lives shall I seek to preserve?

3. Is it better that we, as a family unit, all die together, or that some family members perish while others survive?

4. Is it preferable to give my son or daughter to a passing Turk or Kurd, knowing that he or she will thereby lose all consciousness of their Armenian as well as religious identity—but thereby survive—or is it preferable that they die? [84]

How are the choices they describe like the "choiceless choices" that Langer writes about?

Systematic rape and forced prostitution were not specifically subject to international law until the creation of the International Criminal Tribunal for the Former Yugoslavia included them in its mandate in 1993. The first conviction for rape as a crime against humanity came in February of 2001 in a case where Muslim women were systematically raped by Bosnian Serb soldiers. Why do you think it took so long for crimes against women to be recognized and prosecuted?

Reading 7 — CRIES RINGING IN MY EARS

Viscount Bryce's collection *Treatment of Armenians in the Ottoman Empire 1915-16* includes dozens of eye-witness accounts of the Armenian Genocide, some of them from survivors, others by witnesses. In the book, all of the accounts are published anonymously, but there was a classified key to each person's identity. The following letter was written by a women from the United States who was traveling with her husband by train. Her train had a three-hour stop in the town of Kara Hissar.

> We took a carriage at the station and drove to the home of an Armenian doctor there—a well educated, fine young doctor, whom we had met on our previous visit to Kara Hissar. We found his wife and two small children at home, but the doctor had been taken a year ago to work for the wounded Turkish soldiers.
>
> The wife had heard of the exiling of all the Armenians from different towns around her, and so she was packing a few things to take with her when her hour came to go. That hour arrived while we were in her home. All the Armenians were ordered to be at the station in twenty-four hours, to be sent—where? They did not know, but they did know that they had to leave everything—the little homes they had worked for for years, the few little things they had collected—all must be left to the plunder of the Turks.

Post card of Kerasund before the Genocide.

> It was one of the saddest hours I ever lived through; in fact, the hours that followed on the train, from Kara Hissar to Constantinople, were the saddest hours I ever spent.
>
> I wish I could picture the scene in that Armenian home, and we knew that in hundreds of other homes in that very town the same heart-breaking scenes might be witnessed.
>
> The courage of that brave little doctor's wife, who knew she must take her two babies and face starvation and death with them. Many began to come to her home—to her, for comfort and cheer, and she gave it. I have never seen such courage before. You have to go to the darkest places of the earth to see the brightest lights, to the most obscure spot to find the greatest heroes.
>
> Her bright smile, with no trace of fear in it, was like a beacon light in that mud village, where hundreds were doomed.
>
> It was not because she did not understand how they felt; she

was one of them. It was not because she had no dear ones in peril; her husband was far away, ministering to those who were sending her and her babies to destruction.

"Oh! There is no God for the Armenians," said one Armenian, who, with others, had come in to talk it over.

Just then a poor woman rushed in to get some medicine for a young girl who had fainted when the order came.

Such despair, such hopelessness you have never seen on human faces in America.

"It is the slow massacre of our entire race," said one woman.

"It is worse than massacre!" replied another man.

The town crier went through all the streets of the village, crying out that anyone who helped the Armenians in any way, gave them food, money or anything, would be beaten and cast into prison. It was more than we could stand.

"Have you any money?" my husband asked the doctor's wife. "Yes," she said; "a few liras; but many families will have nothing."

After figuring out what it would cost us all to reach Constantinople we gave them what money we had left in our small party. But really to help them we could do nothing, we were powerless to save their lives....

It was with broken hearts that we left the town, and hardly had we started on our way when we began to pass one train after another crowded, jammed with these poor people, being carried away to some spot where no food could be obtained. At every station where we stopped, we came side by side with one of these trains. It was made up of cattle-trucks, and the faces of little children were looking out from behind the tiny barred windows of each truck. The side doors were wide open, and one could plainly see old men and old women, young mothers with tiny babies, men, women and children, all huddled together like so many sheep or pigs—human beings treated worse than cattle are treated.

About eight o'clock that evening we came to a station where there stood one of these trains. The Armenians told us that they had been in the station for three days with no food. The Turks kept them from buying food; in fact, at the end of these trains there was a truck-full of Turkish soldiers ready to drive these poor people on when they reached the Salt Desert or whatever place they were being taken to.

Old women weeping, babies crying piteously. Oh, it was awful to see such brutality, to hear such suffering.

They told us that twenty babies had been thrown into a river as a train crossed—thrown by the mothers themselves, who could not bear to hear their little ones crying for food when there was no food to give them.

One woman gave birth to twins in one of those crowded trucks, and crossing a river she threw both her babies and then herself into the water.

Those who could not pay to ride in these cattle-trucks were forced to walk. All along the road, as our train passed, we saw them walking slowly and sadly along, driven from their homes like sheep to the slaughter.

A German officer was on the train with us, and I asked him if Germany had anything to do with this deportation, for I thought it was the most brutal thing that had ever happened. He said: "You can't object to exiling a race; it's only the way the Turks are doing it which is bad." He said he had just come from the interior himself and had seen the most terrible sights he ever saw in his life. He said: "Hundreds of people were walking over the mountains, driven by soldiers. Many dead and dying by the roadside. Old women and little children too feeble to walk were strapped to the sides of donkeys. Babies lying dead in the road. Human life thrown away everywhere."

The last thing we saw late at night and the first thing early in the morning was one train after another carrying its freight of human lives to destruction....

The crying of those babies and little children for food is still ringing in my ears. On every train we met we heard the same heart-rending cries of little children.[85]

CONNECTIONS

❧ The author writes that she was "powerless" to save the lives of the Armenians she encountered yet she struggled to respond morally to the atrocities she witnessed. Where do you see evidence of her struggle? How does she respond?

❧ How would you describe the differences between a bystander to injustice and a witness to injustice?

❧ Today people all over the world "witness" ethnic cleansing and the results of genocide and famine on television, the internet, and in the press. What should be done? Why do some people take action in response or to prevent further atrocity while others do not?

❧ How would you respond to the German officer who told the author: "You can't object to exiling a race; it's only the way the Turks are doing it which is bad"?

Reading 8 — TARGETING THE GREEKS AND THE ASSYRIANS

Although many of the Young Turk measures were directed specifically at the Armenians, other non-Muslim populations, including the Assyrians and the Greeks of the empire faced deportation and murder. Although Greece won its independence from the Ottoman Empire in 1828, territorial disputes left many people who identified themselves as Greek or Pontian subject to Ottoman rule. Those Hellenist or Greek Ottomans that remained in the empire were viewed with suspicion. In response to the Balkan war of 1912–1913 there were massive boycotts of Greek Ottoman businesses that spread to other Christians, including Armenians. In the aftermath of Greek victory thousands of ethnic Turkish refugees fled and resettled in Turkey. As the war broke out Talaat, Young Turk Minister of the Interior, told the Greek Patriarch that "there was no room for non-Muslims" in the Ottoman Empire.

Greek and Armenian refugee children from Anatolia, near Athens, Greece.

Thea Halo, an author and daughter of a Pontian [Greek] survivor of the genocide, writes that "there were three separate groups of Greeks in Turkey: the Ionians, who lived in the Western coastal regions facing Greece; the Kappadokans, those from the area of the ancient Greek cities of Anatolia now known as Cappadocia; and the Pontians, who lived in the Pontic Mountains along the Black Sea and on its southern shores. But the term Pontian has come to encompass the struggles and tragedies of all the Greeks of Turkey."

In her book, *Not Even My Name*, Halo, using official documents, outlines the evolution of anti-Greek measures under the Young Turks.

14 May 1914 Official document from Talaat Bey, Minister of the Interior to Prefect of Smyrna: The Greeks, who are Ottoman subjects, and form the majority of inhabitants in your district, take advantage of the circumstances in order to provoke a revolutionary current, favorable to the intervention of the Great Powers. Consequently, it is urgently necessary that the Greeks occupying the coastline of Asia Minor be compelled to evacuate their villages and install themselves in the vilayets of Erzerum and Chaldea. If they should refuse to be transported to the appointed places, kindly give instructions to our [Muslim] brothers, so that they shall induce the Greeks, through excesses of all sorts, to leave their native places of their own accord. Do not forget to obtain, in such cases, from the emigrants certificates stating that they leave their homes on their own initiative, so that we shall not have political complications ensuing from their displacement.

31 July 1915 German J. Lepsius: "The anti-Greek and anti-Armenian persecutions are two phases of

Courtesy of Martin Gilbert, from *The First World War: A Complete History*, revised edition (Henry Holt: New York, 2003)

GREECE AND THE OTTOMAN EMPIRE

Though Greece won its independence from the Ottoman Empire in 1828, many Greeks still lived within the Empire's borders. On July 31, 1915 German missionary and scholar Johannes Lepsius warned, "the anti-Greek and anti-Armenian persecutions are two phases of one programme."

one programme—the extermination of the Christian element from Turkey."

16 July 1916 Austrian consul at Amisos Kwiatowski to Austrian Foreign Minister Baron Burian: "on 26 November Rafet Bey told me: 'we must finish off the Greeks as we did with the Armenians. . . .' On November 28 Rafet Bey told me: 'today I sent squads to the interior to kill every Greek on sight.' I fear for the elimination of the entire Greek population and a repeat of what occurred last year." (the Armenian Genocide).

13 December 1916 German Ambassador Kuhlman to Chancellor Hollweg in Berlin: "Consuls. . . report of displacement of local population and murders. Prisoners are not kept. Villages reduced to ashes. Greek refugee families consisting mostly of women and children being marched from the coasts to Sebastea. The need is great."

19 December 1916 Austrian Ambassador to Turkey Pallavicini to Vienna lists the villages in the region of Amisos that were being burned to the ground and their inhabitants raped, murdered or dispersed.

20 January 1917 Austrian Ambassador Pallavicini: "the situation for the displaced is desperate. Death awaits them all. I spoke to the Grand Vizier and told him that it would be sad if the persecution of the Greek element took the same scope and dimension as the Armenian persecution. The Grand Vizier promised that he would influence Talaat Bey and Enver Pasha."

31 January 1917 Austrian Chancellor Hollweg's report ". . . the indications are that the Turks plan to eliminate the Greek element as enemies of the state, as they did earlier with the Armenians. The strategy implemented by the Turks is of displacing people to the interior without taking measures for their survival by exposing them to death, hunger, and illness. The abandoned homes are then looted and burnt or destroyed. Whatever was done to the Armenians is being repeated with the Greeks." [86]

Until the summer of 1917 official persecution of Greek Ottomans was tempered by foreign policy considerations. Greece, under the rule of King Constantine, remained neutral as the war waged on. When the Special Organizations began to deport Greek Ottomans in the early days of the war, the Greek Premier warned that the Greek government might take reprisals against the Turkish subjects of Greece. Further tempering Turkish treatment of its Greek population was the attitude of the German leadership; a number of high ranking German military and civilian officials lobbied on the behalf of Greek Ottomans.

Vahakn Dadrian explains:

In December 1917, for example Marshal Liman von Sanders alerted the German Ambassador Bernstorff about an order by war minister Enver who wanted "the deportation of virtually all Greeks of the coast to inland areas...." Enver had prepared a list of five categories for the deportation order. Sanders "had personally intervened and had succeeded because he had threatened to resign." The German Foreign Office supported the efforts of Sanders and Ambassador Bernstorff, and let it be known that it "advised strongly against the deportations...." All the while, however, "the plundering and burning down of a large number of Greek villages ... and the forcible relocation of 70,000 Greeks from the Littoral, stretching from Bafra [on the Aegean Sea] to Tirebolu [on the Black Sea] continued; many of the victims in all likelihood died due to the privations they incurred.

To demonstrate his solidarity with the deported Greeks, German emperor William II authorized the allocation of 10,000 Deutsche Marks to be used as relief money for the needs of the deported Greeks." [87]

In July 1917 Greece joined the Allies and declared war on the Central Powers of Austria-Hungary, Germany, and Turkey. As war broke out between Greece and Turkey, Ottoman Greeks lost their leverage. According to Thea Halo, during and especially after World War I some 360,000 Pontian Greeks were systematically deported and killed and one and a half million were sent into exile.

Throughout the war, another Ottoman Christian minority, the Assyrians were also subject to genocide. Estimates of Assyrian deaths range from 75,000 to 150,000.

CONNECTIONS

‣ How is your understanding of the Armenian Genocide influenced by examining the persecution of the Greeks and Assyrians?

‣ How do you explain the difference in the way German officials responded to the treatment of Greeks and Armenians? What does it say about the way German officials defined their "universe of obligation"?

‣ Some historians believe that many Ottoman Greeks were saved from death through the outside intervention of the Greek and German governments. Neither the Assyrians nor the Armenians had a country of their own, and those concerned with their plight either failed to use their power or were unable or unwilling to directly intervene in the deportation and murder. Who is responsible for groups that do not have their own state? How can their safety be protected?

NOTES

61. Robert Melson, *Revolution and Genocide*, pp. 169–170.
62. Quoted in Samantha Power, *A Problem from Hell: America and the Age of Genocide* (New York: Basic Books, 2002), p. 6.
63. The Permanent Peoples' Tribunal, "Verdict of the Tribunal," Gerard Libaridian, ed. in *A Crime of Silence: The Armenian Genocide* by The Permanent Peoples' Tribunal (London, Zed Books, 1985), pp. 215–217.
64. Deborah Dwork and Robert Jan van Pelt, *The Holocaust: A History* (New York: W.W. Norton & Co., 2002), p. 35.
65. Vahakn N. Dadrian, "The Naim-Andonian Documents," *International Journal of Middle East Studies* 18 (August 1986), p. 329.
66. Dadrian, "Naim-Andonian Documents," p. 359.
67. Reproduced in Leslie Davis, *The Slaughter House Province: An American Diplomat's Report on the Armenian Genocide, 1915–1917* (New Rochelle, NY: Aristide D. Caratzas, 1989), pp. 188–190.
68. Dwork and van Pelt, *The Holocaust*, p. 35.
69. *Armin T. Wegner and the Armenians of Anatolia* (Milan: Edizioni Angelo Guerini e Associati, 1996), p. 96.
70. Power, *Problem From Hell*, p. 2.
71. Krikoris Balakian, *Hai Koghkotan*, (Beriut: Plenetta Printing, 1977) trans. Peter Balakian and Anahid Yeremian, ms. in progress, pp. 35, 36, 41.
72. Ibid.
73. Dadrian, *History of the Armenian Genocide*, p. 251.
74. Dwork and van Pelt, *The Holocaust*, p. 38.
75. Vahakn Dadrian, *German Responsibility in the Armenian Genocide: A Review of the Historical Evidence of German Complicity* (Watertown, MA: Blue Crane Books, 1996), p. 19.
76. Dadrian, *History of the Armenian Genocide*, p. 262.
77. Dadrian, *German Responsibility*, pp. 56–57.
78. Bryce, *Treatment of the Armenians*, available at *http://www.cilicia.com/bryce/a01.htm#German*
79. Dadrian, *History of the Armenian Genocide*, p. 259.
80. Armin T. Wegner available at *http://armenian-genocide.org/photo-wegner/deportees-walking.html.*
81. *http://www.armenian-genocide.org/sampledocs/br-12-26-16-text.htm*, from the British Public Record Office, FO 371/2768/1455/folios 454–458
82. Dadrian, "The Secret Young-Turk Ittihadist Conference," p. 185.
83. Bryce, *Treatment of Armenians* (London: Doniguian & Sons, 1916), pp. 92–93
84. Donald Miller and Laura Touryan Miller, "Women and Children of the Genocide," in Richard Hovanissian ed. *The Armenian Genocide: History, Politics, Ethics* (New York: St. Martin's Press, 1992), p. 166.
85. Bryce, *Treatment of the Armenians*, available at *http://www.cilicia.com/bryce/a12.htm#108.*
86. Thea Halo, *Not Even My Name* (New York: Picador, 2000), pp. 123–125.
87. Dadrian, *German Responsibility*, pp. 230–231.

"You are a Jew; these people are Christians. The (Muslims) and the Jews always get along harmoniously....What have you to complain of? Why can't you let us do with these Christians as we please?"
—Talaat, Minister of the Interior to U.S. Ambassador Morgenthau

Chapter 5

THE RANGE OF CHOICES

IN *A PROBLEM FROM HELL: AMERICA AND THE AGE OF GENOCIDE*, SAMANTHA POWER WRITES: "WE HAVE ALL been bystanders to genocide. The crucial question is why.... The answers seemed to lie in the critical decisions—and decisions not to decide—made before, during, and after the various genocide."[88] This chapter focuses on the choices made by a wide range of people in response to the genocide—from diplomats to missionaries to ordinary Turks and even members of the Young Turk party. Although some people were actively involved in the genocide—issuing orders, escorting the deportations, attacking women and children, and rounding up Armenian men and executing them—many others either witnessed part of the process, or heard stories about what was happening. Confronted with massive injustice, people had to make a decision. What role would they assume? Would they speak out, and if they did, who would they speak to? Would they risk their lives to rescue men, women, or children? Would they go about their lives, pretending they were unaware? Did they believe the anti-Armenian propaganda? Did they choose to believe it?

Often scholars of history classify people's involvement with injustice into categories, such as bystander, perpetrator, victim, resister, or rescuer. These labels reflect the complexity of human behavior. There is a wide range of choices people can make in the face of quickly moving events. Often people who are in one role at one time choose to respond differently in another. People who once had the opportunity to make a choice often lose those opportunities as time passes. Writing about individuals who spoke up during genocide, Samantha Power created a new category, "upstanders," people who stand up to get others to take notice and make a difference. While the people Power writes about were unable to stop the process of genocide, their choices often saved lives. The actions of "upstanders" remind us that if the warning signs are recognized early enough prevention is possible.

During the second decade of the twentieth century, the Armenian massacres were widely publicized. Many people, inside and outside of the Ottoman Empire, were aware of the persecution of the Armenians, Greeks, and Assyrians. What influenced the ways people responded to that knowledge? While some people halfway around the world chose to become deeply involved in trying to protect the victims of the genocide, others who directly witnessed the murder of innocent people did little or nothing.

Albert Camus, a French writer who joined the resistance during World War II, wrote about the choices people make in the face of injustice:

> I know that the great tragedies of history often fascinate men with approaching horror. Paralyzed, they cannot make up their minds to do anything but wait, and one day the Gorgon monster devours them. But I should like to convince you that the spell can be broken, that there is an illusion of impotence, that strength of heart, intelligence and courage are enough to stop fate and sometimes reverse it.[89]

This chapter explores responses to the Armenian Genocide and highlights the stories of how individuals challenged silence and indifference.

Reading 1 ~ REMEMBERING RESCUE

Although many people were aware of the massacres of Armenians, very few reached out to save others. Yet the stories of ordinary Turks who did what they could to save Armenians are recorded in the stories of survivors. Too often, the stories are of nameless individuals, and, as historian Richard Hovannisian observed: "Altruism during the Armenian Genocide of 1915 is a subject that has not been studied." He and his colleagues are working to understand the complex motivation of individuals who saved Armenians during the genocide. Scholars at the Zoryan Institute, an Armenian research organization that works to educate people about the genocide and Armenian life, believe that much can be learned from sharing the stories of Turkish rescuers.

As the leaders of the Ottoman Turkish government in 1915 were rounding up the Armenians in the Ottoman Empire for mass deportation and slaughter, a number of Turks risked their own lives to help Armenians escape certain death. There is no way to know today how many such individual acts of courage and humanity occurred in those tragic times. Our sources of information are largely anecdotal: family histories transmitted orally, autobiographies and personal memoirs, and the oral testimonies of survivors.

These acts of heroism and kindness stand in stark contrast to the cruelest savagery displayed by the perpetrators of the Armenian Genocide. Their importance is great, for several reasons. First, they are additional evidence of the Armenian Genocide. Secondly, they illustrate that, while there was indeed a genocide, not all Turks supported it. Thirdly, these stories serve to reassure us of the human potential for courage and virtue. While these stories do serve as evidence of goodness, they can not and should not be used to counterbalance the record of evil in some quantitative manner, as there are relatively few documented examples. The quality of goodness they evidence, however, may give some comfort to us all.

What did these people do? As Armenians were being rounded up, forced to sell all their possessions, save what they could carry, for a tiny fraction of their worth, and led off to what was certain death, some individual Turks hid them in their homes, while others helped them escape to safety. It must be noted that these Turks did so in the full knowledge that to be caught helping an Armenian meant summary execution.... In such highly charged circumstances, one can only imagine today the difficulty of helping Armenians escape to a safer location, or keeping secret the fact that a group of Armenians was hidden in one's home. Providing food for them, giving them privacy for bathing and other necessities of life, were all fraught with mortal danger.

Why did they do it? One can only speculate. We know in some cases it was because of long-standing personal friendships. Yet, there are many cases where Turks helped Armenians who were strangers. It seems that basic human decency was a key element, although there are cases where some benefit to the rescuer was involved (e.g., bribes, labor, sexual exploitation, marriage to the rescuer's chil-

dren), as well as forced conversion to Islam.[90]

Members of Kourken Sarkissian's family were among those that were rescued by Turks:

I am the son of genocide survivors. My father is now 90, my mother 82. His father was hanged, his mother raped and killed, and of the nine children in the family, only he and his five year old brother survived.

The story of my mother's family was different, atypical, but not to be neglected for that reason. My maternal grandfather was hanged in front of his family, which included his pregnant wife, my grandmother, and four children between the ages of two and eight.

A Turkish businessman, Haji Khalil, had been my grandfather's partner, and had promised to care for his family in case of misfortune. When a disaster greater than anything either of them could have imagined struck, he kept his promise by hiding our family in the upper story of his house for a year. The logistics involved were extremely burdensome: including my grandmother's niece, there were seven people in hiding. Food for seven extra mouths had to be purchased, prepared and carried up undetected once a night and had to suffice until the next night. Khalil's consideration was such that he even arranged for his two wives and the servants to be absent from the house once a week so that my grandmother and her family could bathe.

When two of the children died, he buried them in secret. He took tremendous risks and his situation was precarious, because his servants knew what he was doing. Had he been caught sheltering Armenians, he would almost certainly have shared their fate. Luckily, his household was loyal and discreet, and so I was one of the few children of my generation and neighborhood to grow up with uncles and aunts, all of whom remember the Turk Haji Khalil—may God bless his soul.

I grew up in the predominantly Armenian districts of Aleppo and Beirut, attended Armenian schools and joined Armenian organizations like the Zavarian movement. The dream of a free, independent Armenia and of the nightmarish genocide perpetrated by the Turks became the obsessions of my life. Both from Armenian organizations and from other survivors I learned that Turks had been inhuman monsters, and indeed many had

Courtesy of the Armenian National Institute

**An Armenian Orphan
after the genocide.**

behaved as such. Yet the memory of Haji Khalil was also part of my consciousness, and so I grew up with a dichotomy, knowing the story of a humane Turkish man, his family and household.

This internalized duality taught me that truth and justice cannot be had easily; they must be searched for . . . . I want to extend my hand to the people of Turkey, to ask them to remember that though at one time their state was led by mass murderers, they also had their Haji Khalils, and that it would honor the memory of the latter to acknowledge the overwhelming truth of the genocide, to express regrets, so that the healing process may begin between our two peoples. Because without this healing mass extermination as a tool of political dominance may become more common in the future.[91]

CONNECTIONS

✦ Is it important to understand the motivation of rescuers? Do their actions speak louder than any words or explanations they might share?

✦ Often entire groups of people are blamed for mass atrocities like the Armenian Genocide. In an essay titled "Intervention and Shades of Altruism during the Armenian Genocide", Richard Hovannisian writes:

> *Even in the extreme circumstances of 1915, there were thousands of Turks, Kurds, and others who opposed the persecution of the Armenians. Some of them tried to intervene. The testimony of the victims attests to the fact that kindness and solace were manifest amid the cruelty and suffering, and that the human spirit was never fully extinguished.*

How do these stories of break down generalizations and stereotypes? How do they help the healing process?

✦ Knowing the story of Haji Khalil taught Sarkissian that "truth and justice cannot be had easily; they must be searched for." How can stories like Sarkissian's and Khalil's broaden our perspective on how all people understand truth and justice?

✦ Kourken Sarkissian says "I want to extend my hand to the people of Turkey, to ask them to remember that though at one time their state was led by mass murderers, they also had their Haji Khalils." What does he hope will happen through the acknowledgment of Turkish rescuers?

⌐

Reading 2 ⌐ TRYING TO MAKE A DIFFERENCE

Ahmed Riza, an early leader of the Young Turks and a member of the Ottoman parliament during and after the genocide, and Ali Suad Bey, the governor general of Deir-el-Zor found themselves, as Turkish politicians, witnesses to the unfolding genocide as well as being part of a government that was responsible. What could they do to stop the atrocities? What were the risks of taking a stand?

At the outset of the genocide in 1915, the Ottoman parliament introduced two bills: The Temporary Law of Deportation, which authorized the deportation of the bulk of Turkey's Armenian population, and The Temporary Law of Expropriation and Confiscation, which allowed the government to confiscate Armenian cash and property and resell it for profit.

There was no debate on the Law of Deportation. It was approved by the cabinet. However, the Temporary Law of Expropriation and Confiscation came up for debate during the fall sessions of the Ottoman parliament in 1915. The debate gave Senator Ahmed Riza an opening. He argued that the proposed law violated basic constitutional protections and pleaded for the government to assume responsibility for the people who were being deported.

Courtesy of the Armenian National Institute

1915, deported Armenian family—two older couples and two young children—living under a tent in the desert.

Senator Riza pleaded with his government to allow the deportees, "hundreds of thousands of whom, women, children and old people, are helplessly and miserably wandering around the streets and mountains of Anatolia, to return to their original places of residence or to settle wherever they wish before the onset of winter." He then submitted a draft bill that proposed to postpone the Temporary Law's application until after the end of the war, arguing that the Temporary Law was, "contrary to...the Ottoman Constitution.... [I]t is also inimical to the principles of law and justice."[92] Riza's actions provoked a strong backlash and ultimately no action was taken on Riza's proposal. Despite the pressure he faced, Riza continued to speak out forcefully. In a later session of parliament, Riza once again took up the issue of confiscated Armenian property. He argued:

> It is unlawful to designate the Armenian assets and properties as "abandoned goods" for the Armenians, the proprietors, did not abandon their properties voluntarily; they were forcibly...removed from their domiciles and exiled. Now the government through its officials is selling their goods. . . . Nobody can sell my property if I am unwilling to sell it. . . . If we are a constitutional regime functioning in accordance with constitutional law we can't do this. This is atrocious. Grab my arm, eject me from my village, then sell my goods and properties, such a thing can never be permissible. Neither the conscience of the Ottomans nor the law can allow it.[93]

In December 1916, Riza continued his resistance when he took on the special organization, which had become primary actors in the genocide. Without raising questions about its actions directly, Riza argued that the law allowing convicts to enroll in the special organization degraded the military. He argued that:

> Our nation's respect for the military, its esteem of and affection for the military corps, is great. Those who are enrolled in it are [expected to] not only protect its rights, but also its honor. . . .

> Parents, who learn of the presence in the army of murderers and criminals, do not want to send their offspring to it; even if they did, they would do it with [feelings of] loathing and disgust. . . . [The convicts'] immorality and wicked attitudes can, however, be contagious for their companions, and corrupt the sense of morality in the Army." [94]

After the war, Riza's first speech in the new Ottoman Senate publicly exposed the dimensions of the massacres. He declared:

> All Ottomans, irrespective of race and creed, shall equally benefit from [the blessings of] justice and freedom during the reign of his Imperial Majesty [the new Sultan, Vahdeddin.] The Sublime Highness, His Imperial Majesty, will not allow that the orphans and widows of those Armenians who were savagely killed off, those Arabs who were hanged and exiled, be overwhelmed by miseries on this earth. There shall be no more people weeping and moaning in places of exile.[95]

Riza wasn't the only Ottoman politician to try to make a difference. Many Armenian survivors describe the heroic acts of Turks, some of whom were in positions of power, who tried to save their lives. Several witnesses recorded the efforts of a Turkish governor, Ali Suad Bey, to save the lives of Armenians who had been deported and placed under his supervision in Deir-el-Zor [now part of Syria]. An American eye-witness believed that Ali Suad Bey's example makes it clear that, "even if one is prepared for a moment to admit a reason of state for the mass-deportation of the Armenians … it was surely not necessary for the Turkish authorities to betray basic humanity."[96] He recalled:

> A few months ago, 30,000 Armenians in various camps outside of the town were … under the protection of the governor, Mutessarif Ali Suad Bey…. I would like to remember this man's name, who has a heart, and to whom the deportees are grateful, for he tried to lighten their miseries…. The mitigating circumstances, under which the Armenians of Der-el-Zor existed, became the cause for a denunciation at the Central Authorities in Constantinople. The "guilty" Ali Suad Bey was sent to Baghdad and replaced by Zekki Bey who is well known for his cruelty and barbarism. I was told horrible things that happened under the rule of the new governor... Ali Suad Bey, this rare example of a Turkish official, had lodged about 1,000 children in a large house, where they were fed at the cost of the municipality.[97]

CONNECTIONS

✤ What risks did Ahmed Riza and Suad Bey take in order to help victims of the massacres? Would you consider them heroes? How do their actions influence the way you think about the choices made by their peers to remain bystanders?

✤ What kinds of arguments did Ahmed Riza use to try to win support in the Ottoman Parliament? Did they appeal to conscience or law? Which arguments do you find most powerful?

✤ Did Ahmed Riza's and Suad Bey's actions change policies? Were they able to save lives? Did their actions make a difference?

✤ Ahmed Riza argued that guilt for the massacres of the Armenians belonged to Turkey alone because the killing was a political crime committed by the Ottoman state. If a crime is committed by a state, who should be responsible for pursuing justice?

Reading 3 — OFFICAL POLICY

During the war, German diplomats balanced their personal feelings about the treatment of Armenians with their professional duties. Their reports revealed the attitudes of Young Turk officials toward the Armenians.

Despite intimate knowledge of the Young Turks' intentions, the German Ambassador Baron von Wangenheim pronounced that diplomats had no right to interfere in Turkey's wartime decisions. After being prodded to protest the treatment by the American ambassador, Henry Morgenthau, Wangenheim replied: "I shall do nothing whatever for the Armenians."[98] As time went on and the killing escalated, some of the consular officials tried to find a way to make their disapproval public, without success. Morgenthau observed: "Of course no Germans could make much impression on the Turkish Government as long as the German Ambassador refused to interfere. And, as time went on, it became more and more evident that Wangenheim had no

German ambassador Baron von Wangenheim

desire to stop the deportations."[99] On October 25, 1915, Wangenheim died and was replaced in November by Count Paul von Wolff-Metternich. Almost immediately Wolff-Metternich looked for ways to protest Turkish treatment of the Armenians. In December 1915, he wrote the reich chancellor [a top government official] in Germany that he would like to take a "firmer stance" against the way the Armenians were being treated:

> Our annoyance about the persecution of the Armenians should be clearly expressed in our press and an end be put to our gushings over the Turks. Whatever they are accomplishing is due to our doing; those are our officers, our cannons, our money. Without our help that inflated frog would be slowly deflated. There is no need to be so afraid in dealing with the Turks. It is not easy for them to switch sides and make peace....
>
> In order to achieve any success in the Armenian question, we will have to inspire fear in the Turkish government regarding the consequences. If for military considerations we do not dare to confront it with a firmer stance, then we will have no choice but, with further abortive protests which tend rather to aggravate than to be of any use, to stand back and watch how our ally continues to massacre.[100]

The reich chancellor rejected Wolff-Metternich's proposal, objecting, "public reprimand of an ally in the course of a war would be an act which is unprecedented in history. Our only aim is to keep Turkey on our side until the end of the war, no matter whether as a result Armenians do perish or not."[101] German Ambassador Wolff-Metternich was recalled to Germany on October 3, 1916, at the request of Ottoman Minister of War Enver, who complained about the ambassador's protests about the treatment of the Armenians.

Inside Germany, reports on the genocide were severely censored to portray their ally, Turkey, in a favorable light. Historian Deborah Dwork writes that the situation troubled at least one reporter.

> *Harry Sturmer, a German correspondent in Constantinople for the major newspaper Kolnische Zeitung, understood that his government's silence and lack of action amounted to complicity. A veteran of many German military operations, Sturmer was no stranger to the brutality and the misery of war. The murder of Armenians was not a military action, however, and Sturmer knew the difference and knew that his country knew the difference. "The mixture of cowardice, lack of conscience, and lack of foresight of which our Government has been guilty in Armenian affairs is quite enough to undermine completely the political loyalty of any thinking man who has any regard for humanity and civilization." The genocide of the Armenians was "the meanest, lowest, the most cynical, most criminal act of race-fanaticism that the history of mankind has to show," Sturmer lamented. And as far as he was concerned, it embarrassed "every German." He resigned his post and went into voluntary exile in Switzerland.[102]*

CONNECTIONS

❧ Professor Ervin Staub believes that bystanders play a more critical role in events than people realize.

> *Bystanders, people who witness but are not directly affected by the actions of perpetrators, help shape society by their reactions....*

> *Bystanders can exert powerful influences. They can define the meaning of events and move others toward empathy or indifference. They can promote values and norms of caring, or by their passivity or participation in the system they can affirm the perpetrators.[103]*

Germany and the Ottoman Empire had a special alliance. Not only were their armies fighting on the same side, but German officers also assumed the leadership of Turkish forces under the Ottoman minister of war. Would Staub consider them bystanders to the genocide of the Armenians, or did their alliance make them complicit in the crime as well?

❧ The German reich chancellor rejected Wolff-Metternich's proposal, objecting, "public reprimand of an ally in the course of a war would be an act which is unprecedented in history. Our only aim is to keep Turkey on our side until the end of the war, no matter whether as a result Armenians do perish or not."[104] Compare the way the reich chancellor framed his "universe of obligation" with the way Ambassador Woff-Metternich constructed his. What differences do you find most striking?

❧ Harry Sturmer said that the mass murder of the Armenians was "the meanest, lowest, the most cynical, most criminal act of race-fanaticism that the history of mankind has to show." What does he mean by race-fanaticism?

❧ Law professor Martha Minow describes how "role morality"—a way in which individuals adapt their morality to their profession—influences the way individuals respond to injustice. In this reading, how do individuals balance their "role" and their personal conscience? Which roles do you play? How do they influence your actions? How do you balance your role and your own sense of right and wrong?

❧ Many German diplomats feared that Germany would be held accountable for Turkey's crimes. Considering their close alliance, in what ways did Germany share responsibility for the genocide?

⸾

Reading 4 — TAKING A STAND

Turkish officials often told distorted stories of Armenian resistance to justify mass killing. They hoped their stories would lessen sympathy for the Armenians outside of the country. The story of Armenian resistance at Musa Dagh had the opposite effect. The bravery of the Armenians, against overwhelming odds, rallied international support for them.

In April 1915, orders reached the district of Musa Dagh, the six villages at the base of Musa Dagh, the Mountain of Moses, instructing the Armenian population to leave their homes. They knew that deportation meant near-certain death and they had to do something if they were to survive. Reverend Dikran Andreasian, described what happened next.

> Knowing that it would be impossible to defend our villages in the foot-hills, it was resolved to withdraw to the heights of Mousa Dagh, taking with us as large a supply of food and implements as it was possible to carry. All the flocks of sheep and goats were also driven up the mountain side, and every available weapon of defense was brought out and furbished up. We found that we had a hundred and twenty modern rifles and shot-guns, with perhaps three times that number of old flint-locks and horse pistols. That still left more than half our men without weapons.

> It was very hard to leave our homes. My mother wept as if her heart would break. But we had hopes that possibly, while we were fighting off the Turks, the Dardanelles might be forced and deliverance come to the country.

> By nightfall of the first day we had reached the upper crags of the mountain. As we were preparing to camp and to cook the evening meal, a pouring rain set in and continued all night. For this we were ill prepared. There had not been time to make huts of branches, nor had we any tents or waterproof clothing. Men, women and children, somewhat over five thousand in all, were soaked to the skin, and much of the bread we had brought with us was turned into a pulpy mass. We were especially solicitous to keep our powder and rifles dry. This the men managed to do very well.

> At dawn next morning all hands went to work digging trenches at the most strategic points in the ascent of the mountain. Where there was no earth for trench-digging, rocks were rolled together, making strong barricades behind which groups of our sharp-shooters were stationed. The sun came out gloriously, and we were hard at it all day strengthening our position against the attack which we knew was certain to come.[105]

Later that day, the residents of Musa Dagh organized a committee for defense of the six communities. Although they were able to hold off the Turkish soldiers and reinforcements, the Armenians of Musa Dagh found themselves surrounded, cut off by land and sea. The defense committee dispatched a runner to Aleppo with the hopes that he might be able to reach the American Consul, Jesse B. Jackson. Their other hope was of a rescue by sea. In desperation, people suggested sending three swimmers out into the harbor with the hope that one would reach a ship passing by the coast. At the same time a group of Armenian women prepared two very large white flags. One was embroidered with thick black English lettering. It read "CHRISTIANS IN DISTRESS: RESCUE." The other had a large red cross in the center. The flags were hung from tall trees overlooking the harbor.

Reverend Dikran Andreasian described what happened on the morning of the fifty-third day of the siege:

> I was startled by hearing a man shouting at the top of his voice. He came racing through our encampment straight for my hut. "Pastor, pastor," he exclaimed, "a battleship is coming and has answered our waving!—Thank God! Our prayers are heard. When we wave the Red Cross flag the battleship answers by waving signal flags. They see us and are coming in nearer shore!"

> This proved to be the French Guichen, a four-funnel ship. While one of its boats was being lowered, some of our young men raced down to the shore and were soon swimming out to the stately vessel which seemed to have been sent to us from God! With beating hearts we hurried down to the beach, and soon an invitation came from the Captain for a delegation to come on board and explain the sit-

Port Said, Egypt, fall 1915. Armenians originally from Musa Dagh march with their bishop, priests, and deacons in a procession of thanksgiving displaying the signal flag that was instrumental in saving them. They are joined by officials and missionaries.

uation. He sent a wireless to the Admiral of the fleet, and before very long the flag-ship Ste. Jeanne d'Arc appeared on the horizon followed by other French battleships. The Admiral spoke words of comfort and cheer to us, and gave an order that every soul of our community should be taken on board the ships.[106]

Franz Werfel, a Prague-born writer, was inspired by the story and wrote *Forty Days of Musa Dagh*, published in 1933. The novel became a best-seller in Germany and Austria. Despite the popularity of his work, Werfel was forced to flee shortly after Hitler and the Nazis came to power. The American motion picture company Metro Goldwyn Mayer planned to make a movie based on the novel. The plans were scrapped when the Turkish government protested to the Department of State and threatened to ban all American-made films from Turkey if the film was produced.

In the mid 1930s, Jews in Eastern Europe read Werfel's novel as a warning of their own fate. During the Holocaust, copies of the novel are reported to have circulated as a source of inspiration and a call to arms in some of the ghettos to which the Nazis confined the Jews.

CONNECTIONS

- What inspires people to resist against tremendous odds? What forms can that resistance take?

- Accounts of resistance at Musa Dagh do not focus solely on the military strategy. They often highlight details that may seem less important to outsiders; the democratically elected defense council, the nightly church services in which Armenians of various Christian denominations prayed together. How do those details add to your perception of resistance?

- Why do you think the Armenians in Musa Dagh choose to have the flag read "CHRISTIANS IN DISTRESS: RESCUE." Is it important that the words were written in English? Who did they think would respond to their call for help?

- Why would the Turkish government, after the genocide, take such strong measures to suppress the film *Forty Days of Musa Dagh*?

Reading 5 — THE AMERICAN AMBASSADOR IN CONSTANTINOPLE

The Armenian Genocide did not take place without witnesses. Journalists, missionaries, and diplomats from many countries witnessed the genocide or listened to first-hand accounts. The question was, what to do about it? The problem was particularly troubling to Henry Morgenthau, an American businessman and lawyer who served as the American ambassador to the Ottoman Empire. Pulitzer-prize winner Samantha Power describes the choices he faced as his understanding of the genocide grew. In May 1915, the Allies issued a declaration warning the Turks of the consequences of committing "crimes against humanity and civilization." Power notes:

Henry Morgenthau

> *The United States, determined to maintain its neutrality in the war, refused to join the Allied declaration. President Woodrow Wilson chose not to pressure either the Turks or their German backers. It was better not to draw attention to the atrocities, lest U.S. public opinion get stirred up and begin demanding U.S. involvement. Because the Turks had not violated the rights of Americans, Wilson did not formally protest.*

But in Turkey itself America's role as bystander was contested. Henry Morgenthau Sr., a German-born Jew who had come to the United States as a ten-year-old boy and had been appointed ambassador to the Ottoman Empire by President Wilson in 1913, agitated for U.S. diplomatic intervention. In January and February 1915, Morgenthau had begun receiving graphic but fragmentary intelligence from his ten American consuls posted throughout the Ottoman Empire. At first he did not recognize that the atrocities against the Armenians were of a different nature than the wartime violence. He was taken in by Talaat's assurances that uncontrolled elements had simply embarked upon "mob violence" that would soon be contained. In April, when the massacres began in earnest, the Turkish authorities severed Morgenthau's communication with his consuls and censored their letters. Morgenthau was reluctant to file reports back to Washington based on rumors, and the Turks were making it impossible for him to fact-check.

Although he was initially incredulous, by July 1915 the ambassador had come around. He had received too many visits from desperate Armenians and trusted missionary sources to remain skeptical. They had sat in his office with tears streaming down their faces, regaling him with terrifying tales. When he compared this testimony to the strikingly similar horrors relayed via consular cables,

Morgenthau came to an astonishing conclusion. What he called "race murder" was under way. On July 10, 1915 he cabled Washington with a description of the Turkish campaign:

"Persecution of Armenians assuming unprecedented proportions. Reports from widely scattered districts indicate systematic attempt to uproot peaceful Armenian populations and through arbitrary arrests, terrible tortures, whole-sale expulsions and deportations from one end of the Empire to the other accompanied by frequent instances of rape, pillage, and murder, turning into massacre, to bring destruction and destitution on them. These measures are not in response to popular or fanatical demand but are purely arbitrary and directed from Constantinople in the name of military necessity, often in districts where no military operations are likely to take place."

Morgenthau was constrained by two background conditions that seemed immutable. First, the Wilson administration was resolved to stay out of World War I. Picking fights with Turkey did not seem a good way to advance that objective. And second, diplomatic protocol demanded that ambassadors act respectfully toward their host governments. U.S. diplomats were expected to stay out of business that did not concern U.S. national interests. "Turkish authorities have definitely informed me that I have no right to interfere with their internal affairs," Morgenthau wrote. Still, he warned Washington, "there seems to be a systematic plan to crush the Armenian race."

Local witnesses urged him to involve the moral power of the United States. Otherwise, he was told, "the whole Armenian nation would disappear." The ambassador did what he could, continuing to send blistering cables back to Washington and raising the matter at virtually every meeting he held with Talaat. He found his exchanges with the interior minister infuriating.[107]

As Morgenthau became increasingly aware of the conflict between his role as ambassador and his moral outrage, he faced a dilemma. Power elaborates:

Morgenthau had to remind himself that one of the core prerogatives of sovereignty was that states and statesmen could do as they pleased within their own borders. "Technically," he noted to himself, "I had no right to interfere. According to the cold-blooded legalities of the situation, the treatment of Turkish subjects by the Turkish Government was purely a domestic affair; unless it directly affected American lives and American interests, it was outside of the concerns of the American Government." The ambassador found this maddening.[108]

Without support from the American government, Morgenthau had to look for help from private sources. He lobbied his friends at the *New York Times* to give the story prominent coverage and helped raise funds for Armenian relief. Power describes this work and its limitations:

The Congregationalist, Baptist, and Roman Catholic churches made donations. The Rockefeller founda-

tion gave $290,000 in 1915 alone. And most notable, a number of distinguished Americans, none of Armenian descent, set up a new Committee on Armenian Atrocities. The committee raised $100,000 for Armenian relief and staged high-profile rallies, gathering delegations from more than 1,000 churches and religious organizations in New York City to join in denouncing the Turkish crimes.

President Theodore Roosevelt

But in calling for "action," the committee was not urging U.S. military intervention. It was worried about the impact of an American declaration of war on American schools and churches in Turkey. In addition, the sentiment that made committee members empathize with their fellow Christians in Armenia also made some pacifists. In decrying the atrocities but opposing the war against Turkey, the committee earned the scorn of former president Theodore Roosevelt. In a letter to Samuel Dutton, the Armenia committee secretary, Roosevelt slammed the hypocrisy of the "peace-at-any-price type" who acted on the motto of "safety first," which, he wrote, "could be appropriately used by the men on a sinking steamer who jump into boats ahead of the women and children." He continued:

"Mass meetings on behalf of Armenians amount to nothing whatever if they are mere methods of giving a sentimental but ineffective and safe outlet to the emotion of those engaged in them. Indeed they amount to less than nothing. . . . Until we put honor and duty first, and are willing to risk something in order to achieve righteousness both for ourselves and for others, we shall accomplish nothing; and we shall earn and deserve the contempt of the strong nations of mankind."

Roosevelt wondered how anyone could possibly advise neutrality "between despairing and hunted people, people whose little children are murdered and their women raped, and the victorious and evil wrongdoers." He observed that such a position put "safety in the present above both duty in the present and safety in the future." Roosevelt would grow even angrier later in the war, when the very relief campaign initiated to aid the Armenians would be invoked as reason not to make war on Turkey. In 1918 he wrote to Cleveland Dodge, the most influential member of the Armenia committee: "To allow the Turks to massacre the Armenians and then solicit permission to help the survivors and then to allege the fact that we are helping the survivors as a reason why we should not follow the only policy that will permanently put a stop to such massacres is both foolish and odious." [109]

Despite the criticism, Morgenthau continued to work tirelessly to aid the Armenians, including an offer to raise money to relocate survivors to the United States. Yet he remained frustrated that he had not achieved more. "My failure to stop the destruction of the Armenians had made Turkey, for me a place of horror—I had reached the end of my resources."[110]

CONNECTIONS

◈ In May 1915, the Allies decried persecution of the Armenians as a "crime against humanity and civilization." What qualifies as a crime against humanity and civilization? What are the implications of the label? Who is responsible for preventing crimes against humanity and civilization? What do you think are other examples of crimes against humanity and civilization?

◈ Despite Morgenthau's pleas, President Woodrow Wilson was determined to remain neutral during the early days of the war. What are the advantages of remaining neutral during a conflict? During the genocide was it possible to remain neutral and act morally? What actions did Wilson take?

◈ What was Morgenthau's dilemma? What choices were available to him? Why do you think he made the choices that he did?

◈ Morgenthau wrote, "Technically, I had no right to interfere . . . the treatment of Turkish subjects by the Turkish government was a purely domestic affair, unless it directly affected American lives and interests, it was outside of the concerns of the American Government." Do you agree? How do you define American interests?

◈ When does one nation have the right to intervene in the internal affairs of another sovereign nation? The film *Triumph of Evil* examines the role of international intervention and responsibility during the Rwandan Genocide, including the role of the U.S. government and the United Nations.

◈ Former President Theodore Roosevelt was very critical of U.S. neutrality in the face of genocide. That criticism extended to assessment of Armenian relief efforts. In 1918 he wrote: "To allow the Turks to massacre the Armenians and then solicit permission to help the survivors and then to allege the fact that we are helping the survivors as a reason why we should not follow the only policy that will permanently put a stop to such massacres is both foolish and odious." How would you respond to Theodore Roosevelt's critique of Armenian relief efforts?

◈ Samantha Power describes Morgenthau and other people who try to made a difference as "upstanders." What does that term mean to you? What do you think enables people to become "upstanders"?

⌐

Reading 6 — TALAAT AND THE LIMITS OF DIPLOMACY

American Ambassador Henry Morgenthau often met with leaders of the Committee of Union and Progress to protest the treatment of Christians in Turkey. Later he recounted the first time he brought up the plight of the Armenians with the Ottoman Minister of the Interior Talaat. Morgenthau recalled:

Talaat, the Ottoman Minister of the Interior.

I began to talk about the Armenians at Konia. I had hardly started when Talaat's attitude became even more belligerent. His eyes lighted up, he brought his jaws together, leaned over toward me, and snapped out:

"Are they Americans?"

The implications of this question were hardly diplomatic; it was merely a way of telling me that the matter was none of my business. In a moment Talaat said this in so many words.

"The Armenians are not to be trusted," he said, "besides, what we do with them does not concern the United States."

I replied that I regarded myself as the friend of the Armenians and was shocked at the way they were being treated. But he shook his head and refused to discuss the matter. [111]

Morgenthau dropped the subject but continued to raise the "Armenian Question" in subsequent meetings. At another meeting Talaat asked Morgenthau: "Why are you so interested in the Armenians anyway?" Talaat continued:

"You are a Jew; these people are Christians. The [Muslims] and the Jews always get on harmoniously. We are treating the Jews here all right. What have you to complain of? Why can't you let us do with these Christians as we please?"...

"You don't seem to realize," I replied, "that I am not here as a Jew but as American ambassador. My country contains something more than 97,000,000 Christians and something less than 3,000,000 Jews. So, at least in my ambassadorial capacity, I am 97 percent Christian. But after all, that is not the point. I do not appeal to you in the name of any race or any religion, but merely as a human being. You have told me many times that you want to make Turkey a part of the modern progressive world. The way you are treating the Armenians will not help you to realize that ambition; it puts you in the class of backward, reactionary peoples."

"We treat the Americans all right, too," said Talaat. "I don't see why you should complain."

"But Americans are outraged by your persecutions of the Armenians," I replied. "You must base your principles on humanitarianism, not racial discrimination, or the United States will not regard you as a friend and an equal. And you should understand the great changes that are taking place among Christians all over the world. They are forgetting their differences and all sects are coming together as one. You look down on American missionaries, but don't forget that it is the best element in America that supports their religious work, as well as their educational institutions. Americans are not mere materialists, always chasing money—they are broadly humanitarian, and interested in the spread of justice and civilization throughout the world. After this war is over you will face a new situation. You say that, if victorious, you can defy the world, but you are wrong. You will have to meet public opinion everywhere, especially in the United States. Our people will never forget these massacres. They will always resent the wholesale destruction of Christians in Turkey. They will look upon it as nothing but wilful murder and will seriously condemn all the men who are responsible for it. You will not be able to protect yourself under your political status and say that you acted as Minister of the Interior and not as Talaat. You are defying all ideas of justice as we understand the term in our country."

Strangely enough, these remarks did not offend Talaat, but they did not shake his determination. I might as well have been talking to a stone wall. From my abstractions he immediately came down to something definite.

"These people," he said, "refused to disarm when we told them to. They opposed us at Van and at Zeitoun, and they helped the Russians. There is only one way in which we can defend ourselves against them in the future, and that is just to deport them."

"Suppose a few Armenians did betray you," I said. "Is that a reason for destroying a whole race? Is that an excuse for making innocent women and children suffer?"

"Those things are inevitable," he replied.

This remark to me was not quite so illuminating as one which Talaat made subsequently to a reporter of the Berliner Tageblatt, who asked him the same question. "We have been reproached," he said, according to this interviewer, "for making no distinction between the innocent Armenians and the guilty; but that was utterly impossible, in view of the fact that those who were innocent to-day might be guilty to-morrow!" [112]

In later conversations with Talaat, Morgenthau argued that if humanitarian issues weren't of concern, what about economic interests. Talaat replied: "We care nothing about the commercial loss." As much as Morgenthau tried, talk alone was not going to save the remaining Armenian population. Not only was Talaat unmoved, but he tried to influence Morgenthau to give the money raised for Armenian relief to the Turkish government. Another request went even further. In his memoir, Morgenthau recounts the day when Talaat raised a question about Armenian life insurance policies. He explains:

> One day Talaat made what was perhaps the most astonishing request I had ever heard. The New York Life Insurance Company and the Equitable Life of New York had for years done considerable business among the Armenians. The extent to which this people insured their lives was merely another indication of their thrifty habits.

> "I wish," Talaat now said, "that you would get the American life insurance companies to send us a complete list of their Armenian policy holders. They are practically all dead now and have left no heirs to collect the money. It of course all escheats to the State. The Government is the beneficiary now. Will you do so?"

> This was almost too much, and I lost my temper.[113]

CONNECTIONS

☙ What arguments does Morgenthau use to try to persuade Talaat to stop the deportation and mass murder of Armenians? How does Talaat respond to each argument? Considering President Wilson's determination to remain neutral, what other forms of persuasion were available to Morgenthau?

☙ Talaat assumes that Morgenthau, as a Jew, will be unsympathetic toward Christians and inclined to support Muslims. Compare the way Talaat and Morgenthau construct their "universe of obligation"? How does Morgenthau define his identity?

☙ What is a diplomat? What is diplomacy? What strategies do diplomats use to get their way? How do the stories of Ambassador Morgenthau and the German ambassador reflect the limits of diplomacy?

☙ What do the exchanges between Talaat and Morgenthau suggest about the limits of diplomacy in responding to genocide?

☙ Underline words and phrases in this reading that resonate with you. Reflect on them in your journal. How do they help you understand this particular history? What connections are you making to your own life or other history that you have learned? How does this history connect with current events?

☙ In his conversation with Morgenthau, Talaat asked for information on Armenian life insurance policies. Victims of genocide have used the courts to seek justice and reparations from corporations and banks that played a role in the genocide. Research how Holocaust survivors, victims of apartheid, and descendents of slaves from the United States are using the law to seek restitution.

Reading 7 — THE EYES OF THE WORLD

Witnesses to the Armenian Genocide shared their stories in journals, newspapers, and even best-selling books. How did those accounts influence the way people understood the events and the world around them? In an essay entitled "Genocide and Traumatic Memory," American literary scholar Walter Kalaijian probes the way the media's coverage of the Armenian Genocide shaped the public's response.

> *Not just an unprecedented modern horror, the Armenian genocide was also an inaugural media event. The spectacle of concentration-camp internment, death marches, and mass murder—centrally administered throughout the Ottoman Empire under the watchful eye of the German and Austro-Hungarian alliance—was widely reported in the United States and among other Entente nations of Britain, France, and Russia. In America alone, such newspapers and journals as the* New York Times, New York Herald Tribune, Boston Herald, Chicago Tribune, Atlantic Monthly, Nation, Outlook, *and* Literary Digest *covered the story. In diplomatic circles, Viscount Bryce in 1916 submitted a massive government blue paper to the British Secretary of State for Foreign Affairs; edited by Arnold J. Toynbee,* The Treatment of Armenians *archived eyewitness accounts of torture, rape, and mass murder reported by missionaries, Red Cross volunteers, consular officials, German health workers, and Armenian survivors. The previous year, Toynbee had published* Armenian Atrocities: The Murder of a Nation, *which included Bryce's address to the House of Lords appealing for British intervention in the Turkish massacres. Quoting from a 1915* New York Tribune *editorial, Toynbee underscored "German complicity with the Young Turk Genocide." "What Germany has done," according to the* Tribune, *"is to bring us back in the Twentieth Century to the condition of the dark ages." German witnesses who dissented from Germany's denial of the massacres included Dr. Johannes Lepsius, head of the Deutsche Orient-Mission. His Der Todesgang des armenishen Volkes (The Walk into Death March of the Armenian People) had a 1919 print run of twenty-thousand copies, distributed, in part, to the Orient Mission and German Reichstag....*

> *What did it mean in the mid 1910s to pick up, for the first time, any major daily paper around the world and read such headlines as "Armenians Are Sent to Perish in Desert: Turks Accused of Plan to Exterminate Whole Population," "Turks Depopulate Towns of Armenia," and "1,500,000 Armenians Starve"?* [114]

Among the countless newspaper stories on the genocide was front-page coverage in the *New York Times* on October 4, 1915. It was followed up with stories in the October 5 and 6. On the fourth straight day of coverage, October 7, an article appeared on page 3. It read:

> *Viscount Bryce, former British ambassador to the United States, in the House of Lords today said that such information as had reached him from many quarters showed that the figure of 800,000 Armenians destroyed since May was quite a possible number. Virtually the whole nation had been*

wiped out, he declared, and he did not suppose there was any case in history of a crime "so hideous and on so large a scale."

"The death of these people," said Lord Bryce, "resulted from the deliberate and premeditated policy of the gang now in possession of the Turkish government. Orders for the massacres came in every case direct from Constantinople. In some instances local Governors, being humane, pious men, refused to carry out the orders and at least two Governors were summarily dismissed for this reason.

"The customary procedure was to round up the whole of the population of a designated town. A part of the population was thrown into prison and the remainder were marched out of town and in the suburbs the men were separated from the women and children. The men were then taken to a convenient place and shot and bayoneted. The women and children were then put under a convoy of the lower kind of soldiers and dispatched to some distant destination.

"They were driven by the soldiers day after day. Many fell by the way and many died of hunger, for no provisions were furnished them. They were robbed of all they possessed, and in many cases the women were stripped naked and made to continue the march in that condition. Many of the women went mad and threw away their children. The caravan route was marked by a line of corpses. Comparatively few of

Hundreds of articles appeared in newspapers throughout the world describing massacre and deportations.

From Kloian, *Armenian Genocide: News Accounts*

The New York Times

THURSDAY, OCTOBER 7, 1915

(3:4)

800,000 ARMENIANS COUNTED DESTROYED

Viscount Bryce Tells House of Lords That Is the Probable Number of Turks' Victims.

10,000 DROWNED AT ONCE

Peers Are Told How Entire Christian Population of Trebizond Was Wiped Out.

Special Cable to THE NEW YORK TIMES.

LONDON, Thursday, Oct. 7.—The Daily Chronicle's Parliamentary correspondent in the House of Lords says:

"This afternoon Lord Bryce gave a heart-piercing account of the circumstances under which the Armenian people are being exterminated as a result of an absolutely premeditated policy elaborately pursued by the gang now in control of Turkey. He computes that since May last 800,000 Armenians, men, women, and children, have been slain in cold blood in Asia Minor.

"The House of Lords is a very unemotional assembly, but it was thrilled in every fibre at the story of the horrors compared to which even the atrocities of Abdul Hamid pale. As Lord Bryce truly said, there......

"On behalf of these pathetic als of a fine race Lord Bryce r powerful appeal to the neutral n He did not mention America by na it was obvious that this former A sador at Washington had the gre public of the West in mind wh appealed to the conscience of ne and when he said he believed the some crimes which even now in the vulsion of a great war the public ion of the world will not tolerat

"The Armenian question arose question put by Lord Cromer, who a whether statements that German sular officials had been privy to massacres rest on any substantial dence. Lord Cromer thinks that th there may be no trustworthy evid to prove the complicity of the Ger Government and its agents in t terrible atrocities, yet the German (ernment, having regard to its influe in Constantinople, cannot be acqui of moral responsibility unless it can shown that it took vigorous and en getic measures to prevent these crim

"Lord Crewe, replying for the G ernment stated that the British C sular reports bear out the story of massacre and reveal facts of the m horrible character. The condition refugees in Caucasian provinces is pi ous in the extreme.

"We have no official confirmation said Lord Crewe, 'of the allegation that German Consular representativ have not merely looked on but hav possibly managed these horrors. Stat ments to that effect have, however been freely made by American observ ers, and in view of what has happene elsewhere, these cannot be said to b antecedently improbable since July last when we informed the Porte that in dividuals who incited these massacres would be held personally responsible by us, no representations on this subject have been made by our Foreign office to the Turkish Government either directly or indirectly, but they know our views.'"

The Daily News commenting Armenian mas......

the people ever reached their destination.

"The facts as to the slaughter in Trebizond are vouched for by the Italian Consul. Orders came for the murder of all the Armenian Christians in Trebizond. Many Mussulmans tried to save their Christian friends, but the authorities were implacable and hunted out all the Christians and then drove them down to the sea front. Then they put them aboard sail boats and carried them some distance out to sea and threw them overboard. The whole Armenian population, numbering 10,000, was thus destroyed in one afternoon." The Lord Mayor at a meeting at the Mansion House on Oct. 15, will start a fund for the aid of Armenian refugees. Among the speakers will be Lord Bryce, Cardinal Bourne and T. P. O'Connor.[115]

Hundreds of subsequent articles appeared in the *New York Times* and other newspapers and journals throughout the world.

CONNECTIONS

❧ As Professor Walter Kalaijian explains, the Armenian Genocide was covered thoroughly in the press of the 1910s. How does media exposure to genocide and collective violence shape the way people respond to atrocity? Does the awareness of genocide and mass violence lead to action? Do people become desensitized to violence?

❧ Today, more and more people are able to witness genocide and human rights abuses through the media. Does this mean that more people are bystanders to the atrocities? How do you respond to television and newspaper reports of war crimes and genocide?

❧ Collect a few issues of a major daily newspaper. Are there articles and reports of human rights violations? What language do the articles use? On what page do the stories appear?

⤺

Reading 8 ⸺ SAVING THE ARMENIANS

As stories of Turkish atrocities against innocent Armenians spread through the Western press, activists clamored to get their governments to intervene and stop the abuses. In *The Splendid Blond Beast,* Christopher Simpson describes the choice that Djemal Pasha, one of the Young Turk leaders, offered to the Allies.

Djemal Pasha, Ottoman Minister of the Marine.

At the height of the genocide, a factional split among the Young Turks opened the possibility that Turkey might put an end to the massacres in exchange for an agreement from the Associated Powers to abandon their claims on Turkey and the Ottoman Empire. Djemal Pasha, a member of the triumvirate that ruled Turkey, had settled into Damascus and exercised local control of much of what is today Syria, Jordan, and Israel. In late 1915, while Turkish efforts to exterminate Armenians were at their height, Djemal sought out an Armenian emissary and convinced him to carry an offer to the governments of the Associated Powers. If czarist Russia, France, and Britain would back him, Djemal promised, he would undertake a coup d'etat against his Young Turk rivals, end the massacres, and take Turkey out of the war. . . .

The price for the plan was that the European powers would abandon imperial claims for what is today Iraq and Syria and provide reconstruction assistance to Djemal's government after the war. Djemal, for his part, was willing to concede control of Constantinople and the Dardanelles to Russia.

"Djemal appears to have acted on the mistaken assumption that saving the Armenians—as distinct from merely exploiting their plight for propaganda purposes—was an important Allied objective," writes David Fromkin, a historian specializing in Ottoman affairs. *The Russians favored Djemal's plan and for a time assured him that the other Associated Powers would cooperate. But in early 1916, France rejected Djemal's offer and claimed southern Turkey, Syria, and parts of Iraq. Great Britain followed suit, claiming Iraq on the behalf of a local "Iraqi" government created by London. "In their passion for booty,"* Fromkin writes, *"the Allied governments lost sight of the condition upon which future gains were predicated: winning the war... Djemal's offer afforded the Allies their one great opportunity to subvert the Ottoman Empire from within"—and to save innocent lives—"and they let it go."* Nor did the Allies

exploit Djemal's attempted betrayal of his colleagues for propaganda or intelligence purposes. As far as can be determined, the other Young Turks never learned of Djemal's secret correspondence with the enemy, and he remained part of the ruling triumvirate for the remainder of the war.[116]

CONNECTIONS

🖝 Why do you think the Allies decided to reject Djemal Pasha's offer? What factors do you think influenced the thinking of the Allied leaders?

🖝 David Fromkin writes: "Djemal appears to have acted on the mistaken assumption that saving the Armenians—as distinct from merely exploiting their plight for propaganda purposes—was an important Allied objective." What happens to victims of injustice when their cause is exploited for political gain?

🖝 Do stories like this one influence your thinking about who is responsible for the Armenian Genocide? Does it make the leaders of France and Great Britain complicit?

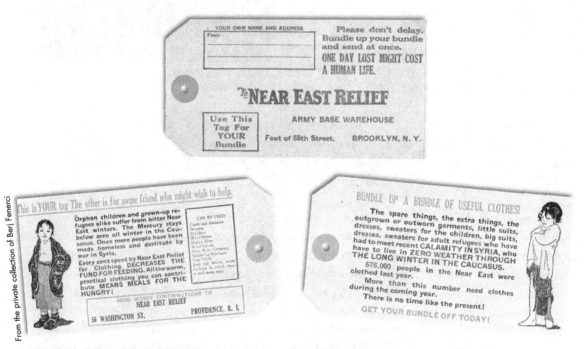

Tags for bundles of food and supplies intended for Armenian, Greek, and Assyrian refugees of the deportations, sent through the Near East Relief foundation.

Reading 9 — ARMENIAN RELIEF

When major disasters occur anywhere in the world, efforts begin immediately to provide relief for the victims. The mass media are able to keep ordinary people from all over the world abreast of the disaster. The Red Cross, Red Crescent, and other nongovernment organizations raise money and send experts and supplies to the location.

The American reaction to the treatment of the Armenians in the Ottoman Empire became one of the largest humanitarian responses in the history of the United States. Fundraising efforts were coupled with a public relations campaign designed to elicit sympathy for the Armenian orphans and refugees. Bureaucracies evolved to handle the distribution of money and materials for the Armenians. In many ways, the relief campaign for the Armenian Genocide provided a prototype for relief work in the twentieth century.

For decades foreign powers condemned the Ottoman Empire for its abuse of minority rights but failed to intervene directly in the affairs of the empire. During World War I, however, foreign observers took measures to provide food and shelter for Armenians, even though they could not convince their own countries to intervene militarily.

Armenian-Syrian Relief "Tag Day" volunteer fundraisers, Haroutune and Vartanoosh Manigian beside their aunt, Aghavni Kazazian, New York City, 1916.

Project SAVE Armenian Photograph Archives, Inc., Photo courtesy of Hermine Manigian.

As early as April 1915, missionaries from Germany and the United States began helping Armenians in various cities of the Ottoman Empire. In September 1915, Ambassador Henry Morgenthau realized the scope of what was happening to the Armenians and urged the U.S. government to help prevent the complete destruction of the Armenian people. In response, the State Department asked the American Board of Commissioners for Foreign Missions to undertake an emergency drive to collect money. James L. Barton and Cleveland H. Dodge founded the American Committee for Armenian and Syrian Relief with the support of President Woodrow Wilson. Through their efforts to raise awareness, the phrase "starving Armenians" became part of everyday speech. The money raised was sent to the American Embassy in Constantinople, which in turn distributed the funds to missionaries and consuls in Turkey. This line of support was temporarily interrupted when the United States entered the war in April 1917. But within a short time the committee, renamed the American Committee for Relief in the Near East (ACRNE) in 1918, reorganized and expanded former operations to include Armenian communities in Russian

Armenia. In 1919, the committee was incorporated by an act of Congress as the Near East Relief (NER).

An article in *The Literary Digest* explained to the public "How Your Gift Is Saving The Armenians":

> *There are no starving Armenians in Yerevan...A building and site for the orphanage have been bought by the committee, and is being enlarged by refugee workmen. Dr. G. C. Reynolds, the veteran missionary from Van... is in charge of orphan relief and the orphanage. He conducted a large orphanage in Van. His purpose, he says, is not by any means to gather all orphans into institutions, but to train a hundred picked boys and later the same number of girls, who may become leaders of the Armenian people. There are hundreds of orphanages being well maintained by the Armenians themselves, through their joint Armenian committee. Something like 7,000,000 rubles every six months is spent by this committee.*
>
> *All the work upon the new orphanage is being done by refugees, from the building of the walls to the construction of the beds and the tables and garments. Other relief work for the children is the furnishing of milk for the babies, and the maintenance of a physician, and the opening of a hospital. . . . In the Yerevan district [Russian Armenia] . . . there are approximately 50,000 persons being aided, directly or indirectly, by the American committee. . . .*
>
> *. . . The outstanding factor in Armenian relief has been the American committee. Its work has been on a large scale, and systematic form. All of it has been supervised by Americans, and the subordinate workers have been men and women trained in American mission schools, and known personally to the missionaries. Professors have not hesitated to become relief agents in villages, or accountants or actual workers in the industrial department. Had it not been for the fact that there were available a force of American board missionaries knowing the language and the land and the people, and with trusted helpers at hand, the wonders that have been wrought in the way of repatriation, rehabilitation, and the maintenance of life, and self respect would have been impossible.*[117]

In July 1918, James L. Barton, the chairman of the American Committee for Armenian and Syrian Relief said that even though $10 million had already been raised and distributed, the need would continue into the postwar years.

One of the most successful strategies of the American Committee for Armenian and Syrian Relief was a national poster campaign. Using strong graphics and minimal text, the images grabbed the public's attention, sent a message, and offered the average citizen an opportunity to make a difference.

Between 1915 and 1930 American relief organizations raised $116,000,000 of assistance, delivering food, clothing, and materials for shelter. The committee also set up refugee camps, clinics, hospitals, orphanages, and vocational training programs. It is estimated that during that time the Near East Relief cared for 132,000 orphans from Tiflis and Yerevan in the Caucasus to Constantinople, Beirut, Damascus, and Jerusalem.

Posters intended to raise awareness for the American Committee for Relief in the Near East.

CONNECTIONS

• Why do you think President Wilson was willing to support humanitarian assistance but unwilling to make a military commitment to intervene to stop the genocide?

• What is necessary to rehabilitate refugees and survivors of genocide? What needs to happen? Who needs to be involved?

• Examine the posters for Armenian relief.

Look at the image, and describe it exactly as you see it.

Notice how the posters use shape, images, and perspective to communicate a message. Look for the way the artist uses symbols. What emotion is the artist trying to evoke?

What is the message? To whom is it directed? Is it a single message? Or do others in your class interpret the work in other ways? Finally, make your own judgement about the poster.

Reading 10 — THE STORY OF AURORA MARDIGANIAN AND "RAVISHED ARMENIA"

Articles and accounts of the treatment of Armenians in the Ottoman Empire were widely read in the United States and Europe. One of the most popular accounts of Armenian suffering was *Ravished Armenia*. The book and the film that followed, records the story of Aurora Mardiganian, a teenage survivor, living in the United States in the care of Nora Waln, the publicity secretary of the American Committee for Armenian and Syrian Relief. *Ravished Armenia* was a huge success, educating ordinary Americans about atrocities across the globe. On February 15, 1919, the *New York Times* reported that "many persons prominent in society attended a private showing of 'Ravished Armenia.'" It continued:

The first half of the picture consists of four reels of scenes showing Armenia as it was before Turkish and German devastation, and led up to the deportation of priests and thousands of families into the desert. One of the concluding scenes showed young Armenian women flogged for their refusal to enter Turkish harems and depicted the Turkish slave markets.

Aurora Mardiganian, whose experiences in Armenia furnished the story on which the picture was founded, and who was injured in an accident that occurred during the making of the picture, was carried into the ballroom on a chair. . . .

"The whole purpose of the picture is to acquaint America with ravished Armenia," said Mrs. Harriman, "to visualize conditions so that there will be no misunderstanding in the mind of any one about the terrible things which have transpired. It was deemed essential that the leaders, social and intellectual, should first learn the story, but later the general public shall be informed. It is proposed that before this campaign of information is completed, as many adults as possible shall know the story of Armenia, and the screen was selected as the medium because it reaches the millions, where the printed word reaches the thousands."[118]

Aurora Mardiganian

Courtesy of the Academy of Motion Picture Arts and Sciences.

Screenings of the film often climaxed in a personal appearance by Aurora Mardiganian herself, who had been given English lessons to help transform her into a spokesperson for her people. Audiences were moved by what they saw and it helped enlist impassioned supporters of the Armenian cause. The attention had its downside. Anthony Slide, author of *Ravished Armenia and the Story of Aurora Mardiganian* writes about the effect of the publicity on Mardiganian herself.

The pressure was taking its toll on the teenager. In Armenia, she had led a relatively sheltered existence. She had witnessed the horrors of genocide, but was unprepared for the rigors of American society. Its code of behavior was alien to a girl from a different continent and a different culture. She had become a movie star with all the accompanying trappings, but it was unsought-for fame.[119]

Aware of the mounting tension, Mardiganian's guardians hired a chaperone and then later seven impersonators to help cover the relentless schedule of speaking engagements. Before long it became too much, Mardiganian made her last public personal appearance with the film in May 1920 and then slipped into a quiet life. Slide writes:

In the 1920s, interest in both the film Ravished Armenia *and an independent Armenia dissipated in the United States. Near East Relief produced one other film,* Alice in Hungerland *(1921), in which an American child goes to the Near East and witnesses conditions there. Aurora Mardiganian made no other film appearances, and expressed no interest in continuing her career as an actress. . . . Because of the horrors she had suffered in Armenia, for many years Aurora Mardiganian could not permit a man to touch her, but in 1929, she married and embarked on a new life as an Armenian-American housewife. She died in Los Angeles on February 6, 1994.*[120]

Although no complete copy of *Ravished Armenia* remains, the film is a testament to the power of movies to educate and build sympathy for a cause.

CONNECTIONS

✤ Why did Harriman and others believe film would capture the public's attention more effectively than words? Do you agree?

✤ What role can film play in shaping public opinion? How does a film make an event more real for some people?

✤ Many of the contemporary reports of the Armenian Genocide played into cultural and religious prejudices and stereotypes by contrasting the image of innocent Christian victims and "fanatical" Muslims. How do you think the identity of the victims and perpetrators of the Armenian Genocide contributed to the public's engagement with the plight of the Armenians? How does the identity of victims of injustice influence the way people respond to human rights abuses today?

✤ Slide describes Mardiganian's fame as "unsought," yet her celebrity status gave the suffering of her fellow Armenians a face with which people could identify. What toll did those experiences take on Mardiganian?

✦ Are all forms of persuasion propaganda? Was *Ravished Armenia* propaganda? What criteria would you use to judge? Can propaganda be used for a good cause? Are there other ways to rally people to a common cause?

⏤

NOTES

88. Power, *A Problem from Hell*, p. xvii.
89. Albert Camus, *Notebooks 1935–1951* (New York: Marlowe & Co, 1998).
90. "Turks Who Saved Armenians: An Introduction," available at *www.zoryan.org*.
91. "The Story of Haji Khalil," available at *www.zoryan.org*.
92. Quoted in Vahakn N. Dadrian, "Genocide as a Problem of National and International Law: The World War I Armenian Case and Its Contemporary Legal Ramifications," *Yale Journal of International Law* 14 (1989), p. 268.
93. Ibid., p. 269.
94. Vahakn N Dadrian, "The Complicity of the Party, the Government, and the Military, Select Parliamentary and Judicial Documents," *Journal of Political and Military Sociology* 22 (Summer 1994), p. 54.
95. Ibid., p. 91
96. Dickran H. Boyajian, *Armenia: The Case for a Forgotten Genocide* (Westwood, NJ: Educational Book Crafters, 1972), p. 123.
97. Ibid., p. 123.
98. Henry Morgenthau, *Ambassador Morgenthau's Story* (Plandome, NY: New Age Publisher, 1975), p. 370.
99. Ibid., p. 373.
100. From the Ambassador in Extraordinary Mission in Constantinople (Wolff-Metternich) to the Reichskanzler (Bethmann Hollweg), German official archive 1915-12-07-DE-001, from *www.armenocide.net*. A Documentation of the Armenian Genocide in World War I.
101. Ibid.
102. Dwork and Jan van Pelt, *The Holocaust*, pp. 39–40.
103. Ervin Staub, *The Roots of Evil: The Origins of Genocide and Other Group Violence* (New York: Cambridge University Press, 1989), pp. 86–87.
104. Ibid.
105. Bryce, *Treatment of Armenians*, pp. 514–515.
106. Ibid., p. 520.
107. Power, *A Problem from Hell*, pp. 5–7.
108. Ibid.
109. Ibid., p. 11.
110. Ibid., p. 13.
111. Morgenthau, *Morgenthau's Story*, p. 330.
112. Ibid., pp. 333–336.
113. Ibid., p. 339.
114. Walter Kalaidjian, "The Edge of Modernism: Genocide and the Poetics of Traumatic Memory," in Jani Scandura and Michael Thurston ed. *Modernism, Inc.* (New York and London: NYU Press, 2001), pp. 109–110.
115. *New York Times*, Oct. 7, 1915, p. 3, available at *http://www.cilicia.com/armo10c-nyt19151007.html*.
116. Christopher Simpson, *The Splendid Blond Beast* (New York: Grove Press, 1993), pp. 30–31.
117. *The Literary Digest*, "How Your Gift Is Saving The Armenians," March 9, 1918, available at *http://www.cilicia.com/armo10c-ld19180309.html*.
118. *New York Times*, February 15, 1919, p. 4.
119. Anthony Slide, ed., *Ravished Armenia and the Story of Aurora Mardiganian* (Lanham, MD: Scarecrow Press, 1997), p. 15.
120. Ibid., pp. 16–17.

"Must the Armenians be once more disillusioned?
The future of this small nation must not be relegated to obscurity
behind the selfish schemes and plans of the great states."
—Armin Wegner, an eyewitness to the Armenian Genocide

Chapter 6

"WHO REMEMBERS THE ARMENIANS?"
Judgment, Memory, and Legacies

THIS CHAPTER EXAMINES THE WAYS VARIOUS INDIVIDUALS AND GROUPS RESPONDED IN THE WAKE OF THE Armenian Genocide. During the war, the Allies promised to hold Turkish leaders responsible for their crimes. After the war, however, international efforts to prosecute perpetrators of the genocide were aborted. In their place were a series of court martials within Turkey. By the time the prosecutions began many of the top leaders of the Committee of Union and Progress had already fled. Although the post-war trials did not fulfill the promise of bringing the perpetrators of the genocide to justice, the evidence collected offers some of the most important documentation of the Armenian Genocide.

A few months before the end of the World War I, at a time when a civil war was raging in Russia, Armenian leaders in Russian Armenia formed their own Republic. President Woodrow Wilson's support for the concept of national self-determination—the idea that groups should rule themselves in their own nation—encouraged the Armenians, and many other ethnic and national groups to seek support to create their own state. The Armenians would need assistance to rebuild after the genocide. Although the Allies made promises, they did little to protect the emerging Armenian Republic. Empowered by the lack of commitment a Turkish nationalist named Mustafa Kemal led troops into the Republic of Armenia. Desperate to save their remaining land, the leaders of the fledgling Armenian Republic were forced to turn to Communist Russia for help, forgoing national independence. Until the break up of the Soviet Union in 1991, Armenia existed as much in memory and diaspora as it did in any one place on the map.

Living scattered across the globe Armenians have struggled to hold on to their identity. Part of that struggle is an effort for acknowledgement of the genocide. An international campaign of genocide denial, often sponsored by the Turkish government, targeting politicians, academics, and diplomats, has attempted to turn what was a known fact into something unrecognizable to the witnesses and survivors of the genocide.

Despite those efforts, the history of the Armenian Genocide continues to influence international law and human rights policy. Raphael Lemkin, a Polish Jew, saw the connection between the crimes committed against the Armenians and the rise of the Nazis in Germany. Lemkin was profoundly frustrated by the failure of the international community to hold leaders of the Young Turk movement accountable after World War I. He worked tirelessly to have "crimes against humanity" recognized as a violation of international law. Indeed it was Lemkin who coined the term "genocide"—a concept that stands as one of the foundations of the international movement for human rights. Although law and language have not been able to prevent genocide on their own, they have set a legal and moral standard making the protection of citizens a concern of not just one country, but the entire world.

Project SAVE Armenian Photograph Archives, Inc., Courtesy of Rev. Vartan Hartunian

Abraham and Shushan Hartunian and their family, Genocide survivors from Marash, Cilician Armenia, Ottoman Empire, pose in front of the camera on board the King Alexander, a Greek ship out of Athens before stepping into a new life on a New York City pier, November 1, 1922.

Reading 1 — A MANDATE FOR ARMENIA?

By November 1917 a revolution in Russia brought down the czar and replaced the monarchy with a Bolshevik state. At the same time refugees from the genocide poured across the border from Turkey into Russia. On May 28, 1918, in what had been Russian Armenia, surviving Armenians organized an independent republic. At the same time, Armenians as well as other peoples and nations—Arabs, Kurds, Bulgarians, Greeks, Serbs, and Zionist Jews—claimed parts of the Ottoman Empire. Historian Richard Hovannisian describes the optimism that many Armenians felt as the war came to an end.

Armenian deportees returning home to Marash from exile. Marash, Cilician Armenia, Ottoman Empire, 1919. Photo by E. Stanley Kerr, medical missionary.

Project SAVE Armenian Photograph Archives, Inc., Courtesy of Vartan Hartunian

The surrender of the Ottoman Empire and the flight of the Young Turk leaders in October 1918 evoked thanksgiving and hope among the Armenian survivors. The prospect of compatriots returning to the homeland from all over the world, some refugees and survivors of the genocide, and others longtime exiles from the days of Abdul-Hamid, excited imaginations. Every Allied power was pledged to a separate autonomous or independent existence for the Armenians in their historic lands. A small republic had already taken form in the Caucasus and now gradually expanded as the Turkish armies withdrew from the area. There were, of course, major obstacles to its incorporation of Turkish Armenia because the population had been massacred or driven out and the Turkish army still controlled the region. In drawing up the Mudros Armistice, British negotiators had required Turkish evacuation of the Caucasus but gave up their initial intent to demand also the clearance of Turkish Armenia, although they reserved for the Allies the right to occupy any or all of the region in case of disorder, an option they never exercised. Nonetheless, to the Armenians and their sympathizers, it seemed that the crucifixion of the nation would be followed by a veritable resurrection.[121]

Allied leaders began to map out the future of the region at the Paris Peace Conference in 1919. Attempting to organize the peace and mediate further conflict was the newly formed League of Nations. Article 22 of the Covenant of the League of Nations provided mandatories or protectorates, through which larger countries promised to support the developing states.

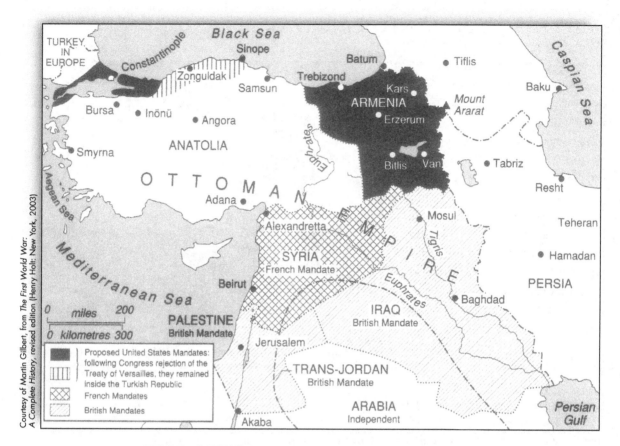

Courtesy of Martin Gilbert, from The First World War: A Complete History, revised edition (Henry Holt: New York, 2003)

THE OTTOMAN EMPIRE MANDATES

A map depicting mandates that were to be created from former Ottoman Territory after the end of World War I.

The article read in part:

> *Certain communities formerly belonging to the Turkish Empire have reached a stage of development where their existence as independent nations can be provisionally recognized subject to the rendering of administrative advice and assistance by a Mandatory until such time as they are able to stand alone. The wishes of these communities must be a principal consideration in the selection of the Mandatory.*

In July 1919, President Wilson sent Major General James Harbord to investigate the status of Armenians living in Turkey and the emerging Armenian Republic and to consider whether the United States should accept an mandate over the territory. Both the report and the League of Nations itself set off a debate about the role of the United States in foreign affairs. In his report Harbord listed reasons for and against taking on a mandate for Armenia. Included here are excerpts from his report:

REASONS FOR	REASONS AGAINST
As one of the chief contributors to the formation of the League of Nations, the United States is morally bound to accept the obligations and responsibilities of a mandatory power.	The United States has prior and nearer foreign obligations, and ample responsibilities with domestic problems growing out of the war.
The Near East presents the greatest humanitarian opportunity of the age—a duty for which the United States is better fitted than any other—as witness Cuba, Puerto Rico, Philippines, Hawaii, Panama, and our altruistic policy of developing peoples rather than material resources alone.	Humanitarianism should begin at home. There is a sufficient number of difficult situations which call for our actions within the well-recognized spheres of American influence.
America is practically the unanimous choice and fervent hope of all the peoples involved.	The United States has in no way contributed to and is not responsible for the conditions, political, social, or economic, that prevail in this region. It will be entirely consistent to decline the invitation.
America is already spending millions to save starving people in Turkey and Transcaucasia and could do this with much more efficiency if in control. Whoever becomes a mandatory for these regions we shall be still expected to finance their relief, and will probably eventually furnish the capital for material development.	American philanthropy and charity are world wide. Such policy would commit us to a policy of meddling or draw upon our philanthropy to the point of exhaustion.
America is the only hope of the Armenians. They consider but one other nation, Great Britain....For a mandatory America is not only the first choice of all the peoples of the Near East but of each of the great powers, after itself. American power is adequate; its record is clean; its motives above suspicion.	Other powers, particularly Great Britain, and Russia, have shown continued interest in the welfare of Armenia....The United States is not capable of sustaining a continuity of foreign policy. One Congress cannot bind another. Even treaties can be nullified by cutting off appropriations.
The mandatory would be self-supporting after.... five years. The building of railroads would offer opportunities to our capital. There would be great trade advantages.	Our country would be put to great expense, involving probably an increase of the Army and Navy.... It is questionable if railroads could for many years pay interest on investments in their very difficult construction. The effort and money spent would get us more trade in nearer lands than we could hope for in Russia and Rumania.
It would definitely stop further massacres of Armenians and other Christians, give justice to the Turks, Kurds, Greeks, and other peoples.	Peace and justice would be equally assured under any other of the great powers.

Continued on next page

REASONS FOR	REASONS AGAINST
America has strong sentimental interests in the region—our missions and colleges.	These institutions have been respected even by the Turks throughout the war and the massacres: and sympathy and respect would be shown by any other mandatory.
If the United States does not take responsibility in this region, it is likely that international jealousies will result in a continuance of the unspeakable misrule of the Turk.	The peace conference has definitely informed the Turkish government that it may expect to go under a mandate. It is not conceivable that the League of Nations would permit further uncontrolled rule by that thoroughly discredited government.
"And the Lord said unto Cain, 'Where is Abel, thy brother?' And he said, 'I know not; am I my brother's keeper?'" Better millions for a mandate than billions for future wars.	The first duty of America is to its own people and its nearer neighbors.[122]

The last point, which Harbord presented without an opposing view read:

Here is a man's job that the world says can be better done by America than by any other. America can afford the money; she has the men; no duty to her own people would suffer; her traditional policy of isolation did not keep her from successful participation in the Great War. Shall it be said that our country lacks the courage to take up new and difficult duties?

Without visiting the Near East it is not possible for an American to realize even faintly the respect, faith, and affection with which our country is regarded throughout that region. Whether it is the world-wide reputation which we enjoy for fair dealing, a tribute perhaps to the crusading spirit which carried us into the Great War, not untinged with hope that the same spirit may urge us into the solution of great problems growing out of that conflict, or whether due to unselfish and impartial missionary and educational influence exerted for a century, it is the one faith which is held alike by Christian and [Muslim], by Jew and Gentile, by prince and peasant in the Near East. It is very gratifying to the pride of Americans far from home. But it brings with it the heavy responsibility of deciding great questions with a seriousness worthy of such faith. Burdens that might be assumed on the appeal of such sentiment would have to be carried for not less than a generation under circumstances so trying that we might easily forfeit the faith of the world. If we refuse to assume it, for no matter what reasons satisfactory to ourselves, we shall be considered by many millions of people as having left unfinished the task for which we entered the war, and as having betrayed their hopes.[123]

After consideration, the United States did not take on a mandate for Armenia.

CONNECTIONS

- Richard Hovannisian writes that Armenians and their supporters believed "the crucifixion of the nation would be followed by a veritable resurrection." The words "crucifixion" and "resurrection" refer to Christian spiritual beliefs. What images do the words evoke? Why do you think he chose to use them in this context?

- The Paris peace conference created new countries in what is now called the Middle East as well as new structures to prevent war. Many contemporary conflicts in the Middle East and the Balkans trace their roots to this period. Research how the decisions made in 1919 echo in the headlines today.

- Which of Harbord's arguments do you find most persuasive? Rank the arguments and justify your rankings.

- Consider Henry Morgenthau's comments from his editorial "Shall Armenia Perish?" which was published on February 28, 1920:

  If America is going to condone these offenses, if she is going to permit to continue conditions that threaten and permit their repetition, she is party to the crime. These people must be freed from the agony and dangers of such horrors. They must not only be saved for the present but either thru governmental action or protection under the League of Nations they must be given assurance that they will be free in peace and that no harm can come to them.[124]

  How do his comments compare with those of Harbord?

- How might Harbord's arguments be applied to a foreign policy decision today? Consider the two statements:

  The United States should always participate in efforts to build new nations with the hope of building democratic states.

  The United States should not involve itself in nation building.

  With which statement do you most agree? Why? Another way to discuss this is through a barometer. Stand in a line representing a continuum between the two statements. Participants should stand closest to the position they agree with most. Discuss why you have choosen your position and listen to the arguments made by others. Move along the barometer as your thinking changes.

- U.S. President Woodrow Wilson promoted the idea of "self-determination" in which groups would be able to decide their own future and form their own government. Why did Wilson believe it would reduce conflict? What new challenges were raised by the concept of self-determination? Would the world be safer if all groups had the right to form their own nation?

❧ Consider how foreign policy decisions are made today. How are arguments made for or against intervention? Are the arguments similar to those made in the Harbord report? How has the language changed? Are the arguments moral or are they political?

❧ Much of the present day Middle East grew from Ottoman mandates. Research other mandates and countries that grew out of the Paris Peace Conference in 1919. Which countries took on mandates? Have the border issues that grew from the collapse of the Ottoman Empire been resolved?

⌣

Reading 2 — CRIMES AGAINST HUMANITY AND CIVILIZATION

After the Mudros Armistice in October 1918 which officially ended the war in the Ottoman Empire, the Allied leaders knew that somebody had to be held accountable for the massacres. In an article titled "The Trial of Perpetrators by the Turkish Military Tribunals: The Case of Yozgat," German scholar Annette Höss described the challenges in bringing the perpetrators of the Armenian Genocide to justice.

The Turkish military defeat in the latter part of 1918 posed serious problems for succeeding governments of the Ottoman Empire. The victorious Allies were expected to impose harsh peace terms upon . . . Turkey, especially because of the mistreatment of prisoners of war and the genocidal massacres against the Armenians. In fact, on 24 May 1915 the Allies had solemnly warned the Turkish authorities of the dire consequences of these massacres which they termed "new crimes of Turkey against humanity and civilization." Consequently, the arrest, trial, and punishment of the culprits was a central issues in Turkish internal and external politics following the Mudros Armistice. . . .

The ruling class of Turkey was divided into two camps after the signing of the armistice. One still adhered to the Ittihadist ideology, while the other repudiated the Ittihadists and sided with the

An article from the New York Times on July 13, 1919 describing the Turkish court-martials for Djemal, Enver, and Talaat.

From Kloian, *Armenian Genocide: News Accounts*

The New York Times

SUNDAY, JULY 13, 1919

(1:2)

TURKEY CONDEMNS ITS WAR LEADERS

Court-Martial Gives Death Sentence to Enver Pasha, Talaat Bey, and Djemal Pasha.

ALL THREE MADE ESCAPES

Djavid Bey and Alusa Metssa Get 15 Years at Hard Labor for Part in the War.

CONSTANTINOPLE, July 11.—Enver Pasha, Talaat Bey, and Djemal Pasha, the leaders of the Turkish Government during the war, were condemned to death today by a Turkish court-martial investigating the conduct of the Turkish Government during the war period.

Enver and his two leading associates in the Young Turk Government fled from Turkey several months ago, and their whereabouts is uncertain.

Djavid Bey, former Minister of Finance, and Alusa Mussa Ki...

Henry Morgenthau, American A[mbas]sador at Constantinople, and Sir Louis M[...] the British Ambassador at the same [...] have left no doubt in their dispatches, [...] articles, and interviews of the guilt o[f the] Young Turk leaders which has just [been] proclaimed with sentences pronounced [by the] Turkish court-martial ordered by the Grand Vizier Damad Ferid Pasha, and [con]vened by Ahmed Abouk Pasha, the Ministe[r of] War.

It is the climax of a long series [of] prosecutions undertaken by the officials of [the] new régime to clear the skirts of the Turk[ish] people from blame for joining in the war a[nd] for the Armenian, Greek, and Syrian atrocit[ies] and deportations. It reached its practic[al] climax on April 12, when Kemal Bey, form[er] Minister of Food and C[...]

Allied Powers, which took charge of parts of the Ottoman capital. . . . In order to impress and molli-fy the victors, therefore, the postwar Turkish government set out to institute court-martial proceed-ings against the top leaders of the Ittihadist party, many of whom had also functioned as cabinet min-isters. Seven leading Ittihadists—Talât [Talaat], Enver, Jemal [Djemal], Shakir, Nazim, Bedri, and Azmi—had already fled the country.

The Allied Powers were pledged to punish the organizers of the genocide and showed considerable interest in the prosecution. As the political situation in Turkey began to change, however, some of the Allies became more cautious. It was Great Britain which actually pursued the prosecution. The main interest of the British was punishment of officials responsible for the ill-treatment of British prison-ers of the war and only secondarily those involved in the Armenian massacres.

There were three different levels at which the formation of courts-martial were considered in early 1919: a sub-commission of the Paris Peace Conference, the British High Commission at Constantinople, and the Turkish cabinets under Izzet Pasha and Damad Ferid Pasha. At the peace conference the delegates dealt with the problems of international law and how the regulations could be applied in the case of Turkey. . . .

The fact that seven Young Turk leaders had fled from Turkey [to Germany] at the end of 1918 required rapid action by the British High Commission and the new Turkish government. This result-ed in numerous arrests in early 1919. A special court-martial was established on 8 January on the basis of an imperial decree of 16 December. . . . Interestingly enough, these sessions were open to the public, an uncommon practice in cases of court-martial. . . .

Although the courts-martial began promisingly, the results were disappointing. . . . The most important trials were as follows: Yozgat (5 February-7 April 1919), Trebizond (26 March-17 May 1919), Ittihadist Leaders (28 April-17 May 1919), and Cabinet Ministers (3 June-25 June 1919). Preparations were made for many other trials . . . but only a few were actually held. . . . Interruption of the trials was not because of lack of evidence but because of political developments in Turkey. As the Kemalist movement spread, the work of the courts-martial slowed and ultimately was suspended.

The evidence used in the court-martial proceedings in 1919 was collected through two commissions: The Fifth Committee of Parliament and the Mazhar Inquiry Commission. The Fifth Committee of Parliament initiated the investigation into the massacres. . . .

In the fourteen hearings of the committee, thirteen ministers, and two Sheikhs-ul-Islam were inter-rogated. A number of documents, including top-secret orders and instructions regarding the mas-sacres, were procured.[125]

The sultan disbanded the Fifth Committee before a vote was taken on their findings but the Mazhar Inquiry Commission continued its work. In less than two months the commission collected written and oral evidence, including telegraphic orders for the deportations and the massacres. In mid-January 1919, the commission submitted dossiers on 130 subjects to the court-martial.[126]

At the trial of the Ittihad leaders in Constantinople, the prosecutors explained to the court: "The disaster visiting the Armenians was not a local or isolated event. It was the result of a premeditated decision taken by a central body . . . and the excesses which took place were based on oral and written orders issued by that central body."[127] In absentia, Talaat, Djemal, and Enver were found guilty and sentenced to death. Just after the verdict was handed down, leaders of the new Ottoman government asked to have the triumvirate extradited from Germany but the request was ignored. In the meantime, nearly 400 functionaries were arrested, and the trials continued while most of the top party officials lived in exile. Under pressure from Turkish nationalist Mustafa Kemal and his supporters, the court martials were brought to a close in January, 1921.

After the trials, the British high commissioner in Constantinople wrote: "The Court Martial has been such a dead failure that its findings cannot be held of any account at all, if it is intended to make responsibility for deportations and massacres a matter of inter-Allied concern."[128] Seemingly alone in their desire to press on with trials, the British considered creating a special court to try Ottoman war criminals but ultimately took no action.

Over thirty years after the start of the Armenian Genocide, Sir Harley Shawcross, the British chief prosecutor at the Nuremberg trials, which followed the fall of the Nazis, declared that the World War I genocide of the Armenians became a foundation for the Nuremberg Law recognizing crimes against humanity.

CONNECTIONS

⭢ On May 24, 1915, the Allied Powers warned that the Turkish leaders would be held responsible for the crimes they committed. What is the danger in threatening prosecution but not following through?

⭢ What is justice? Who should have been held accountable for the Armenian Genocide? After all the years that have passed, is justice still possible? What would need to happen? Who would need to be involved?

⭢ What made it difficult for the Ottoman government after World War I to sustain a vigorous prosecution of its war criminals?

⭢ The Indictment of the Constantinople Military Court (April 27, 1919) read:

The . . . investigation has disclosed that the Ittihad [Young Turk] Party had two faces. One of these was its well-known external face, that is, a Party acting in accordance with its by-laws; the second was the secretive, conspiratorial, traitorous Ittihad acting with criminal intent on oral and secret instructions . . . the history of the Party has been marked by an unending chain of massacres, pillage and abuse. That Party is responsible for the crimes committed. . . . [129]

What kinds of evidence would be needed to establish these charges?

✦ The post-apartheid South African government responded to the mass violence of apartheid very differently from the government of post-war Turkey. While the post-apartheid government formed the Truth and Reconciliation Commission, nationalists led by Mustafa Kemal worked to erase the memory of the Armenian Genocide. What does the term "truth and reconciliation" imply? What is reconciliation? Can there be reconciliation without an acknowledgement of the truth? To learn more about the South African Truth and Reconciliation Commission, download the study guide *Facing the Truth* from the Facing History and Ourselves web site and view the film with your class.

✦ The Nuremberg International Tribunal at the close of World War II placed leading Nazi war criminals on trial. Professor Richard Hovannisian has argued that the Holocaust might have been prevented if the Allied Powers after World War I had upheld the decision to establish an international tribunal for the perpetrators of the Armenian Genocide. See his comments in the videotape of the 1985 Facing History Conference, *The Impact of Nuremberg*, available at the Facing History Resource Center. What are the dangers when injustice is neither confronted nor acknowledged?

↩

Reading 3 — WAR, GENOCIDE, AND HUMAN RIGHTS

At the Paris Peace Conference at the end of World War I, advocates for an international standard for human rights believed the newly formed League of Nations would uphold basic standards for the fair and equal treatment of people from all over the world. Human rights scholar Paul Gordon Lauren describes the dreams and frustrations of those that hoped to ensure that the horror of World War I and the atrocities of the Armenian Genocide would never happen again.

A 1919 political cartoon from Punch magazine, depicting U.S. President Woodrow Wilson with an olive branch, representing the League of Nations.

The human rights of minorities . . . attracted considerable attention and care at the Paris Peace Conference. Humanitarian intervention as a means of protecting religious or ethnic minorities from persecution, of course, had arisen well before the war; but concern had been greatly intensified by the recent experience with genocide against the Armenians and other wartime loss of human life. To make this issue even more acute, the very act of establishing new states created sizable numbers of new minorities within their frontiers, thereby raising serious questions about their rights. If any of these governments persecuted those populations under one guise or another who had just been joined to their states, genuine threats could be posed to both domestic and international stability. "Nothing," acknowledged [U.S. President] Wilson at a plenary meeting of the peace conference "is more likely to disturb the peace of the world than the treatment which might in certain circumstances be meted out to minorities." The realization thus very slowly began to emerge (although it would take the experience of another world war to be appreciated more fully) that violations of human rights at home ran perilous risks of jeopardizing world peace abroad. This could be seen in the large number and wide-ranging scope of proposals submitted to the conference by private citizens, nongovernmental organizations, and official representatives in the name of protecting the rights of minorities. They argued for the right of minorities for the preservation of their culture and ethnic character, the right of equality of all before the law, and the right of freedom of worship and religion. "All citizens," urged one proposal, "without distinction as to race, nationality, or religion, shall enjoy equal civil, religious, political and national rights." The most critical factor in all of these proposals, of course, was not their assertion of rights, but rather their call for responsibilities. That is, all the proposals strongly urged members of the international community to cross that important intellectual and political threshold imposed by strict definitions of national sovereignty and now establish that they possessed a collective responsibility beyond their own borders to guarantee protection for the rights of minorities.[130]

At Paris, negotiators forged an international structure for the protection of the rights of minorities in a series of agreements called the Minority Treaties. Questions also arose around the issue of the human right to life and food, as seen in the commitment of the 1919 legislation that created the American Relief Administration (ARA) and the ongoing efforts for victims and refugees of the Armenian Genocide. The talk of rights went beyond issues of identity; provisions for the rights of labor were written into binding peace treaties as well.[131] For all the accomplishments, many felt ignored. The Minority Treaties did not cover the rights of minorities living in Asia, Africa, the Middle East, Latin America, the United States, and Canada, or islands of the Pacific. Furthermore, the principle of self-determination, used by advocates of the Armenian Republic, did not seem to apply to colonial possessions.

Lauren believes that despite the many disappointments, the Paris Peace Conference built an important precedent for the international human rights movement.

> *The many exaggerated expectations, often encouraged by political leaders themselves, that somehow all the sacrifices made in wartime would be rewarded and thereby suddenly transform the nature of rights around the globe did not materialize. . . . On the other hand . . . never before in history had a peace conference produced so many treaties about the right of self-determination, the right of minorities to be protected, the right to enjoy life by receiving assistance, and the rights of the laboring classes, or produced an international organization formally charged with guaranteeing these particular rights. Never before had the global community made such a direct connection between peace and justice, or been willing to acknowledge such extensive responsibilities.*

The rights of Armenians, as individuals and as a nation, whose plight had been an important warning to the world, would be one of the first tests of the commitment of the new international system.

CONNECTIONS

↩ President Wilson believed, "Nothing is more likely to disturb the peace of the world than the treatment which might in certain circumstances be meted out to minorities." What does he mean? What is the relationship between the treatment of groups within a nation and war? Can you think of examples that support Wilson's argument?

↩ Who was responsible for the Armenian Genocide? Who was guilty? How important is it to have those questions answered?

⚬ One of the challenges in preventing abuses of human rights is the question of enforcement. How can human rights be enforced? Whose responsibility is their enforcement?

⚬ Paul Gordon Lauren writes about the many disappointments at the Paris Peace Conference, including the rejection of a Japanese proposal to ban racial discrimination. He states: "Never before had the global community made such a direct connection between peace and justice." What criteria would you use to evaluate the effort? What precedents did it set for the field of human rights?

⚬ How did indignation about the mistreatment of Armenians evolve from concerned individuals and groups to become an essential foundation for international law and human rights?

⌐

Research post-World War II efforts to prevent collective violence including the Universal Declaration of Human Rights.   You may also visit the archive of Facing History and Ourselves' online forum *Engaging the Future: Religion, Human Rights, and Conflict Resolution.*

Reading 4 — THE ARMENIAN REPUBLIC AND THE NEW TURKEY

Even before the Paris Peace Conference at the end of World War I, President Woodrow Wilson articulated a new vision for the world. At the outset of U.S. involvement in the war, Wilson argued that action was needed to "make the world safe for democracy." His new idea went further. Wilson articulated a principle of national self-determination in which small nations would be granted independence from the old empires. Before the end of the war, Wilson laid out fourteen points, which would be central to his vision. The twelfth point spoke directly to the Armenians:

> *The Turkish portions of the Ottoman Empire should be assured a secure sovereignty, but the other nationalities which are now under Turkish rule should be assured an undoubted security of life and an unmolested opportunity of autonomous development.*[132]

Wilson's ideas influenced the treaties that were negotiated in Paris and after the war. The Treaty of Sevres, which was signed nearly two years after the armistice, required that Turkey recognize the Armenian Republic and allowed President Wilson to set the boundary between Turkey and Armenia within limits of the four eastern Ottoman provinces of Trebizond, Erzerum, Bitlis, and Van.

©Hulton Archive

Mustafa Kemal also known as Kemal Ataturk.

Despite international support, the survival of the small Armenian nation was almost immediately threatened by Mustafa Kemal. As a young man, Kemal had helped the Young Turks overthrow the sultan and had solidified his record as a nationalist during the war. Stung by the surrender of the Turkish army in 1918 and by the occupation of the Turkish ports by British, French, and Greek forces, Mustafa Kemal rejected the terms of the peace, which carved a number of states from Ottoman territory. Mustafa Kemal's message caught on among nationalists who were bitter over the loss of land and angered by what they perceived as further meddling in Turkey's internal affairs. In 1920, he set up an opposition government in Ankara, and the Kemalists (his followers) soon gained so much support that they were able to influence policy in the capital. As Kemal planned an invasion of the Armenian Republic in the Caucasus, he knew he could count on the support of Turkish troops. Historian Richard Hovannisian writes that the fledgling Armenian Republic was unable to defend itself against the invasion of the Turkish army.

*The Allied Powers looked on with a mixture of distress and res-
ignation as the Turkish armies advanced into the heart of the
republic and in December forced the Armenian government to
repudiate the terms of the Sevres settlement, renounce all claims
to Turkish Armenia, and even cede the former Russian
Armenian districts of Kars, Arahan, and Surmalu, including
Mount Ararat, the symbolic Armenian mountain. . . . Desperate
and forlorn, the crippled Armenian government had no choice
other than to save what little territory was left by opting for
Soviet rule and seek the protection of the Red Army.*[133]

Sano Halo (left) and her family, Syria, 1925.

Emboldened by their victory, Turkish nationalists set out to
deport the remaining Armenians and Christians in the
Ottoman Empire. In her daughter's book, *Not Even My Name*,
Sano Halo, a Pontian Greek, remembers the day in 1920
when Turkish soldiers appeared in her village, forcing her
family into exile. After an arduous journey during which she
lost her family, Halo recalls crossing the border into Syria.

*Each day a new group of Christians rolled past our house in creaky wagons, or walked alongside
donkeys piled high with bundles.*

*On the fifth day, we started on our own journey south to Aleppo. The trip was long and tedious, but
could not compare to the forced march with my family. At least there were no corpses on the road,
and we had enough food and money to keep us, even if it was not in great abundance.*

*Our wagon bumped along the dry, pitted road as we crossed the border that marked the end of Turkey
and the beginning of Aleppo. . . . It was the first time since I left my home, a million years ago it
seemed, that I took time to think about what happened and realize my loss. I looked back one last
time toward the country that had been a great joy to me in my first years of life; the country that had
become the cause of all my sorrows. . . .*[134]

Nearly two years after Halo's family was forced to flee, British, Italian, and French ships evacuated thousands of Greek and Armenian nationals from the city of Smyrna in 1922, leaving Turkey nearly purged
of its Christian minorities. While the Allies argued about who was to blame, Kemal ousted the sultan on
November 1, 1922. Unwilling to resume fighting, and aware of the economic benefits of normalizing
relations with Turkey, Allied leaders negotiated a new treaty with the Kemalist government. After these
successful negotiations that culminated in the Treaty of Lausanne, Kemal and his supporters declared
the birth of the Turkish Republic on October 29, 1923. To fulfill the treaty, Greece and Turkey exchanged

minority populations, uprooting Turks in Greece as well as far more Greeks in Turkey.

CONNECTIONS

◆ What is "self-determination"? Who should have the power to determine which people or groups should be given their own nation?

◆ Can you imagine a country where everybody would be the same? What conflicts would be eliminated? What new challenges would you anticipate? What would be lost?

◆ According to Kemal, what threat did the Armenians represent in a new Turkey?

◆ Wilson's plan for the border between Armenia and Turkey granted Armenia over 16,000 square miles of land including access to the Black Sea. The plan was announced on November 22 after Kemal's army had advanced well into the Armenian Republic. Christopher Walker writes that Wilson's plan "was predicated upon the notion that right and justice prevail in the world, not force, cunning and self interest. As such, it served no purpose."[135] What would it have taken for Wilson's plan to become a reality? Why do you think Walker believes "it served no purpose"? Do you agree?

◆ What is ethnic cleansing? In what ways did the Treaty of Lausanne condone ethnic cleansing?

©Hulton Archive

Turkish crowds in Smyrna, 1922, at the symbolic end of the Christian presence in the Ottoman Empire.

Reading 5 — ACQUITTING THE ASSASSIN

In 1918, Talaat Pasha fled Turkey for Germany, Turkey's ally during the war. By March 1921, he was living in Berlin with his wife under an assumed name. There, Talaat became the center of a group of Turkish nationalists and led an active social life. On March 16, Soghomon Tehlirian, a 24-year-old Armenian survivor of the genocide, shot and killed Talaat and wounded Talaat's wife. Tehlirian showed no remorse for the murder. He told police: "It is not I who am the murderer. It is he [Talaat]."

After Talaat's death, the press mourned him as a loyal friend to Germany. In early June, when the trial began, it was widely believed that the German courts would enact the harshest punishment on Tehlirian, especially since Germany had been sympathetic to the Young Turks and had provided refuge for several Turkish leaders after the war.

Soghomon Tehlirian

Courtesy of Project SAVE Armenian Photograph Archives, Inc., Courtesy of Faith Cass

Tehlirian's lawyers planned a two-part defense. First, they would argue that Tehlirian was temporarily insane at the time of the murder. To support his claim, Tehlirian told the court that two weeks before the murder his mother, who had been killed during the genocide, appeared to him in a vision, exhorting him to kill Talaat as an act of revenge for the atrocities committed against the Armenian people. The second part of the strategy was to put the victim on trial.

To support their case, Tehlirian's lawyers were able to get support from two prominent Germans, Johannes Lepsius, who had recently published a book about the atrocities perpetrated against the Armenians by the Turks, and General Liman von Sanders, the former leader of the German military mission in the Ottoman Empire. Testifying in Tehlirian's defense, Lepsius detailed the systematic plans for what he called the elimination of the "Armenians in Armenia." Lepsius testified to Talaat's role in the massacres of the Armenians and told the court that he had physical documentary evidence to prove his allegations. Lepsius' overview was followed by the testimony of General von Sanders, who described the callousness of German military officials who watched the massacre of Armenians but failed to intervene. During the trial, five messages with Talaat's signature were entered into evidence including one in which Talaat ordered that Armenian children who were living in orphanages after the murder of their parents be killed "in order to eliminate further danger from antagonistic elements."[136]

After one hour of deliberations Tehlirian was acquitted.

In an editorial titled "They Simply Had to Let Him Go," the *New York Times*, outlined the jury's dilemma.

By acquitting the young Armenian who shot dead Talaat Pasha on the street in a Berlin suburb where that too eminent Turk was quietly living, the court before which he was tried practically has given, not only to this young man, but to the many others like him and with like grievances, a license to kill at discretion any Turkish official whom they can find in Germany.

That was going rather far. Of course, death was about the least of the punishments for his innumerable and most atrocious crimes that was deserved by Talaat Pasha. The world's atmosphere is the more safely and pleasantly breathed now that he is gone, and there will be little sympathy with his fate or regret for his loss. The fact remains, however, that he was assassinated, not put to death with the judicial formality that is the right of even such as he, and to hold, as the German jurors did, that his taking off was "morally right" both reveals a queer view of moral rightness and opens the way to other assassinations less easily excusable than his or not excusable at all.

And yet—and yet—what other verdict was possible? An acquittal on the ground of insanity, the usual device of jurors who do not want to punish a killing of which they approve, would have been more than ordinarily absurd in the case of a man as obviously sane as this Armenian is, and to have hanged him, or even to have sent him to prison, would have been intolerably to overlook his provocation. The dilemma cannot be escaped—all assassins should be punished; this assassin should not be punished. And there you are! The solution lies further back and long ago, when German officers in Turkey permitted the massacres of Armenians, though they had the power to prevent them.[137]

CONNECTIONS

☙ What was the German court's dilemma? Should the court have acquitted Tehlirian? How do you decide?

☙ Who did Tehlirian's lawyers believe was responsible? Who did the prosecution believe was responsible? Who did the *New York Times* believe was responsible? What arguments could be made in each case? Whom do you hold responsible? Explain your thinking.

☙ Historians now believe that Tehlirian was working with Operation Nemesis, a secret committee of Armenian radicals who, in the absence of international justice, plotted to target individual Turkish leaders they held responsible for the genocide. Does that information alter your thinking about Tehlirian's acquittal?

☙ What is the danger of letting people like Tehlirian, and his compatriots in Operation Nemesis take the law in their own hands? What is lost when a man like Talaat dies without a public trial?

☙ How did the failure of international efforts to hold the leaders of the genocide responsible affect Tehlirian's actions?

Reading 6 — REWRITING HISTORY

Turkish soldiers posing for a picture during World War I.

The three men considered most responsible for the Armenian Genocide—Talaat, Enver, and Djemal—escaped from Turkey at the end of World War I with the help of the German government. They were tried in absentia by a Turkish military tribunal, convicted of war crimes, and sentenced to death. Nevertheless, the tribunal sentences were never carried out, since Talaat and the other principal authors of the genocide remained outside Turkey and the Allied Powers made little effort to hunt them down.

Talaat's memoirs, published after his death, contain the core arguments that have been used by those that have sought to rewrite the history of the Armenian Genocide. Although it is important to compare conflicting interpretations, by analyzing data, identifying sources, and reading critically before making judgment, it is not legitimate scholarship to give credence to denial or intentional distortion or falsification, to revise the history beyond the recognition of its survivors. Israel Charny, editor of the *Encyclopedia of Genocide*, describes denial as a celebration of the crimes of genocide. He believes that killing the record of the truth of the genocide is also killing recorded human history.[138]

Talaat's narrative of the history is crafted to explain away the systematic nature of Young Turk attacks on Armenians. In the opening section, Talaat argues that Turkey had tried to remain neutral at the outset of World War I. A series of political events, Talaat continues, left Turkey with no choice but to join the Germans against Great Britain, France, and Russia: Turkey needed to preserve its own interests against encroachments of the Russians. Moreover, Talaat maintained that there were no deliberate plans for the massacres of Armenians. He wrote:

> *I admit that we deported many Armenians from our eastern provinces, but we never acted in this matter upon a previously prepared scheme. The responsibility for these acts falls first of all upon the deported people themselves. Russia, in order to lay hand on our eastern provinces, had armed and*

equipped the Armenian inhabitants of this district, and had organized strong Armenian bandit forces in the said area. When we entered the great war, these bandits began their destructive activities in the rear of the Turkish Army on the Caucasus front, blowing up the bridges, setting fire to the Turkish towns and villages and killing the innocent [Muslim] inhabitants, regardless of age and sex. They spread death and terror all over the eastern provinces, and endangered the Turkish Army's line of retreat. All these Armenian bandits were helped by the native Armenians. When they were pursued by the Turkish gendarmes, the Armenian villages were a refuge for them. When they needed help, the Armenian peasants around them, taking their arms hidden in their churches, ran to their aid. Every Armenian Church, it was later discovered, was a depot of ammunition. In this disloyal way they killed more than 300,000 [Muslims], and destroyed the communication of the Turkish Army with its bases.

The information that we were receiving from the administrators of these provinces and from the commander of the Caucasian Army gave us details of the most revolting and barbarous activities of the Armenian bandits. It was impossible to shut our eyes to the treacherous acts of the Armenians, at a time when we were engaged in a war which would determine the fate of our country. Even if these atrocities had occurred in a time of peace, our Government would have been obliged to quell such outbreaks. The Porte, acting under the same obligation, and wishing to secure the safety of its army and its citizens, took energetic measures to check these uprisings. The deportation of the Armenians was one of these preventative measures.

I admit also that the deportation was not carried out lawfully everywhere. In some places unlawful acts were committed. The already existing hatred among the Armenians and [Muslims], intensified by the barbarous activities of the former, had created many tragic consequences. Some of the officials abused their authority, and in many places people took preventative measures into their own hands and innocent people were molested. I confess it. . . . I confess . . . that we ought to have acted more sternly, opened up a general investigation for the purpose of finding out all the promoters and looters and punished them severely.

But we could not do that. Although we punished many of the guilty, most of them were untouched. These people, whom we might call outlaws, because of their unlawful attitude in disregarding the order of the Central Government, were divided into two classes. Some of them were acting under personal hatred, or for individual profit. Those who looted the goods of the deported Armenians were easily punishable, and we punished them. But there was another group, who sincerely believed that the general interest of the community necessitated the punishment alike of those Armenians who massacred the guiltless [Muslims] and those who helped the Armenian bandits to endanger our national life. The Turkish elements here referred to were short-sighted, fanatic, and yet sincere in their belief. The public encouraged them.... They were numerous and strong. Their open and immediate punishment would have aroused great discontent among the people, who favored their acts. An endeavor to arrest and to punish all these promoters would have created anarchy in Anatolia at a time when we greatly needed unity. It would have been dangerous to divide the nation into two camps, when we needed strength to fight outside enemies. We did all that we could, but we preferred to postpone the solution of our internal difficulties until after the defeat of our external enemies. . . .

These preventative measures were taken in every country during the war, but, while the regrettable results were passed over in silence in the other countries, the echo of our acts was heard the world over, because everybody's eyes were upon us.[139]

CONNECTIONS

+ What strategies help historians distinguish between conflicting versions of the same historical event? Why is it important to make judgment and recognize that not all historical accounts are equally valid?

+ How does Talaat try to rationalize the mass murder of the Armenians? What strategies does he use? What language do you find striking? Whom does he hold responsible for the deaths?

+ *Takvim-i-Vekayi*, the official gazette of the Turkish government carried reports on the trials of the Young Turk leaders including the indictment of the military court from April 27, 1919. A passage from the indictment counters many of Talaat's claims.

> *The disaster visiting the Armenians was not a local or isolated event. It was the result of a premeditated decision taken by the central body . . . and excesses which took place were based on oral and written orders issued by that central body. . . .The truth is that Talaat, Enver and Jemal ordered the massacres willingly. In a cipher [telegram] dated July 11, 1915, signed by Talaat Bey, and addressed to the Governors of Diarbekir province of the Urfa district, Talaat ordered the burial of all corpses left along the roads, that they may not be thrown into ditches, caves, lakes or rivers; that it was necessary to burn all the effects of the dead.*

> *This operation has been confirmed by another secret telegram sent by Jemal [Djemal] Pasha, Commander in Chief of the 4th Army in Syria, dated July 1, 1915, addressed to the Governor of Diarbekir. . . . In it, Jemal advised the Governor General to circulate false rumors that "dead bodies found in rivers were possibly those of Armenians who had revolted."*[140]

Compare Talaat's version of events with the excerpt from the indictment. Notice the choice of language of the indictment. How does it counter Talaat's claims? After reading the indictment, which words or phrases do you find most significant?

Reading 7 — THE LEGACY OF A WITNESS

Armin Wegner personally witnessed the brutality of the Armenian Genocide, and it changed him forever. After he first learned about the atrocities he risked his life to document the destruction of the Armenian population of the Ottoman Empire.

Wegner was born in Wupperthal, Germany, in 1886 and died in Rome, Italy in 1978. As a young man with the German army, he witnessed the Armenian Genocide and took graphic photographs of what he saw. For the rest of his life, he devoted his efforts as a writer, photographer, and poet to human rights.

At the outset of the World War I, Wegner enrolled in the army as a volunteer nurse in Poland. When Turkey joined the alliance with Germany, he was sent to the Middle East as a member of the German Sanitary Corps. Wegner used his leave in the summer months to investigate rumors about the Armenian massacres. Horrified by what he witnessed, Wegner went to work. Serving under German Field Marshal von der Goltz, commander of the sixth Ottoman Army in Turkey, he traveled throughout Asia Minor, photographing the Armenian deportations and the unburied remains of the dead. Deliberately disobeying orders meant to prevent news of the massacres from spreading, Wegner arranged for evidence of the genocide, including photographs, documents, and personal notes to reach contacts in Germany and the United States. Before long, Wegner's mail routes were discovered, and the Turkish government asked the German army to place him under arrest.

Reassigned to the cholera wards, Wegner became seriously ill the fall of 1916 and was sent from Baghdad to Constantinople in November 1916, all the while hiding photographic images of the atrocities in his belt. Wegner was recalled to Germany in 1916. Back home he continued to raise consciousness about the Armenian massacres. In 1919, Wegner published his eyewitness accounts of the atrocities in *The Way of No Return: A Martyrdom in Letters.*

By that time, the map of Europe and Asia was very different from what it had been before the war. The large multinational empires had been broken apart, and new independent nation states were created in their place. The Armenian Republic in Russian Armenia was one of these new states.

Wegner, a German citizen, wrote an open letter to President Wilson calling on the Allied governments to fulfill their obligations to support the nascent Armenian Republic.

> *I appeal to you at the moment when the Governments allied to you are carrying on peace negotiations in Paris, which will determine the fate of the world for many decades.*

> *But the Armenian people is only a small one among several others; and the future of greater and more prominent states is hanging in the balance. And so there is reason to fear that the importance of a small and extremely enfeebled nation may be obscured by the influential and selfish aims of the great*

Courtesy of the Armenian National Institute

A photograph taken by Armin Wegner in 1915 documenting a burial service in a deportation camp.

European States, and that with regard to Armenia there will be a repetition of neglect and oblivion of which she has so often been the victim in the course of her history....

In the Berlin Treaty of July 1878, all the six European Great Powers gave the most solemn guarantees that they would guard the tranquility and security of the Armenian People. But has this promise ever been kept? Even Abdul Hamid's massacres failed to refresh their memory, and in blind greed they pursued selfish aims, not one putting itself forward as the champion of an oppressed people. In the Armistice between Turkey and your Allies, which the Armenians all over the world awaited with anxiety, the Armenian Question is scarcely mentioned.

Shall this unworthy game be repeated a second time, and must the Armenians be once more disillusioned? The future of this small nation must not be relegated to obscurity behind the selfish schemes and plans of the great states. . . .

Mr. President, pride prevents me from pleading for my own people. I have no doubt that, out of the depths of its sorrow, they will find the force to co-operate, making sacrifices for the future redemption of the world.

But, on behalf of the Armenian Nation, which has been so utterly humiliated, I venture to intervene, for if, after this war, it is not given reparation for its fearful sufferings, it will be lost forever.[141]

By 1921, the Armenian Republic was lost. When Kemalist forces invaded the small republic, its leaders turned to the new Russian Bolshevik government for protection. Just a few years later, Wegner reeled in horror when the Nazis came to power in his own country, bringing with them a vile racism that Wegner found familiar. In the months after Hitler became chancellor of Germany, anti-Jewish legislation swept the country. Unable to remain only a witness, Wegner delivered a letter, through intermediaries, to Hitler pleading for an end to the persecution of the Jews to save the soul of Germany. Nazi officials had Wegner arrested but it did not silence him. He continued to try to speak out to protect the Jews from the brutal end suffered by the Armenians he had photographed.

In 1966, on the fifty-first anniversary of the Armenian Genocide, Wegner described the frustration of being a witness to an atrocity that had been nearly forgotten.

> This is what happened to the witness who tried to have their tragedy and their end known. He continued to bear the burden of his promise to remember the dead once back in the West. But no one listened anymore.

> Fifty years have passed. The people of even larger nations have experienced great suffering. The witness remains, full of shame and feeling a little guilty for he has seen things that one can see without risking one's life. Does this not perhaps mean that he must die like one who has seen the face of God?

> There is silence all about him. In whatever direction he turns, he knocks on closed doors. "We have our own sorrow!" they think or say. "We bear the tragedies of our own people. Why should we torment ourselves with the pain of others, long forgotten?"

> They want to live without worry or sorrow, and go through life knowing nothing about the violence and troubles of the preceding generation. At the beginning of the Twenties, when the witness of these horrors foresaw that the same thing could occur in the West, and illustrated what he had seen with numerous photographs and all the documentation that he could collect from the extermination camps, those that came to know of these things in Germany and in neighboring countries were seized with fear but thought, "The Arabian desert is so far away!"[142]

CONNECTIONS

✢ Wegner describes himself as a witness to the Armenian Genocide. What are the responsibilities of people who have witnessed an injustice? When are they relieved of those responsibilities?

✢ Wegner's photographs are housed at the United States Holocaust Memorial Museum. Samples from the collection may be viewed on line at *http://www.armenian-genocide.org/photo-wegner/index.htm*. After viewing the photographs, discuss their impact. How do they add to your understanding of the genocide?

- Wegner tried to save Jews from the same end that met the Armenians. Imagine if the world had paid attention. What lessons should have been learned from this history?

- How does Wegner describe the world's responsibility towards the Armenian people to President Wilson? What arguments does he make for U.S. intervention? Which do you personally find most convincing? Least effective? Which arguments do you imagine would resonate with the President?

- Wegner writes about the reactions he gets when he reminds people of the treatment of the Armenians in the Ottoman Empire. People responded, "We have our own sorrow.... We bear the tragedies of our own people. Why should we torment ourselves with the pain of others, long forgotten?" How would you answer those comments?

- What lesson does Wegner hope to impart when he reminds readers that when people learned of the Armenian Genocide in Germany they "were seized with fear but thought, 'The Arabian desert is so far away'"?

- Photographs serve as a powerful record of human rights abuses. James Natchwey, a contemporary photojournalist, has used his camera to awaken the moral conscience of people throughout the world. *War Photographer*, a film on Natchwey, is available from the Facing History and Ourselves library.

Reading 8 — REMEMBRANCE AND DENIAL

Even at the very beginning of the Armenian Genocide, plans were already under way to distort the facts about the massacres.[143] The posthumous release of Talaat's memoirs set a pattern of rationalization and deflection of responsibility that has continued into the twenty-first century. After the Treaty of Lausanne in 1923 effectively ended all talk of the "Armenian Question," Turkey concentrated on building a modern state and used all means to suppress any memory or mention of the genocide. Mustafa Kemal Pasha, who took the name Ataturk—father of the Turks, was the leader of the new Turkish Republic and insisted that there had been no systematic mass murder of the Armenians. The Allied Powers remained silent in the face of the historical revisionism. United in their anti-Communism, they viewed Ataturk's Turkey as a strategic ally against the newly formed Soviet Union, which had come to include what was left of historic Armenia. At the same time, all efforts of the immediate postwar Turkish government to prosecute war criminals for brutalities against Armenians were forgotten; records were buried in the archives and closed off to scholars unsympathetic to the new Turkish policy of denial.

Deniers and revisionists have used many different strategies and many different arguments while attempting to turn what was everyday knowledge into myth. By the 1960s, deniers hoped to take advantage of a climate of openness. They argued that teachers, journalists, and public officials should "tell the other side of the story." At the same time, deniers worked to censor United Nations reports by blocking mention of the genocide and by countering resolutions in the United States that would have recognized April 24 as a national day of remembrance of the Armenian Genocide.[144]

In the 1980s, deniers expanded their work to universities and other academic institutions. In 1982, a grant from the Turkish government helped to create the Institute of Turkish Studies in Washington, D.C. At the time of its inception through 1994, the Institute's executive director was Dr. Heath Lowry. Through his work at the institute, Lowry advised the Turkish ambassador to the United States about the work being done by scholars of the Armenian Genocide. The ambassador, in turn, used his position to intimidate authors who dared write about the genocide. It is possible that nobody would have found out if Lowry's notes to the ambassador hadn't ended up in a letter mailed to Robert Jay Lifton, author of *The Nazi Doctors*.[145]

Lifton, a prominent psychiatrist and historian whose work often investigates the roots of violence, wrote about the Armenian Genocide in his book about doctors who participated in the Holocaust. Lowry's letter tried to refute Lifton's scholarship on the Armenian Genocide by concentrating on his footnotes. Lowry wrote to the ambassador, "our problem is less with Lifton than it is with the works upon which he relies. Lifton is simply the end of the chain."[146] Lowry drafted a letter to Lifton for the ambassador to sign, declaring: "I was shocked by references in your work . . . to the so-called 'Armenian Genocide,' allegedly perpetrated by the Ottoman Turks during the First World War."[147] By accident, Lifton received both the memo and the draft letter, and a letter from the ambassador that was almost a word for word copy of Lowry's draft.

Lifton and his colleagues questioned why. Why do deniers deny a history that is overwhelmingly supported by historical evidence, including primary sources, eyewitness accounts, testimony of the perpetrators, survivor recollections, convictions in post-war Turkish courts, and physical evidence? Lifton wondered if it is possible that the deniers believe their own distortions and considered what it means if they do not. Were they denying the genocide simply to advance their careers? In an article examining the ethics of denial, Lifton and his colleagues wrote:

A petition signed by prominent scholars commemorating the Genocide.

> *"Careerism" is a complicated phenomenon, but for our purposes we would identify two forms ... that it may take: one that is oriented toward material goals, and one that involves the satisfactions that go with power. Both share the "thoughtlessness" that Hannah Arendt saw as the essence of the "banality of evil": an imaginative blindness that prevents one from reflecting upon the consequences from one's actions. . . . Arendt also speaks of a "willed evil," and the second type of careerism is not far removed from this: not simply the obliviousness to hurt, but the calculated infliction of hurt.[148]*

In 1998, Lifton was one of more than a hundred prominent scholars who signed a petition circulated by Peter Balakian as an effort to counter denial efforts by commemorating the genocide and deploring the Turkish government's denial of this "crime against humanity."

> *Denial of genocide strives to reshape history in order to demonize the victims and rehabilitate the perpetrators. Denial of genocide is the final stage of genocide. It is what Elie Wiesel has called a "double killing." Denial murders the dignity of the survivors and seeks to destroy remembrance of the crime. In a century plagued by genocide, we affirm the moral necessity of remembering.[149]*

CONNECTIONS

✤ Why do you think the Turkish government has invested so much money and energy in denying the reality of the Armenian Genocide? What does it require of a nation to face the truth of its past errors? What actions can nations take to face their own histories of collective violence and genocide?

We Commemorate the Armenian Genocide of 1915 and Condemn the Turkish Government's Denial of this Crime Against Humanity

Courtesy of the Armenian National Institute

❧ What are the ways in which individuals can respond to denial? What options does a prominent scholar like Lifton have that aren't available to the average citizen?

❧ In the past, denial efforts have prevented some public recognition of the Armenian Genocide, but at the same time scholars have continued to study the history and write about it. Are there ways to measure the impact of denial? What would they be?

❧ Lifton and his colleagues, Smith and Markusen, suggest reasons why people might deny the Armenian Genocide. Can you think of others?

❧ Lifton and his colleagues write that behind some denial there is "the 'thoughtlessness' that Hannah Arendt saw as the essence of the 'banality of evil': an imaginative blindness that prevents one from reflecting upon the consequences of one's actions." What do they mean? Do you agree?

❧ What is the difference between the "thoughtlessness" of banal evil and "willed evil"? Do the differences alter the action or simply the motivation behind them? Who do you find more responsible, someone who is thoughtless or someone who acts intentionally? Who is more dangerous?

❧ The authors of the petition wrote that "in a century plagued by genocide" there is a "moral necessity of remembering". What makes something a moral necessity?

❧ The scholars and writers who signed the statement believe that "denial is the final stage of genocide." What does denial accomplish? For whom?

❧ Why is it important to acknowledge past attrocities? How can acknowledgement of injustice influence victims, perpetrators, bystanders, and their descendents?

❧ The Turkish government attempts to resist official recognition of the Armenian Genocide. Despite that pressure, a growing number of countries now formally recognize the history. The United States is not one of them. In the fall of 2000, the House Foreign Relations Committee approved a resolution acknowledging the Armenian Genocide and sent it to the full House for a vote. The State Department and the Clinton Administration prevented the resolution from coming to a vote in the face of threatened military and economic retaliation from the Turkish government, and this was repeated in the administration of George W. Bush. What would acknowledging the genocide accomplish? Is the decision to formally recognize the genocide a moral or a political decision?

↩

Refer to *Facing History and Ourselves Holocaust and Human Behavior* for a story about U.S. Senator Robert Dole's efforts to bring attention to the Armenian Genocide.

Reading 9 — DENIAL, FREE SPEECH, AND HATE SPEECH

Scholar and philosophy professor Henry Theriault believes that denial of the Armenian Genocide is tantamount to hate speech. Theriault explains:

> *In recent decades, the international denial campaign has intensified in reaction to growing calls for acknowledgement of and restitution for the genocide. Beyond activities by diplomatic leaders and staff, the Turkish government since the 1960s has spent millions of dollars in the United States on denialist public relations and political lobbying. The Turkish government and its supporters have also funded chairs at prestigious United States universities awarded to prominent deniers. Typical denial arguments contend that documentation of the genocide is inconclusive, biased, or falsified, that the genocide was actually a civil war or mutual conflict in which the Turks were also killed and for which Armenians likewise bear responsibility; or that Armenian deaths in 1915 and after were not the result of a deliberate, centrally-orchestrated extermination program.*
>
> *In the United States and elsewhere, Armenian organizations and activists as well as comparative genocide, Holocaust, and Armenian Studies scholars have done much to teach the public about this tragedy. Yet, active denial backed by political blackmail has blocked general recognition and restitution.*[150]

Theriault believes that academic and historical openness have created a climate of relativism, in which all versions of the past are treated as equally valid. This, he argues, has contributed to a failure to recognize the serious consequences of denial on Armenian individuals and on the Armenian community and has played into the hands of those that willfully deny the historical facts. "Academic relativism," as Theriault understands it, "is the belief that any viewpoint held by a scholar declaring expertise is automatically a credible perspective."[151] Deniers, then, are able to claim expertise and despite the overwhelming documentation of the genocide, relativists "retreat into a neutrality that accepts all parties to the 'debate' as equally worthy simply by their status as academics. As a consequence, they avoid the Armenian Question in teaching and writing because they believe the history uncertain, or they promote in their classrooms and other forums a two-sided approach that validates denial."[152] Furthermore, their attitude influences other researchers and educators.

Theriault notes: "At its most extreme, academic relativism takes the form of historical relativism. Historical relativists believe that, where there are competing versions of historical periods or events, there is no ultimate fact of the matter. Each perspective or side is as accurate as the other." This is a problem because people often fail to consider the overwhelming evidence. As Theriault reminds us: "There is a wealth of it [evidence] showing unequivocally that the Turkish government carried out a premeditated, centrally-planned, systematic program to exterminate its Armenian subjects. A properly critical attitude would distinguish between the failure to be aware of compelling evidence because one has not investigated the issue adequately and a genuine shortfall of evidence."[153]

In the meantime, denial has consequences. Theriault reasons that "deniers are 'accessories after the fact of genocide,' who have so far prevented an international political and legal process affirming the genocide, requiring appropriate restitution, and curbing further Turkish mistreatment of Armenians."[154] One outgrowth of the failure is that people in Turkey are able to reap benefit from the land and money belonging to victims of the Armenian Genocide. There is also psychological harm that the genocide and its subsequent denial caused the victims, their descendents, and the larger Armenian community, as well as the impact on individual identity that is caused by preventing people from being able to properly mourn the dead. Professor Theriault writes: "Deniers operate as agents of the original perpetrators [of the genocide], pursuing and hounding victims through time. Through these agents, the perpetrators reach once again into the lives of the victims long after their escape from the perpetrators' physical grasp."[155]

Deniers have disrupted efforts to commemorate the Armenian Genocide and hounded those that tried to speak about the genocide publicly. Theriault notes that often these deniers hide behind the First Amendment.

Deniers often complain that their free speech rights are suppressed when their views do not appear alongside published statements about the genocide or if in public forums these statements are given more attention than denialist claims. Such protests distort the meaning of freedom of speech. The right does not guarantee access to the podium during a discussion of the genocide, publication of a response to a newspaper or scholarly article on the genocide, or automatic inclusion of denial sources next to information on the genocide in school curricula.

New York City, Fifth Avenue at 42nd Street, April 24, 1975. Armenian Martyrs' Day; Armenians march in front of the New York Public Library.

Professor Theriault argues that until the harm done by denial is stopped, there should be regulation of denial based on current regulations that restrict hate speech. Theriault proposes:

> *Legal restriction of public dissemination of denial of the Armenian Genocide would entail a law barring denial and setting penalties for it or authorizing civil suits against deniers. The law need not determine particular statements to be counted as denial but rather offer general guidelines for determining this. Because universities, colleges, scholarly associations, and sometimes school systems have greater latitude in setting limits in hate speech than Congress or a lower-level legislature, they could ban denial in the absence of laws doing so. . . . Crucial for anyone found guilty of denial would be an order to cease and desist. A just remedy would in addition require a statement affirming the genocide as a historical fact.*[156]

CONNECTIONS

❧ Theriault writes: "At its most extreme, academic relativism takes the form of historical relativism." What is relativism? How is relativism different from being open to other possibilities?

❧ According to Theriault, what are the consequences of denial?

❧ Create a working definition for the term "hate speech." How is hate speech different from a matter of opinion? How does Theriault compare hate speech and genocide denial?

❧ Theriault and others believe that "academic relativists" become bystanders while denial does real harm to individuals and the larger society. Revisit your definition of bystander. What arguments could be made to support Theriault's claim that academic relativists are bystanders?

❧ What is the purpose of a debate? What ground rules are useful to ensure that a debate leads to understanding? Do deniers follow those rules?

❧ How can educators validate multiple points of view without creating an atmosphere in which every comment is understood as equally true?

❧ What arguments does Theriault use to make the case for prohibiting denial? What other arguments would you add? Does his proposal raise concerns for you? What are they? Create a structured debate of Professor Theriault's proposal in your class. First agree on some ground rules. Divide the class into three groups. One group should brainstorm arguments in support of Theriault's proposal. Another should brainstorm arguments against the proposal. The third group, the judges, should try to work on a rubric to score the debate.

Reading 10 — DEMANDING JUSTICE

Where does justice come from? Is it achieved? Is it obtained? How do you know when it is fulfilled? Nafina Hagop Chilinguirian, scholar Peter Balakian's grandmother, did not rely on international treaties and tribunals to right the wrongs that had been done to her family. Rather, she took legal action to express her personal outrage.

Chilinguirian survived a death march during which her husband, a U.S. Citizen, was killed. After the war, the United States government supported claims against foreign governments for the loss of life or injury suffered by citizens of the United States. Since Chilinguirian's husband had been a U.S. citizen, she reasoned that she was entitled to compensation for his loss, the loss of his property, and the loss of nearly their entire family. With the help of a lawyer in Newark, New Jersey, Chilinguirian filled out an application seeking the support of the U.S. government for her claims against Turkey. She answered Question 63 on the form by detailing the facts and circumstances surrounding her husband's death.

At 1 August 1915, our parish in Diarbekir was besieged by the gendarmes under the command of the Vali of Diarbekir. The same day with the menace of death they removed us, the Armenians. We could take by us only our ready money, if it was easy to take, our birth and marriage certificates; my husband Hagop Chilinguirian's Naturalization Paper and Passport; all our other goods were left behind. The Turk officers

Courtesy of Peter Balakian

The Chilinguirian family, circa 1914. Nafina is seated in the middle. Her brothers and sisters in the photograph were murdered in August 1915.

of the Turkish government and by their allowance the Turk people plundered and captured our goods left behind. The deporter gendarmes separated the men from the women, and binding them to each other, they carried all of us to an unknown direction. After three days journey, they killed one by one the man deportees of whom only a few were saved. So were killed mercilessly my brothers and sisters, and other relatives mentioned in the answer 55. My husband in spite of that he was a citizen of the U.S.A., was forced to be deported with us, his Naturalization paper and Passport being taken of him by the gendarmes. As he was feeble and indisposed, being subjected to such conditions, and seeing our relatives killed unhumanly, he could not support the life, and died, leaving me a widow with my two orphan daughters named Zivart 7 years old and Arshalois 5 years old. We, the remaining of the deportees, women and children, were forced to walk without being allowed even to buy some bread to eat. Frequently we were robbed by Turks and the gendarmes, as if they would carry us safely to our destiny which was entirely unknown to us. So for thirty two days we were obliged to wander through mountains and valleys. Fatigue and hunger enforced by the whip of the cruel gen-

darmes, diminished the number of the deportees. After many dangers whose description would take much time, a few women and children, included I myself, arrived at Aleppo, Syria, in the beginning of September 1915. Since then I am supported by the Hon. Consulate of U.S.A. in Aleppo, Syria. The deportation itself and the fiendish steps taken against the Armenians in general being well known by the civilized world, I do not mention other evidence concerning this matter. Only I assert that 1) The Turkish government is responsible for the losses and injuries happened to me, because I am a human being and a citizen of U.S.A., I am under the support of human and International law. 2) That the circumstances being very extraordinary, and our deportation unawares, it was impossible to have by me the documentary evidences concerning my losses and injuries; but my co-deportees, saved of death by any way, witness that I am the very owner and proprietor of the said losses and injuries occurred. Herewith I attach their affidavit.[157]

Chilinguirian's total claim for was $167,750. Among the items and property lost which she enumerated in her claim were the names of 13 family members, the contents of a dry goods store, jewels, and money. No action was taken on Chilinguirian's claim despite her husband's status as a U.S. citizen. In fact, no one in the Balakian family spoke of it until Peter Balakian's aunt pulled the yellowed document from a drawer in the 1980s.

CONNECTIONS

✤ What forms can justice take? If Chilinguirian had received compensation for her claim would that have been just? Would she have obtained justice?

✤ One strategy in pursuing justice for the victims of mass atrocity and their descendents has been to insist on reparations, including financial compensation, after mass atrocities. Do you think Armenian descendents of the genocide are entitled to reparations?

✤ In January 2004, almost 90 years after the Armenian Genocide, the New York Life Insurance Company agreed to settle 2,400 unpaid claims and pay $20 million to the descendants of those who were killed. What are the limits of financial compensation as a means toward justice and healing?

✤ The crimes of the Armenian Genocide were perpetrated under the Ottoman Empire. In 1923, the empire was replaced by the Republic of Turkey. Should the current Turkish Republic be financially accountable for reparations to Armenians? What should be done about the countless individuals who benefited by obtaining confiscated Armenian goods and property? Do those that have benefited from atrocity have a responsibility towards the victims and their descendents?

✤ In the 1980s, the United States Congress voted reparations for Japanese Americans interned in camps during World War II. Why do you think these claims were finally honored while a claim after World War I has remained dormant for eight decades?

Reading 11 ⁓ MEETING THE PAST

After massive popular demonstrations throughout Soviet Armenia in 1965, the fiftieth anniversary of the genocide, Soviet leaders were compelled to commission architects S. Kalashian and L. Mkrtchian to build a monument on a hilltop in Yerevan. Every year, on April 24—the anniversary of the beginning of the Armenian Genocide—thousands of people come to the monument to remember the history.

In *Passage to Ararat*, Michael J. Arlen writes about his struggle to come to terms with his dead father and their identity as Armenians. Arlen travels to what was then Soviet Armenia and is assigned a guide, Sarkis, who brings him to the genocide memorial shortly after he arrives. At the time, Arlen feels disconnected from the genocide and the need to remember. Throughout his visit to Armenia, Arlen is conflicted about his relationship to Armenian history and culture. Before returning to the United States, Sarkis takes him back to the monument for a second visit, it is there that he is able to come to terms with his identity.

How strange it is to finally meet one's past: to simply meet it, the way one might finally acknowledge a person who had been in one's company a long while. So, it's you.

I was standing by myself beneath the overhanging slabs of the monument, looking into the fire. I remember thinking that if I had a flower in my hand I would gladly have thrown it into the fire, but that I hadn't remembered to pick one. My eyes went out to the open fields beyond the fire, the fields

© Dave Bartruff/CORBIS

People stand around the eternal flame that burns as part of a monument to the victims of the Armenian Genocide, ca. 1980s Yerevan, Armenia.

of yellow flowers. I thought that it didn't matter about the flower; I thought suddenly that I was home. It was the flattest, simplest, lightest of feelings. I thought, So this is what it's all about.

And then I felt my father's hand in mine. It was so strong a feeling that today I can almost (but not quite) recover that imaginary touch. But what I responded to was not merely the "touch"—I had felt that before at many moments in my life. One of the key memories of my childhood had been a nearly tactile recollection of being pulled by the hand (were we running? walking?) by my father down an unremembered street—an unremembered time except for the pull of the hand, even his face out of sight, his expression unknown, only his arm extending from a dark overcoat.

But I knew that this time it was different, and as I stood there I knew that it would always be different (as it has been). For the hand I felt was not pulling me; it was the hand of a man which I had briefly held in my own one afternoon in New York, the hand of my father dying. His hand had been so small—smaller than mine—and I remember how the feel of this hand had been such a shock to me then (more than his fading speech, or pale features, or struggle of recognition): the hand of my father, who was releasing me, releasing himself from me, and me from him (if either thing were possible between fathers and sons). And I had not known how to grip him back. But here his hand was again. I felt that hand in mine. I felt somehow I had brought him here—to this place. I didn't know what else I felt or knew, but I wept, large tears streaming down my face. I wasn't even sure for what. Nor did it feel bad. On the contrary it felt quite natural.[158]

CONNECTIONS

✦ What does it mean to come to "finally meet one's past"? How is it different from knowing what happened in the past?

✦ What is it about being at the monument that allowed Arlen to reconnect with his father and their Armenian identity?

✦ How do individuals and nations heal after genocide? Is it possible?

✦ At the Armenian Genocide Memorial in Yerevan it is customary to place flowers around the eternal flame. How do you interpret that ritual? What is its meaning? What rituals for remembering the past do you participate in? How do memorials inform how you think about the past? Do they inform how you think about your role in society?

To learn more about memorials and monuments, visit Facing History and Ourselves online module *Memory, History Memorials* at www.facinghistory.org.

Reading 12 — THE CRIME OF GENOCIDE

Journalist and human rights activist Samantha Power writes that the trial of Soghomon Tehlirian stirred up deep moral reflection in Raphael Lemkin, a 21-year-old Polish Jew studying linguistics at the University of Lvov. He raised the issue with a law professor. Power describes the exchange.

> Lemkin asked why the Armenians did not have Talaat arrested for the massacre. The professor said there was no law under which he could be arrested. "Consider the case of a farmer who owns a flock of chickens," he said. "He kills them and this is his business. If you interfere, you are trespassing."
>
> "It is a crime for Tehlirian to kill a man, but it is not a crime for his oppressor to kill more than a million men?" Lemkin asked. "This is most inconsistent."
>
> Lemkin was appalled that the banner of "state sovereignty" could shield men who tried to wipe out an entire minority. "Sovereignty," Lemkin argued to the professor, "implies conducting an independent foreign and internal policy, building schools, construction of roads . . . all types of activity directed towards the welfare of people. Sovereignty cannot be conceived as the right to kill millions of innocent people." But it was states, and particularly strong states, that made the rules.[159]

Lemkin set about to change the rules. After all, they had not worked for the Armenians. The international community first failed to intervene as innocent Armenians were slaughtered. Then it lacked the political will to prosecute those responsible. Maybe, he thought, if there was a law that made mass murder a crime without state boundaries, people like Tehlirian would not fill the vacuum with the need for revenge.

During the 1920s Lemkin became a lawyer and drafted a law challenging the issue of state sovereignty. In 1933, the same year that the Nazis came to power in Germany, Lemkin planned to present his ideas before an international criminal conference in Madrid.

Courtesy of the American Jewish Historical Society New York, NY and Newton Centre, MA

The U.S. War Department I.D. card of Raphael Lemkin

Power writes:

> Lemkin drafted a paper that drew attention to both Hitler's ascent and to the Ottoman slaughter of the Armenians, a crime that most Europeans either had ignored or filed away as an "Eastern" phenomenon. If it happened once, the young lawyer urged, it would happen again. If it happened there, he argued, it could happen here. If the international community ever hoped to prevent mass slaughter of the kind the Armenians

had suffered, he insisted, the world's states would have to unite in a campaign to ban the practice. With that in mind, Lemkin had prepared a law that would prohibit the destruction of nations, races, and religious groups. The law hinged on what he called "universal repression," a precursor to what today is called "universal jurisdiction": The instigators and perpetrators of these acts should be punished wherever they were caught, regardless of where the crime was committed, or the criminals' nationality or official status. The attempt to wipe out national, ethnic, or religious groups like the Armenians would become an international crime that could be punished anywhere, like slavery and piracy. The threat of punishment, Lemkin argued, would yield a change in practice.[160]

Unable to present the legislation in person, Lemkin was disappointed by the response his paper received. One delegate to the conference wrote that crimes of this sort occurred "too seldom to legislate." Others wondered why these issues should concern them at all. Despite the setback, Lemkin pushed on, presenting his legislation at law conferences in Budapest, Copenhagen, Paris, Amsterdam, and Cairo. Samantha Power notes that Lemkin "was not the only European who had learned from the past. So, too, had Hitler."

She explains:

Six years after the Madrid conference, in August of 1939, Hitler met with his military chiefs and delivered a notorious tutorial on a central lesson of the recent past: Victors write the history books. He declared:

"It was knowingly and lightheartedly that Genghis Khan sent thousands of women and children to their deaths. History sees in him only the founder of a state. . . . The aim of war is not to reach definite lines but to annihilate the enemy physically. It is by this means that we shall obtain the vital living space that we need. Who today still speaks of the massacre of the Armenians?"[161]

In 1939, Lemkin, a Jew, fled when the Nazis invaded Poland. While Lemkin pursued his research in the libraries of Europe, his friends, family, and colleagues found themselves under Nazi rule. Lemkin listened carefully as people throughout the world struggled to find the right words to describe the horrors of Nazi brutality. In the early 1940s, Lemkin was living in the United States, doing what he could to find an audience for his message that the international community had to do something to stop Hitler's crimes. Most people, including Vice President Henry Wallace and President Franklin Roosevelt, listened politely, but the timing was wrong. Some simply failed to respond.

Perhaps he was using the wrong language. He knew his legal reasoning was sound, but how could he get people to pay attention? Before Lemkin met with Roosevelt, one of the president's aides suggested that he summarize his proposals in a one-page memo. How was he to do that? How do you "compress the pain of millions, the fear of nations, the hopes for salvation from death" into one page, Lemkin asked. After hearing Winston Churchill tell the world: "We are in the presence of a crime without a name," Lemkin, a former student of linguistics, came to believe that if he could find the right name people would listen.

Power writes:

> *"Mass murder" was inadequate because it failed to incorporate the singular motive behind the per-*
> *petration of the crime he had in mind. "Denationalization," a word that had been used to describe*
> *attempts to destroy a nation and wipe out its cultural personality, failed because it had come to mean*
> *depriving citizens of citizenship. And "Germanization," "Magyarization," and other specified words*
> *connoting forced assimilation of culture came up short because they could not be applied universal-*
> *ly and because they did not convey biological destruction. . . .*
>
> *The word that Lemkin settled upon was a hybrid that combined the Greek derivative geno, meaning*
> *"race" or "tribe," together with the Latin derivative cide, from caedere, meaning "killing."*
> *"Genocide" was short, it was novel, and it was not likely to be mispronounced. Because of the word's*
> *lasting association with Hitler's horrors, it would also send shudders down the spines of those who*
> *heard it.*[162]

In his book *Axis Rule in Occupied Europe*, Lemkin documented the way the Nazis used the legal system to turn society inside out. In the book he describes genocide as a "coordinated plan of different actions aiming at the destruction of essential foundations of the life of national groups, with the aim of annihi-lating the groups themselves."[163] It did not mean that the groups had to be physically annihilated to suf-fer. It implied cultural destruction as well as mass murder.

During World War II, the word "genocide" was included in *Webster's New International Dictionary*. On December 3, 1944, a *Washington Post* editorial claimed that genocide was the only word that properly described the murder of Jews at Auschwitz. While these were signs of progress, Lemkin was not simply trying to create new language, instead, he was trying to use language as a tool to make mass atrocity a violation of international law. In a letter to the *New York Times* on November 8, 1946, Lemkin wrote:

> *It seems inconsistent with our concepts of civilization that selling a drug to an individual is a mat-*
> *ter of worldly concern, while gassing millions of human beings might be a problem of internal con-*
> *cern. It seems also inconsistent with our philosophy of life that abduction of one woman for prosti-*
> *tution is an international crime, while sterilization of millions of women remains an internal affair*
> *of the state in question.*[164]

As the Nuremberg trials unfolded in the aftermath of the Nazi Holocaust, Lemkin was there to push for his legislation making genocide a crime against humanity. It was at Nuremberg that he learned that at least 49 members of his family were killed by the Nazis. More determined than ever, Lemkin listened as one of the British prosecutors explained to a Nazi defendant that in the indictment he was being charged "among other things, with genocide." Samantha Power notes: "This was the first official mention of genocide in an international legal setting."[165]

After Nuremberg, Lemkin went to the newly formed United Nations. In a climate of optimism, Lemkin lobbied UN delegates nonstop. On December 11, 1946, the General Assembly unanimously passed a resolution defining genocide as "the denial of the right of existence of entire human groups" which is "contrary to moral law and the spirit and aims of the United Nations." The resolution went further; it asked a committee to draft a treaty banning the practice. Two years later, with Lemkin acting as one-man lobby, the United Nations passed the Convention on the Prevention and Punishment of the Crime of Genocide, which declares "genocide, whether committed in time of peace or in time of war, is a crime under international law which [the United Nations] undertake to prevent and to punish."

Since that ratification of the genocide convention, war criminals have been prosecuted both by domestic and international courts. In 2002, the United Nations established a permanent international criminal court to try the crime of genocide and other cases of massive abuse of human rights.

CONNECTIONS

☙ After learning about the treatment of Armenians in the Ottoman Empire, Lemkin failed to understand why the Armenians did not have Talaat arrested. Lemkin's law professor argued that Turkey did not break any laws. To explain, he asked Lemkin to "consider the case of a farmer who owns a flock of chickens," he said. "He kills them and this is his business. If you interfere, you are trespassing." How would you respond to the analogy presented by the professor? Does it work as a framework to consider ways to respond to the intentional murder of over a million people?

☙ Power writes that after the Armenian Genocide few people understood that the problem was universal. Even after terrible crimes befall people in faraway places, most of us fail to imagine that something similar could happen where we live. Why?

☙ What did Lemkin hope to accomplish by making mass murder an international crime? Why was it so hard for him to persuade people to act on his proposals?

Survivors of the Rwanda Genocide, 1994.
Tutsi refugees on the road to Kabgayi.

© Gilles Peress, Magnum Photos

☙ In 1939 Hitler asked: "Who today still speaks of the massacre of the Armenians?" What did Hitler learn from the way the world responded to the Armenian Genocide? What have you learned from this study about preventing mass violence?

☙ How does finding language focus attention on a problem? Samantha Power, a scholar of genocide and human rights, states that during the blood bath in Rwanda U.S. officials were careful not to use the word *genocide*.

> *Even after the reality of genocide in Rwanda had become irrefutable, when bodies were shown choking the Kagera River on the nightly news, the brute fact of the slaughter failed to influence U.S. policy except in a negative way. American officials, for a variety of reasons, shunned the use of what became known as "the g-word." They felt that using it would have obliged the United States to act, under the terms of the 1948 Genocide Convention. They also believed, under-standably, that it would harm U.S. credibility to name the crime and then do nothing to stop it. A discussion paper on Rwanda, prepared by an official in the Office of the Secretary of Defense and dated May 1, testifies to the nature of official thinking. Regarding issues that might be brought up at the next interagency working group, it stated,*
>
> > *1. Genocide Investigation: Language that calls for an international investigation of human rights abuses and possible violations of the genocide convention. Be Careful. Legal at State was worried about this yesterday—Genocide finding could commit [the U.S. govern-ment] to actually "do something." [Emphasis added.]*[166]

Would it made a difference if the president had declared the events in Rwanda as genocide? Why do you think the U.S. officials were reluctant "do something"?

☙ Article 2 of the Genocide Convention defines genocide as:

> *"any of the following acts committed with intent to destroy, in whole or in part, a national, ethnical, racial or religious group, as such:*
>
> *"(a) Killing members of the group;*
>
> *"(b) Causing serious bodily or mental harm to members of the group;*
>
> *"(c) Deliberately inflicting on the group conditions of life calculated to bring about its physical destruction in whole or in part;*
>
> *"(d) Imposing measures intended to prevent births within the group;*
>
> *"(e) Forcibly transferring children of the group to another group."*

Some people claim that each of the following is an example of genocide:

The destruction of the Native American population by various colonial powers and later the United States.

The enslavement of Africans in the United States.

Iraq's treatment of the Kurds before and after the first Gulf War.

The suffering of the people of East Timor during the 1980s and 1990s.

The mass murder of Bosnian Muslims during the 1990s.

Research one of these cases or another case of which you are aware. Using the definition offered by the Genocide Convention, decide whether it was genocide. Present your findings to the class. Do your classmates agree with your assessment? What difficulties did you encounter in trying to reach a consensus on what constitutes genocide?

NOTES

121. Richard Hovannisian, "Historical Dimensions of the Armenian Question: 1878–1923," in Richard Hovannisian ed. *The Armenian Genocide in Perspective* (New Brunswick, NJ: Transaction Publishers, 1991), pp. 32–33.
122. Major General Harbord, in a report October 16, 1919, Senate Document 266, Congressional Record May 29, 1920, available in Dickran H. Boyajian, *Armenia: The Case for a Forgotten Genocide* (Westwood, N.J: Educational Book Crafters, 1972), pp. 197–204.
123. Ibid.
124. Henry Morgenthau, "Shall Armenia Perish?" *The Independent* (February 28, 1920), p. 341.
125. Annette Höss, "The Trial of Perpetrators by the Turkish Military Tribunals: The Case of Yozgat" in Richard G. Hovannisian ed. *The Armenian Genocide: History, Politics, Ethics* (New York: St. Martin's Press, 1992), pp. 208–211.
126. Ibid., p. 211.
127. Kloian, *Armenian Genocide: News Accounts*, p. 316.
128. Gary Bass, *Stay the Hand of Vengeance: The Politics of War Crimes Tribunals* (Princeton, NJ: Princeton University Press, 2000).
129. Excerpted from "Transcript of the Military Court Trial" from Takvim-i-Vekayi, April 27, July 5, 1919. Reprinted in Kloian, *Armenian Genocide: News Accounts*, pp. 314–315.
130. Paul Gordon Lauren, *The Evolution of International Human Rights: Visions Seen* (Philadelphia: University of Pennsylvania Press, 1998), pp. 94–95.
131. Ibid., pp. 96–97.
132. Christopher Walker, *Armenia: Survival of a Nation* (New York: St. Martin's Press, 1990), p. 264.
133. Richard Hovannisian, "Historical Dimensions 1878–1923" in *Armenian Genocide in Perspective*, p. 36.
134. Thea Halo, *Not Even My Name* (New York: Picador, 2000), pp. 202–203.
135. Walker, *Armenia: Survival of a Nation*, p. 316.

136. *New York Times*, June 4, 1921, p. 12.

137. *New York Times*, June 6, 1921, editorial.

138. Israel W. Charny, "The Psychology of Denial of Known Genocides," in Charny, ed., *Genocide: A Critical Bibliographic Review*, vol. 2 (New York: Facts on File, 1991), p. 23, Table 2.

139. Kloian, *Armenian Genocide: News Accounts*, p. 361.

140. Kloian, *Armenian Genocide: News Accounts*, pp. 316, 320.

141. Armin Wegner, "An Open Letter to the President of the United States of America Woodrow Wilson," *in Armin T. Wegner and the Armenians in Anatolia, 1915* (Milan, Italy: Guerini E Associati, 1996), pp. 137, 138, 143, 145.

142. Ibid., "The Blue Light," p. 168.

143. Christopher Walker, "World War I and the Armenian Genocide," in Richard Hovannisian ed. *The Armenian People: from Ancient People to Modern Times*, vol. 2 (New York: St. Martin's Press, 1997), p. 251.

144. Roger W. Smith, Eric Markusen, and Robert J. Lifton, "Professional Ethics and Denial of the Armenian Genocide," in Richard Hovannisian ed. *Remembrance and Denial: The Case of the Armenian Genocide* (Detroit: Wayne State University Press, 1999), p. 273.

145. Ibid., pp. 271, 274–275.

146. Ibid., p. 278.

147. Ibid., p. 279.

148. Ibid., p. 288.

149. "Statement by Concerned Scholars and Writers," April 24, 1998, available at *http://www.armenian-genocide.org/Affirmation.22/current_category.3/affirmation_detail.html*.

150. Henry C. Theriault, "Denial and Free Speech: The Case of the Armenian Genocide," in Richard Hovannisian ed. *Looking Forward, Moving Backward: Confronting the Armenian Genocide* (New Brunswick, Transaction Pub., 2003) pp. 231–262.

151. Ibid.

152. Ibid.

153. Ibid.

154. Ibid.

155. Ibid.

156. Ibid.

157. Quoted in Balakian, *Black Dog of Fate*, pp. 202–203.

158. Arlen, *Passage to Ararat*, pp. 253–255.

159. Power, *A Problem from Hell*, pp. 17,19.

160. Ibid., pp. 19–20.

161. Ibid., p. 23.

162. Ibid., pp. 41, 42.

163. Ibid., p. 43.

164. Ibid., p. 48.

165. Ibid., pp. 48–49.

166. Samantha Power, "Bystanders to Genocide: Why the United States Let the Rwandan Tragedy Happen," *The Atlantic Monthly* (September, 2001), available at *http://www.theatlantic.com/issues/2001/09/power.htm*.

INDEX

CPSIA information can be obtained
at www.ICGtesting.com
Printed in the USA
JSHW050435040621
15425JS00011B/51

9 781940 45726